Town Meeting

Town Meeting

PRACTICING DEMOCRACY
IN RURAL NEW ENGLAND

Donald L. Robinson

University of Massachusetts Press
Amherst & Boston

LC 2010044988
ISBN 978-1-55849-855-6 (paper); 854-9 (library cloth)

Designed by Jack Harrison
Set in Monotype Dante with Bernard Condensed display type
Printed and bound by Thomson-Shore, Inc.

Library of Congress Cataloging-in-Publication Data

Robinson, Donald L., 1936–
Town meeting : practicing democracy in rural New England / Donald L. Robinson.
p. cm.
Includes bibliographical references and index.
ISBN 978-1-55849-855-6 (pbk. : alk. paper) — ISBN 978-1-55849-854-9 (library cloth : alk. paper)
1. Municipal government—New England—Citizen participation—History.
2. Political participation—New England—History. 3. Direct democracy—New England—History.
I. Title.
JS431.R63 2010
320.8'50974—dc22
2010044988

British Library Cataloguing in Publication data are available.

To Molly

AND TO

Susan Todd
Buz Eisenberg
and Stuart Harris

CITIZENS PAR EXCELLENCE

Contents

Illustrations follow pages 84 and 162

Maps

Acknowledgments

While I was serving as a member of Ashfield's select board, from 1991 to 2000, people would ask whether I intended to write a book about my experiences. I was not being disingenuous when I answered in the negative; I was working at the time on a book about framing Japan's postwar constitution.

Work on this book began in the 2003/2004 academic year. I was a faculty associate that year of the Kahn Institute at Smith College, headed then by Marjorie Senechal, later by Rick Fantasia and Rosetta Cohen. With Catharine Newbury, I led a small group of students and faculty members who met weekly to pursue an interdisciplinary inquiry titled "Problems of Democracy." Colleagues Pat Coby, Sam Intrator, Steve Tilley, Paula Giddings, and Bob Buchele, among others, joined in that project. The attention and interest of these friends gave me a tremendous boost right at the start.

By 2005, my thoughts were beginning to take shape. I asked John Bowman, an incisive critic, to read a raw draft. John's comments helped me to find my way. Anonymous reviewers for potential publishers were sometimes brutal, but they steered me away from mistakes and into fruitful lines of inquiry. Other colleagues at Smith College, especially Neal Salisbury, Dan Horowitz, Howard Nenner, and Rob Weir, suggested valuable resources and perspectives.

The most important contributions have come from neighbors and friends in Ashfield. Peter Wiitanen was unstinting in sharing his vast knowledge of the history of Ashfield properties. Dave Fessenden took several photographs and skillfully helped me to arrange the galleries of illustrations. Faye Whitney responded graciously to repeated requests for information and guidance. Stuart Harris and his mother, Norma Harris, shared their profound sense of place and people. Grace Lesure and Nancy Garvin shepherded me through the wonderfully rich holdings of the Ashfield Historical Society. Dave Newell provided access to his extensive research on Ashfield's founding period. Janet Swem drew on her mastery of the town's finances to correct my account of the sewer project. Maryellen Cranston, our estimable town clerk, and her assistant, Nancy Dunne, responded cheerfully to many inquiries.

Also helpful at critical junctures were Eleanor Ward, Mary Fitz-gibbon, Ruth Craft, Buz Eisenberg, Phil Pless, Bill Perlman, Dianne and Dick Muller, Tom and Sandy Carter, Thom Gray, Lester Garvin, Alden and Audrey Gray, Nancy Hoff and Laura Bessette, Phil Nolan, Mollie Babize, Susan and Dick Todd, Kit Nylen and her late husband, Bob, and countless others. Unfailingly supportive and accommodating were Phyllis Kirkpatrick, co-chair of the Ashfield History Project, and board members Lynn Dole, Harry Keramidas, and Liz Castro. I particularly wish to thank Dianne Muller, Phyllis Kirkpatrick, Bill Perlman, Alden Gray, and Cynthia and Tom Cranston for reviewing drafts at various stages.

Elsewhere, I had generous assistance from Barbara Fell-Johnson at the Hampshire Law Library, Jonathan Benoit and David Whitesell of the American Antiquarian Society in Worcester, and David Bosse of the Pocumtuck Valley Memorial Library.

In finding the University of Massachusetts Press as my publisher, I have been fortunate indeed. Clark Dougan and Bruce Wilcox believed that my rather un-gainly manuscript would ultimately work and made an important contribution in persuading me to drop a chapter comparing Ashfield and ancient Athens. Mary Bellino proved to be far more than a copy editor. She was demanding when she needed to be, yet more than once, when I was about to scream with frustration, she found a source I had lost or helped me to clarify a tangled thought. Some have told me that the days of expert editorial support are past, but the publishers of this book have proven them wrong.

Let me at this point insert the usual disclaimer on behalf of people men-tioned in these acknowledgments. None of them should be blamed for errors of fact, misinterpretations of meaning, or offenses against good taste. For flaws that remain despite their efforts, I alone am responsible.

Smith College provides vital encouragement and strong support for the scholarly projects of its faculty members. I depended especially on Susan Bourque, peerless provost, and her associate, John Davis; Pam Skinner, who has for many years guided me through the resources available at and through the William Allan Neilson Library; and Liane Hartman, Pat Billingsley, and Sandy Bycenski, wizards of information technology.

Finally, special thanks to dear friends who sustained me with their confi-dence and warm encouragement: Barbara and Dean Alfange, Ginny and Henry Paige, and Leona and Shep Forman. Above all, thanks to my beloved wife and best friend, Molly, who loves Ashfield as much as I. She has worked hard on this book, combing out inaccuracies and vestiges of ill temper. For irritations that remain despite her valiant efforts, most people in Ashfield know enough not to blame her.

TOWN MEETING

Introduction

This is a book about the practice of democracy. It focuses on Ashfield, Massachusetts, a rural town of about two thousand inhabitants in the foothills of the Berkshires, in western New England. Ashfield governs itself by a process known generally as town-meeting democracy. It is one of 262 towns in the Commonwealth of Massachusetts that still practice this form of direct democracy.

In 2002 the town of Plymouth, Massachusetts, voted to stick with its town-meeting form of government, rather than switch to a mayor-and-council format. A glossy new magazine, *CommonWealth,* published by an organization called MassINC, commented that the vote in Plymouth represented a victory for "tradition" over the need for stronger, more centralized, professional management.[1]

The same issue of *CommonWealth* contained a glitzy section called "Mapping Massachusetts Politics." It identified ten areas in the state and described their demographics, party loyalties, "big questions," and performance in past primary elections. Each of the ten was given a cute name. Franklin County, where Ashfield is located, was identified as part of "Vacationland," which also included most of adjacent Berkshire and Hampshire counties ("most of the western third of the state"), as well as Cape Cod and the islands (Martha's Vineyard and Nantucket), Gloucester, Cape Ann, and the North Shore. So much for the "western third of the state" and its place in the consciousness of the aspirant classes in the

Boston area. Ashfield has grown used to disdain emanating from the state capital.[2] Anyone who has been a delegate to a statewide political convention knows the experience of being seated high in the balcony, far from the pit where the decisions are made.

On the other hand, Ashfield residents have another experience as well, one that most citizens of the United States never have: the practice of direct democracy in a public jurisdiction. For all its trials and tribulations, democracy is their pride and joy. Other Americans may experience a form of democratic governance in other institutions or organizations. Some church congregations govern themselves democratically, choosing their pastors and officers and deciding on budgets by vote of the membership. Trade unions and businesses sometimes operate that way, and so do some communes. From experiences such as these, many of us develop at least some general familiarity with Robert's Rules, along with a deeply ingrained resistance to autocratic leadership.

Still, towns that are governed by town meetings are different from these other democratically run organizations. A municipality (a town or a city) is a *jurisdiction*. Its corporate actions have the force of law and are enforceable by the state's courts and police departments. As an adult resident, you are not free to choose whether or not to join. If you live in Ashfield, you are a constituent.[3] Once the town takes formal action, you must obey. Town meeting has declared it unlawful to allow a dog to run unleashed, or to play amplified music that can be heard between 11 p.m. and 7 a.m. from 150 feet away, and it has set fines for violating these ordinances. The town assesses taxes, and if you do not pay them on time, the town can add interest to the amount you owe, and if you continue not to pay, the town can begin proceedings to take your property. The local police, who operate in part under regulations set by town meeting, enforce these laws. In other words, if you live in Ashfield, you are under the jurisdiction of its government. It is your responsibility to obey decisions made by an assembly of its citizens.

That last statement needs one major qualification. Ashfield is incorporated under the laws of Massachusetts, and Massachusetts exists in a federal system in which the Constitution, federal laws, and treaties are "the supreme Law of the land." As we will see throughout this book, these supervening authorities, both federal and state, often impinge on Ashfield and bring its government to account, forcing it to act in ways that are contrary to the will of its constituents. This has been true since the town's founding in the mid-eighteenth century. With that qualification, however, the citizens of Ashfield enjoy—and sometimes endure—the sovereignty of a government controlled by a majority of their own number.

Why would anyone outside of Ashfield care about the operation of such an anomaly? Ashfield is so small, and only similar towns in New England still practice this form of government. Why would most Americans care about what happens in these places?

The answer is that Ashfield embodies an enduring American ideal. Abraham Lincoln said at Gettysburg that Americans are dedicated to "government of the people, by the people, for the people." That was a radical formulation of our commitment, our national project, but Lincoln's rhetoric holds it steadily before us. As we have seen, it has been scaled down; for most of the country, most of the time, it applies mainly to elections, making us more a republic than a democracy.[4] Nevertheless, our fascination with public opinion polls alone suggests that we aspire to more. We feel that government should respect our opinion between elections. Even the Federalist Papers, although they are sometimes dismissive of democracy, hold up the ideal of "popular government." This implies respect for the opinion, values, and interests of the people.[5] American democracy has always yearned in the direction of greater popular participation. Every amendment to the Constitution, especially those expanding the franchise, has pulled in that direction. So, historically, have most major reform movements.

Ashfield claims our interest as a place where democracy is practiced in ways unusual for most of the United States, where grassroots citizens perform as a government of general jurisdiction. That is the subject of this book.

Why Tocqueville celebrated town-meeting democracy

In 1830, Alexis de Tocqueville came from post-Revolutionary France to New England. His ostensible mission was to study America's penal system, but his own private agenda was far more ambitious: to examine the course of democracy in the United States. He believed that the spread of democracy was a "providential fact." He wanted to understand what it meant for culture, as well as for politics and government. The product of his studies has been called "the best book ever written on democracy and the best book ever written on America."[6]

Shortly before leaving France, Tocqueville attended lectures by François Guizot at the Sorbonne that described how the independence of France's far-flung medieval estates provided space and incentive for the development of initiative and self-reliance. Burghers assembled and deliberated on their affairs, taxed themselves, elected magistrates who judged persons accused of crimes and punished those found guilty. In other words, these medieval Frenchmen governed themselves; they were practically sovereign. Guizot went on to recount how turbulence and rioting in these incipient polities contributed to a demand for centralization under royal authority. This antidemocratic development, in Guizot's opinion, was not only inevitable but beneficial.

Tocqueville, Guizot's young auditor, was not so sure. He realized that France's medieval communes presented a "bizarre blend of oppression and liberty." But for him they were important incubators of local liberties and potential counterweights to France's stifling, centralized bureaucracy. He believed that something precious had been lost when royal centralization and administration replaced local initiative and responsibility.[7]

When Tocqueville arrived in Boston fifteen months later, Guizot's lectures were still fresh in his mind. Guizot had argued that liberty could rest only on a centralized, monarchical foundation made possible by the sacrifice of local action. What Tocqueville found in New England offered a prima facie rebuttal to this notion.

It was in Boston, in conversations between September 20 and 29, 1831, with Josiah Quincy Jr., the president of Harvard, and Jared Sparks, a young historian and Harvard's future president, that Tocqueville learned about New England's townships and began to develop the notion that their "indigenous 'communal spirit'" was a critical source of democracy in America.[8] His conversations with Sparks were particularly important for him. The two young men had met three years earlier in Paris, when Sparks was doing research in French archives for a history of American foreign relations. In Boston, Tocqueville questioned Sparks closely, and then peppered him with letters of inquiry as he and his fellow traveler

Gustave de Beaumont ventured west to Pittsburgh and Cincinnati and made their perilous way, through a bitterly cold and dangerous winter passage down the Ohio and Mississippi rivers, to Memphis and New Orleans. Initially one source among many, Sparks became virtually a collaborator on Tocqueville's study of the development and practice of democracy in New England.[9]

Sparks stressed the critical importance of a community's origins. New England, he said, owed her freedom to the circumstances of her original foundation. "We arrived here as republicans, as religious enthusiasts. . . . Those who want to imitate us should consider that our history is unprecedented." In the United States, Sparks told his French visitor, it is dogma that the majority is always right. Sometimes, though, a majority will attempt to oppress the minority. Fortunately we have the governor's veto and, above all, the power of judges to refuse to apply an unconstitutional law. These provide a safeguard against democracy's passions and mistakes.

This "casual remark" by Sparks led to what Hugh Brogan, the author of a well-respected biography of Tocqueville, has called Tocqueville's "most serious mistake": his exaggeration of the danger of tyranny of the majority (that is, the tendency of the majority to abuse its power).[10] Another conversation in Boston, this one with a state senator, led Tocqueville to muse further that it was "even more difficult to establish municipal institutions . . . than great political assemblies." "When I say municipal institutions," he wrote, "I wish to speak not of the forms, but of the very spirit that gives them life. The habit of treating all matters by discussion, and of directing them all, even the smallest, by means of majorities, this habit is acquired with greater difficulty than all the rest. But it alone makes governments that are truly free."[11] In America, Tocqueville observed, "free habits have created free political institutions." In France, "free political institutions [would have] to create the habits." Tocqueville did not, at this stage, consider whether the latter development was indeed possible. It certainly would not be easy, as French political development in the nineteenth century sadly demonstrates.

From his sources in Boston, Tocqueville had gotten the impression that the practices he found in New England had migrated westward, as pioneers from New England moved to the frontier.[12] Alas, by the time he reached Cincinnati a month later, he began to realize it was not true. Nowhere out west was he finding "communal institutions that appear to me to operate with such vigor in New England."[13] Now he wished he had studied more carefully "the principles, forms and methods of action" he had found in the towns of New England.[14]

That is exactly my goal in the pages that follow.

What we mean by "democracy"

Some who have written about town-meeting democracy in New England have claimed that it is "real democracy," implying that other forms are somehow less truly democratic.[15] Certainly the term *democracy* is elastic, covering many phenomena, some of which simply do not deserve the name, such as the Democratic People's Republic of Korea (North Korea). But to suggest that the United States or the Commonwealth of Massachusetts are not "real democracies" is to invite a quarrel over terms.

Since the mid-1980s there has been much work devoted to refining the term *democracy*.[16] It is possible now to speak with some precision about how social scientists, at least, are using the word.

When we call a system of government "democratic," we normally mean that

- those in a position to make policy owe their power to an election;
- elections are competitive;
- anyone qualified to vote is eligible to run for public office;
- the franchise is universal (for adults, without discrimination based on gender, race, or ethnicity);
- votes count equally;
- the rights of free speech, association, and communication are protected.

No polity fulfills these criteria perfectly. In comparative studies of democracy worldwide, the United States usually ranks somewhere in the middle. Analysts note, for example, that legislators and chief executives are elected, but elections are not competitive in many states, and votes Americans cast for president (because of the electoral college) or for senator (because the states' populations vary) are not of equal weight.[17]

Candid observers recognize that democracy in the United States is imperfect. We are always trying to reform it. But notice one thing about the discussion so far. We have been talking about government by elected representatives. Sometimes such governments are called "republics," to distinguish them from direct democracies. Here is where the advocates of "real democracy" want to chime in. As soon as we admit the need to govern by elected representatives, they argue, we have given away something precious. (For more on this point, see the Conclusion.) Unless the people—all the adult people—have the ultimate say about the undertakings of government, and unless they can express that determination directly, we do not have true democracy.

How far do we want to take this point? Are we saying that the whole polity, acting directly, should make and closely oversee the implementation of foreign policy? How about judicial functions? Should the assembly as a whole conduct criminal trials? What about the regulation of modern markets? Should assemblies of citizens do that?

For democrats, the important thing for citizens is to retain control over all governmental functions. Arguments for delegating certain tasks to elites based on supposed expertise are anathema. Stepping around the sophistication of lawyers, radical democrats insist that the people, acting directly, must articulate the will of the regime at all phases of the process. Even if citizens do not themselves perform administrative or judicial functions, they must insist that assemblies of citizens are the incarnation of the regime's will, the ultimate authority in all respects.

An introduction to Ashfield

Most people who know it today think of Ashfield as a salubrious place, with glorious springtimes followed by soft lazy summers and spectacular autumns.[18] Winters, though, are cold and hard, with icy roads and subzero temperatures. "Mud season" in the spring is particularly awful and seemingly interminable. Most of us today are equipped to deal with these hazards and trials. The highway department keeps the roads paved, plowed, and salted.[19] Homes are insulated and reliably heated, and mud rooms absorb most of the damage in March and April.

Our predecessors were not so fortunate. Winters were full of danger. Infectious diseases—influenza, pneumonia—were commonplace, and

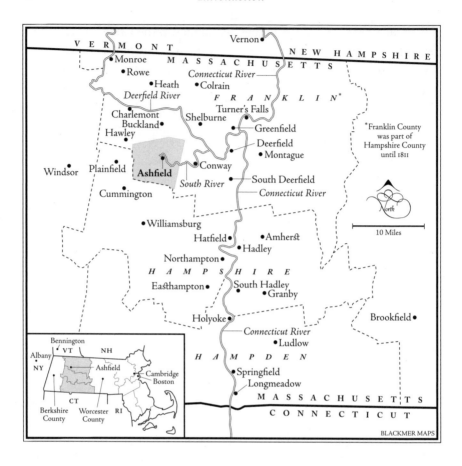

epidemics were practically an annual occurrence. They struck infants and toddlers most severely. Gravestones in the town's cemeteries bear witness to the staggering toll.

Ashfield Lake, a lovely gem in the middle of the village, strangely embodies the town's haunted past. It looks perfectly benign now.[20] There is a wee beach; teenagers fish near the dam that holds back the lake's water. But there are also echoes of earlier tragedies. In May 1827, seven young men were reportedly washing sheep in the lake when their overloaded skiff filled with water and sank. Four of them drowned: fifteen-year-old William and thirteen-year-old Robert Gray, eighteen-year-old Aaron Lyon (cousin of the famed educator Mary Lyon), and twenty-eight-year-old Arnold Drake. Aaron's father, David, a deacon, saw the boat sinking from the shore. Attempting a rescue, he drowned as well.[21] Once you hear this story, the lake never looks quite the same again.

To picture what life was like in Ashfield when the patterns of town-meeting democracy were set, we need to remember that it was above all a rural place. There were waves of migration out of town, especially during the nineteenth century, as young families went west in search of fortune. But many families lived in town for generations, marrying and giving birth, baptizing and burying their babies, planting and harvesting, birthing and milking their herds, practicing trades, gossiping and quarreling, hiring and dismissing their pastors and schoolteachers, creating neighborhoods. And going to war. We're still doing that, of course, sending young men, and now women, to fight on far-flung battlefields, remembering them in our prayers, sending cookies and jams to remind them of home. In earlier wars, particularly the Civil War, Ashfield sent many more of its precious sons to join the battle. Between 1861 and 1865, eighty-four men from Ashfield fought in Lincoln's armies.[22] Twelve of them died in battle, in rebel prisons, or from wounds or sickness.[23]

We still remember our Civil War veterans, and veterans of other wars, every Memorial Day. At 10 a.m. we gather at Town Hall, in the middle of the village, for a brief ceremony: a selection or two played by the high school marching band or, lately, a band of local musicians; solemnly raising the flag and drawing it back down to half-mast; the pledge of allegiance led by Girl Scouts or Boy Scouts; then forming up into a parade—honor guard and veterans first, followed by the marching band, then the select board and other town officers, fire trucks, various organizations (scouts, for example), and the much-anticipated antique cars, carrying elderly dignitaries. As the parade passes, the spectators (bless them, why else do we march so solemnly?) fall into line at the rear for the half-mile trek east down Main Street, left at the Episcopal church onto Baptist Corner Road, and on to the cemetery. There veterans lead us again in a formal flag-raising and fire off a three-gun salute, followed by a speech by one of the town's capable citizen-orators. Then off again to the stately Civil War monument at the entrance to the Plains cemetery, where schoolchildren read the Gettysburg Address. Then back to the center of town for a chicken barbecue on the lawn of the Congregational Church.

One recent year, during the stop at the Civil War memorial, a local historian gave a carefully researched account of the sons of Ashfield who had died in the Civil War. Many, it turned out, had died not from fatal wounds but in hospitals, where treatment and sanitation were brutally primitive. Noah Gordon, a local novelist with an international reputation, wrote a fine book, *Shaman,* about a doctor in the Civil War.[24] Many of us had read that book and knew the background behind the sad tale of agony at the front and bereavement back home. Many of the surnames of these soldiers—Taylor, Lilly, Eddy, Howes—were familiar to us; several of these families have lost sons in other wars as well, and their descendents are our neighbors and friends.

That's the thing about living in a small rural town: you get a sense of continuity, of inheriting something valuable and beloved. You feel responsible for it. You want to understand it, to feel it. You want to preserve it, to pass it along undamaged.

Perhaps the most amazing thing about Ashfield is that most of those whose families built this legacy seem willing to share it with newcomers. There is no need to be sentimental about this. A few of the old-timers seem to resent newcomers, and some newcomers act as if they have little respect for those who built the community they admire so much.[25] But most people here, old-timers and newcomers alike, try hard to listen and to appreciate their neighbors.

Two fine examples are Ruth and Clayton Craft.[26] They were both born near Ashfield more than eighty years ago. Ruth was a nurse; Clayton worked in social services. They raised three children here. Since the early 1970s they have operated a used-book business out of the barn attached to their modest, beautifully kept home on Baptist Corner Road. Ruth compiled a local telephone book as a fund-raiser for the local Episcopal church. She knows everyone in town—not just their names, but details of their lives. She spends much of the day on the telephone, catching up. Lately she and Clayton have spent many hours near the stove in the local hardware store, gathering gossip. No town ever had a more benign gossip-gatherer than Ruth. She knows when people fall short of her own high standards, but she is remarkably forgiving. She finds something good to say about everyone, and she is notoriously unable to hold a grudge.

Another bridging person is Mary Hall Snow. Born of a multigenerational Ashfield family, Mary attended Radcliffe College, did graduate studies, and worked in the Boston area as a school teacher and social worker. She married John Snow, who taught homiletics (preaching) at Episcopal Divinity School in Cambridge. Throughout their professional lives in the Boston area, the Snows continued to nourish their roots in Ashfield, returning regularly for the summer and holidays. When they retired, they moved permanently into their house on South Street. It has since become a place for special gatherings, as when an esteemed scholar and civil rights leader, Gayraud S. Wilmore, made a stop there on his book tour.[27] Recently Mary Snow served a term on the district school board. For years John wrote a regular column for the monthly *Ashfield News,* and he preached from time to time in the local Episcopal church. John was a quiet man in the pulpit; he read every word from a carefully handwritten text. But I, a seminary graduate myself who has heard many of the greatest preachers of my generation, have never heard anyone in the pulpit more powerful than John Snow. Nearly every sentence he uttered set off an explosion in the mind.[28] Mary and John are strong personalities, but invariably gentle and affirming. They deeply value the town, they cherish it and help to nourish its memories, and they welcome the contributions of newcomers.

The Snows immediately bonded, for example, with Bill Perlman, a man not always easy to love. We will meet Bill many times in these pages, but here let me tell just one story. Bill decided to run for a vacancy on the select board less than a year after he moved to town from New York City. Who was he? Quickly we began hearing about his uncle, a famous attorney in New York City; that Bill had an engineering degree, that he was a skilled musician and storyteller, that he had been active in the civil rights movement. As this information gradually emerged and people began to come to terms with it, Dale Kirkpatrick, who had served an earlier term on the select board, decided to throw his hat into the ring as a write-in candidate. The two men met, privately. They had (Bill reports) what the diplomats call a cordial exchange. The only public issue they discussed was a property-owner's decision to mine gravel from a mound behind his house. A few neighbors objected, but Bill remembers telling Dale that he personally had no objection to that; owners should be free to develop their property. Bill knew there were limits to this principle, but he also knew he wouldn't hear them from a conservative Republican, and in any case, most Ashfield residents, whatever their ideology, would favor laissez-faire in a case like this.

Some people resented Bill's rather brazen candidacy, but others, including the Snows, welcomed it. In any case, he won, decisively. Dale Kirkpatrick's widow remembers that even Dale voted for him. Several years later, when an ugly spasm of anti-Semitism targeted Bill, Dale stood up at a huge public assembly called to respond to the challenge and told with powerful emotion how, as a young soldier, he had been present at the liberation of a concentration camp in Germany. He had vowed then to resist the spirit that led to such atrocities whenever it reared its loathsome head.

A clash of cultures

The surface of Ashfield politics is normally tranquil. Every once in a while, however, ominous rumbles rise from the cultural tensions below the surface. A particularly troubling example began to unfold in May 2004.

Dr. Thomas Cranston, a veterinarian and farmer, had served with distinction for several years as chair of the finance committee, the financial watchdog and principal counterweight politically to the select board. In 2004, he decided to relinquish his seat on the finance committee to run for an opening on the board of assessors. The three-person board oversees the evaluation of local property, which is the basis for distributing the local tax burden among property owners. Cranston himself is a major landowner; he has large agricultural holdings, including several multiacre stands of Christmas trees.[29] He is widely respected for his knowledge of the town. On the board of assessors he joined two other large landowners: Len Roberts, a lumberman, and Mark Graves, who had recently built a public golf course just off Baptist Corner Road.

Normally assessments arouse little controversy in Ashfield. Thus most people were surprised, but not upset, when a form came in the mail, asking residents to list all personal property. After a brief fracas, the board decided not to pursue the survey.

Then some residents began to receive notices of adjustments in the evaluation of their property. This time the reaction was stronger.[30] Boards of assessors have considerable leeway in applying state regulations. For example, separate assessments are made for each parcel of real estate. What is a parcel? According to the state's manual for assessors, "There is no general definition of the term parcel for purposes of property taxation. If the assessors have a reasonable basis for their determination of what is a parcel, an assessment is valid." Addressing what they saw as certain anomalies in Town Hall records, the assessors began combining parcels and recalculating the amount of land assigned to the landowner's dwelling (the latter could not be included as part of the agricultural land that was set aside under state law for reduced taxation; shrinking the dwelling area could expand the amount of land that qualified under that law and reduce an owner's tax burden, redistributing it to other taxpayers in town).[31]

The plot thickened when the *Ashfield News,* the town's monthly newspaper, published a letter of resignation by an aide in the assessors' office. The writer was descended from one of the oldest families in town. There is a plaque in Town Hall honoring her grandfather's long service as town clerk. Over the years, her journalistic accounts of the most complicated and emotional issues in Ashfield politics had come to be touchstones, relied on for their solid information, insight, and balanced judgment. When she hinted, in her carefully worded letter, of dark goings-on in the assessors' office and declared her unwillingness to risk besmirching her family's name by association with them, no one knew exactly what to make of it, but many of us began to pay closer attention.

Bill Perlman, whom we have already met, was by this time back as chair of the select board after a brief hiatus. He determined to take the bull by the horns. He called Cranston before the select board, the one forum in town that is regularly covered by the press, and took him to task. It was an embarrassing ordeal for Cranston himself, not to say shameful for the other assessors, who were suspected, at a minimum, of neglect of duty and carelessness for failing to insist on posted meetings, informative minutes, and recorded votes.[32]

On one level, what we had here was a clash of cultures. Perlman, though a relative newcomer to town, had become thoroughly at home in Ashfield and had given generously of his time and energy, but he is also a modern, urban man. The spirit of modern American law and culture, for better and for worse, is in his bones. Open meetings are no problem for him; he loves them. Are people's foibles likely to be exposed? Bring it on. The assessors were men of a different culture. They believed they were entitled to respect for willingness to perform a valuable but difficult service. Many people are reluctant to serve in elective office, unwilling to endure the exposure and interference with their business interests. Cranston knew the sacrifices very well, not only of time and privacy, but of dollars and cents. As a veterinarian, he suspected that people had taken their business elsewhere because of opposition to decisions he made in public office, but he took the call of citizenship seriously.

In this instance, however, members of the board of assessors seemed to be taking actions that favored themselves at the expense of residents who owned less land than they. They may not have acted with that concern primarily in mind (knowing Cranston, most people found it hard to imagine that was the case), but it would in any case have been the consequence of what they were doing. Assessments are not about the amount of taxes to be raised; they are about the distribution of that burden. As a farmer, Cranston's livelihood is exposed to the vagaries of wind and weather. Farmers are favored by public policy, including the state law that allows them to pay lower taxes on agricultural land. Such laws express a widely shared sympathy and support for what farmers and farm families do and what it stands for, in terms of cherished ways of life and appealing landscapes. Even with this special treatment, however, farmers live a precarious existence, and some of them feel aggrieved.

Whatever one might have thought about the actions the board was taking, however, the changes in parcels and evaluations ought not to have been done without a full public vetting. The board should have held hearings and taken its decisions by recorded vote, in a well publicized meeting. The board had not sufficiently internalized the code of modern administration. It was painful to watch these men and their families exposed to the ruthless gaze of the press, but champions of the rule of law thought there was no alternative.

In December 2007, a special town meeting was called to consider whether the select board should henceforth appoint the assessors (until then, voters elected them). Many town boards are appointed by the select board: conservation, human relations, personnel. In the late 1990s (as we will see in chapter 6), the town converted several other key positions that were viewed as primarily administrative (town clerk, tax collector, treasurer) from elective to appointive.

The question at the 2007 special town meeting was whether the board of assessors was like these other positions: primarily administrative, rather than discretionary. The debate was well-informed and to the point. Cranston did not attend (he was out of town), and his fellow-assessors did not participate much. Perlman also laid low. The select board chair, Lynn Dole, bore the burden of advocacy. She cited a strong recommendation in favor of the change from the regional office of the state's department of revenue. But in Ashfield, that argument stood no chance against the contention that the town's voters were quite capable, through elections, of sorting through the troubles in the assessors' office and correcting them at the ballot box. (No member of the board of assessors who had been serving in 2006, when the disputed actions were brought to light, was still serving on the board in 2008. Two did not run for reelection, and one was defeated at the polls.) The turnout at the 2007 special town meeting was large and the meeting-room charged with emotion, but in the end, by a decisive margin, the proposed change was rejected. Existing procedures had brought the problems to light, and by existing procedures we would guide the board of assessors, reconstituted, if necessary, back to safe ground. We chose in this case to make the assessors directly accountable to the voters, rather than the select board.

Ashfield's social capital

There has been considerable attention lately, among social scientists, to the notion of *social capital* as an essential component of democratic politics. Robert Putnam and his associates have argued, for example, that Northern Italy has it, but Southern Italy does not. In a subsequent book, Putnam argued that the United States used to have it and needs to rebuild it.[33]

What is social capital, on which so much is said to depend? Where do we look for it, how do we measure it, and how is it nurtured or dissipated? Do we find it in bowling leagues, in Little League baseball tournaments, in the parish life of neighborhood churches, in clubs like Rotary and Zonta, in scout troops and the like? Do we look for it in organizations spring-ing up to accomplish ad hoc local projects? Or—especially if we are trying to measure a community's capacity for democratic politics—should we be focusing more specifically on political or governmental manifestations of the instinct to take collective action?[34]

Some inquiries looking for the building blocks of democracy have been broad and inclusive, apparently on the notion that habits developed in the broader social sector carry over into governing. Thus, if people are used to helping one another raise a barn or organize a library or manage the affairs of a parish church, they will develop social connections and skills that carry over into politics and governing. If people are used to banding together for informal projects and socializing, are they not more likely to do it in political life? And are they not likely to rise up in protest or rebel-lion if authorities interfere with their efforts to do that?

But does it actually happen that people trained in voluntary organiza-tions will demand a voice in public government? Can we depend on it? Isn't it possible that people will be neighborly and active in their local communities, but will be mystified about how to have a significant im-pact on local or national politics and gradually lose interest and compe-tence in more explicitly political activities? Unless there are institutions and practices to call them to effective action on public governance, they may begin to feel unengaged, incompetent, and ultimately alienated. To take an example, if we feel that a president's or vice president's consti-tutional doctrines undermine our liberties and drain our nation's moral authority, how can we resist them? How does involvement in a bowling league or church council prepare us for such a fight?

This book proceeds from the notion that governing is a unique form of communal action. It deals with the authoritative acquisition and alloca-tion of resources. It is by its nature coercive. Much depends on whether I think my taxes have been fairly levied, but even if I don't think they have been, I must pay them. If enough of us develop the opinion that our taxes are unfair or unduly burdensome, we may challenge them, in court or through political action. If that fails, and the mood spreads, there may be resistance, and ultimately revolution. This is fundamentally different from whether I choose to join a neighborhood movement to build a base-ball field. I may choose not to join the effort, and my neighbors may shun me for my standoffishness. But they cannot take my money or throw me in jail if I fail to show up for a working-bee on the project.

This is not to deny that there is a connection between a community's inclination toward social interactions and the strength of its political and governmental institutions. Gatherings around the stove at the Ashfield Hardware Store, at the bar at the Lake House, or for Friday dinner at Elmer's Country Store are important occasions in community life. When friends exchange local gossip on the telephone or at the convenience store, information is shared and important links are forged and fortified. There is no doubt that these contacts affect local politics, renewing it, shifting its center of gravity, engaging it with people's instincts and attitudes. But these contacts alone do not make Ashfield a democratic polity. Human beings have always gossiped about life unfolding around them. They did that beyond Eboli and in China during the Cultural Revolution, but no one finds models for democracy in these godforsaken places.[35]

Ashfield's "point of departure"

The Massachusetts Bay colony was a chartered company of the crown of England. As an entity within this framework, Ashfield, which was called Huntstown until 1765, from the start was under various legal and traditional obligations. For example, the provincial legislature oversaw and legalized the distribution of lots. When inhabitants came into contact with other communities—for example, to define the borders between townships—they looked to higher authority, the provincial legislature in Boston, for guidance and resolution. And, on one occasion, the colonial government in Boston sent a small detachment of troops to help defend the settlement from Native Americans.

As a practical matter, however, the town's first British inhabitants were not so much permitted as obliged to take many matters into their own hands. In most things—clearing land, raising houses and barns, exchanging commodities, building roads—as individuals, in households, and as a community, they were on their own. Each proprietor and his family acted for themselves, or they joined with neighbors to take common action. If such a group disagreed about how to proceed, decisions were made, as if naturally, by majority vote.

These settlers came from England. They brought with them certain ingrained habits of self-government at the local level. What is striking, however, is how readily they adapted to the environment they found in America.

Broadly, three forces shape a community's politics: the physical environment, the legal framework, and what Tocqueville called "the habits of the heart."[36] The American frontier in the mid-eighteenth century was physically challenging, marked by rocky soil, harsh winters, and a sometimes menacing indigenous population. The inherited legal framework was English, but in practice on the frontier, it is well characterized by Edmund Burke's term "benign neglect." Into that vacuum Ashfield's settlers moved, energetically and confidently, to build a community according to their own (developing, evolving) sense of fitness.

We will look more carefully at these founding conditions in chapters 1–3. They are important because they form the point of departure for town-meeting democracy as it is experienced in modern Ashfield.[37] A community's founding period is crucial. Attitudes and institutional features can be modified or even swept aside by subsequent events, but they leave an indelible mark on procedures, expectations, and attitudes, and thus exert an enduring influence. In Ashfield's case, it will be part of my argument that the town's roots in colonial New England continue to exert a powerful influence on life in this place, mostly for the good.

This book is built on two propositions: that we can learn a lot about how democratic government is established by examining its origin and foundations in colonial Huntstown and in late colonial and early national Ashfield, and that we can learn a good deal about the practice of democracy by examining its operation in modern Ashfield.

The three chapters in Part I recount the founding of Ashfield (as Huntstown) in the middle of the eighteenth century, examining the ad hoc creation of institutions of government, the conflict between Ashfield's Baptists and the Congregational establishment (in Ashfield and in the province), and the conduct of local government during the American Revolution and in the early national period.

I turn next to an account of Ashfield's transformation, presenting, in chapter 4, a sketch of major changes in its political culture since the founding period, particularly during the 1970s and 1980s. This sets the stage for Part II, where I present a portrait of the seat of government, Town Hall, and then, in five chapters, address some of the questions the town has faced:

Modernizing the structure of government: What happened to control by the people when we adopted reforms designed to produce greater efficiency?

Building a sewer: Can an assembly of the people direct a huge, technical project with reasonable efficiency? Can we tap expertise without losing control? Can we interact with state and federal bureaucracies productively?

Managing coercion: Can the people, acting together, manage the application of force, including violence, in their community?

Educating our children: Can we, in one small town, prepare our children for life in a global economy and culture?

Completing the foundation: Presented with a belated opportunity to establish a town common and provide for its preservation, can we, and should we, impose restrictions on ourselves without violating essential democratic principles?

In a concluding chapter, I consider the implications of democracy as practiced in this small town for the ideal of government of and by the people.

I
ORIGINS

1

Becoming Ashfield

"The past is a foreign country," an appropriate warning for anyone writing history, is particularly apt for Part I of this book.[1] Colonial New England is a foreign country for us, and not just in the technical sense that it was part of the British Empire. Modern observers must be careful about assuming we know it very well, no matter how many documents and books we have studied.

That said, we cannot avoid the effort of trying to understand it, because therein lie the origins of town-meeting democracy. Because those origins explain a great deal about how Ashfield developed, and they manifestly shape its present life, we need to explore them, learning what we can.

Democracy, within limits

In this book I argue that, for better and for worse, democracy—self-government by the people[2]—is a living reality in Ashfield (and in New England towns like it) perhaps more than anywhere in the world at any time in human history. Yet an examination of the history of Ashfield shows that the people of this place have not always controlled their own destiny. Authorities and events originating outside the town have regularly impinged, setting the framework and playing critical roles in shaping outcomes.

In the eighteenth century, the town did not have authority to call itself to a formal meeting. It could not establish a name for itself; to this day, the town bears a name apparently chosen by a royal governor to honor a friend back home in Britain (many of us think that is how Ashfield got its name; no one is sure). Such indignities are an integral part of the story of democracy in this place.

This pattern of limits was apparent from the first moments of the settlement called Huntstown that became Ashfield. People did not simply materialize here and begin governing themselves. When they came, they displaced other human occupants, and they occupied an entity established by law at the provincial capital in Boston. The legislature of the colony of Massachusetts, called the General Court, encouraged settlement by offering rights to land in exchange for soldiers' pay vouchers. The General Court directed that the town be divided into lots and authorized a drawing to distribute the lots to these ex-soldiers or their heirs, who were termed the "proprietors" of the lots.[3] When the proprietors got to quarreling about where their meetings would be held, the General Court intervened by transforming the "plantation" called Huntstown into a town called Ashfield and decreeing that the "inhabitants," not the lot owners, were the rightful constituents of its town meetings. Thus, from the beginning, sovereign authority impinged on the autonomy of both proprietors and settlers.[4]

How the town was planted

The proprietors of the plantation that would become Ashfield met in the 1730s at Weymouth, and later at Braintree, on the coast south of Boston. Weymouth is where Captain Ephraim Hunt had lived, and where, in 1690, he had recruited a band of men to join the colonial militia then seeking to drive the French from Quebec. In lieu of pay, the descendents of Hunt and his men were granted property rights to land in the western part of the colony. In 1739, descendents still living in or near Weymouth held a lottery (authorized by the General Court in 1736) to distribute ownership rights to particular pieces of the land that had been granted to their forebears. The sixty-three lots available at that meeting were in the northeast quadrant of town as it now exists, in the areas now called Baptist Corner and Beldingville.[5]

Gradually the most intrepid among these original lot-owners began to make their way across the commonwealth to scout their acquisitions.[6]

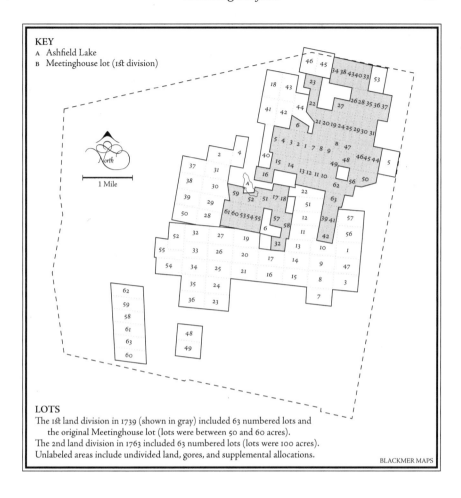

KEY

A Ashfield Lake
B Meetinghouse lot (1st division)

North

1 Mile

LOTS

The 1st land division in 1739 (shown in gray) included 63 numbered lots and the original Meetinghouse lot (lots were between 50 and 60 acres).
The 2nd land division in 1763 included 63 numbered lots (lots were 100 acres).
Unlabeled areas include undivided land, gores, and supplemental allocations.

BLACKMER MAPS

It was not an easy journey. From the Atlantic coast they made their way, either by foot or on horseback, via the Old Bay Path that led from Boston to Springfield. At Brookfield, well east of Springfield, they probably took a trail to the northwest. Many of those first settlers apparently sojourned with kin and friends in the Connecticut River valley, in Hatfield and Hadley, while laying plans to take possession of their lots in the hills to their west. Once ready to proceed, they crossed over the Connecticut River and then forward by marked trees, following the trail blazed by Nathaniel Kellogg, a surveyor, through Deerfield and what is now Conway, to their new property. There may have been a few meadows along the way, the

result of fires set by Native Americans as a hunting technique,[7] but mostly they hacked their way through forests broken only by native hunters,
wild animals, and men like Kellogg.

It is worth emphasizing, by the way, that the area they would be settling
may have been a howling wilderness, as they liked to claim,[8] but it was
certainly not uninhabited.[9] By delineating the differences between settler
and native practices regarding land tenure, the historian William Cronon
has brilliantly shown how colonial laws, practically self-evident to us in
their basic assumptions, were in fact cultural artifacts, and how they became a source of misunderstanding and conflict between the people who
dwelt here, natives and settlers side by side, in the seventeenth and eighteenth centuries. According to native concepts of property, land belonged
to extended families or tribes, and its use was regulated by agreement
between chiefs or sachems. Individuals did not "own" land, in our sense,
nor did tribes. They *used* it, by long-standing agreements with their neighbors. Mostly they used it for temporary lodging and for hunting animals:
deer, bears, wolves, beavers. Reconciling these practices with English notions of private property (owned by individuals, bought and sold, rented
or leased, by explicit contract, for a specific period of time) was not easy,
and it led to murderous misunderstandings.[10]

Not many colonials understood the ways of their neighbors or had
any sympathy for them. Roger Williams, the founder of Rhode Island,
was one exception. In his famous quarrel with the leaders of the Puritan
settlement of Massachusetts Bay, he insisted that title to the land obtained
by negotiation with Native Americans was better than one obtained by
grant from the British crown. The king had committed an "injustice, in
giving the Countrey to his English subjects, which belonged to the Native Indians." The native inhabitants, he argued, had rights derived from
first occupancy and from improvement of the land. They may have used
the land differently from the English: they did not do agriculture in the
European way. Who was to say that one "improvement" was better than
another? If these rights were to be questioned, Williams asked in a devastating twist of argument, then by what right did the king possess the vast
tracts of land reserved as royal game parks in Britain?[11]

Early English settlers in the hills of western Massachusetts often lived
in fear of their Native American neighbors.[12] A raid in June 1755 in Char-

lemont (about fifteen miles northwest of Huntstown) left two men dead, two taken captive, and the rest of the inhabitants thoroughly terrified. One settler escaped from the raid and ran to warn the settlers in Huntstown. The families who were already huddled there, about eleven of them, scurried to the relative safety of Deerfield, on the banks of the Connecticut River.[13] There they sojourned for several months, through the winter, before returning to Huntstown the following spring.[14]

It is not hard to sympathize with the fear of these white people, nor to admire their courage in returning. But the native people had fears of their own. Epidemic disease was one of them.[15] Native Americans, it turned out, had not developed immunities to European diseases. The consequences were felt as early as 1633,[16] when an outbreak of smallpox led to 95 percent mortality in some coastal native villages. Tuberculosis, influenza, and pneumonia tore through native communities like wildfire, and measles, syphilis, typhus, and dysentery wrecked havoc as well. The total population of Native Americans in New England, estimated at about 70,000 when Europeans began to establish permanent settlements, stood at about 12,000 a century later. New Hampshire and Vermont were virtually depopulated by the end of the seventeenth century.

The resulting "biological havoc" created a crisis for native society and culture that can scarcely be imagined.[17] Depopulation bred social disorganization. John Winthrop noted that Indians came to regard the Christian God as very powerful. Many promised to convert if they were spared. As few did survive, this was not a great boon for Christian evangelism. As Winthrop observed with pious satisfaction, however, the epidemics did "make room" for more immigrants and "cleared our title to this place."[18]

Thus it was a gravely weakened, dispirited group of Native Americans who inhabited the forests as English colonists made their way westward. That did not make them less frightening or dangerous, especially when they made common cause with other hostile elements before and during the French and Indian War (1754–1763).[19] A meeting of Huntstown proprietors in 1756 petitioned the General Court to send guards to protect the settlement from native raids. The authorities responded, tardily, with a detachment of about ten men, who stayed in Huntstown probably until 1759.

The first recorded meeting of Huntstown proprietors in western Massachusetts was held in the town of Hadley, about twenty miles southeast of Huntstown on the Connecticut River, on September 2, 1742.[20] During the 1750s, resident proprietors of Huntstown met from time to time in Hadley, or just across the river in Hatfield. Only scant records of these early gatherings survive.

The first proprietors' meeting in Huntstown itself was held in 1754. No record of this meeting survives, but the principal business was apparently determining the ownership of a sawmill. The second, in September 1760, resolved that future proprietors' meetings be held in Huntstown.[21] This was a power play, and consequences immediately followed. Meetings in Huntstown in the spring and summer of 1761 moved forward with plans for settlement, including road-building and the siting of the meeting-house—and, of course, levying taxes on proprietors (not residents) to pay for these improvements and facilities. A few proprietors were residents, but most were absentee landlords.

In September 1761, fed up with paying taxes for improvements far off in the forests, ones they would likely never see nor benefit from directly, the nonresident proprietors staged a counter-coup. At a town meeting held in Huntstown, the proprietors in attendance voted to hold "all future" meetings of Huntstown proprietors in Hatfield, twenty hard miles away.[22]

The meeting must have been stacked with nonresidents; people who lived in Huntstown would not have supported such an inconvenient location. It was difficult in those days to get to meetings within Huntstown, let alone from Huntstown to Hatfield. Trails through the forests were still primitive; so were the means of transportation, and public accommodations on the way were virtually nonexistent. Ashfield's history quotes the "first record of a road laid out in Huntstown":

> We met at [then contiguous] Deerfield, began at the east path, south from the top of Long Hill, which leadeth out to the old sawmill, and in said path until it comes to the path turning out northerly, commonly called Huntstown road, and on said road as it was marked by the town of Huntstown, and now commonly traveled, until it comes unto the west side of Deerfield bounds, and from thence in the northern road unto Thomas Phillips' house in Huntstown, and from thence as the road now goes to the west side of

said Phillips' lot, and from thence in a straight line to Richard Ellis' new house, from thence as the path now goes unto Meeting House hill [now Bellows Hill], unto a beech tree with stones around it, near Heber's[23] fence, the whole road to be ten rods wide.[24]

The decision to move future meetings back to Hatfield reflected a determination to wrest power from those who had already settled in the hills. It is not clear from the record what specifically drove the decision, but actions taken in Hatfield over the next three years indicate that the town's boundaries, the siting of the meetinghouse, and the levying of taxes were among the issues that agitated the men who owned stakes in Huntstown (see also chapter 2).

In December 1761, at the first meeting following the decision to return to Hatfield, the proprietors voted to proceed with the building of a meetinghouse and named a new committee to take charge of the project. The meeting was dominated by "Hatfield men," that is, proprietors who owned lots in Huntstown but had not moved to the hills.[25]

Two years later, in 1763, the proprietors conducted another lottery, this time in Hatfield, to distribute lots on the plain in Huntstown and to the south and west, and also to resell, at auction, land that had previously been claimed but not occupied, to recover delinquent taxes. The town's estimable historian, Frederick G. Howes, says that these buyers of the "second division" planned to build houses on the lots they purchased, move their families, and settle there themselves.[26]

The business of early town meetings

From the beginning, one great challenge of town government was to fill various elective offices. The warrant for the second town meeting after incorporation (in 1765) lists—besides the usual positions, such as selectmen, clerk, and treasurer—others, by title, such as clerk of markets, surveyors of wheat, clapboards, and shingles, field driver, "hoggrief" (hog officer), and fence viewer.

Some of the titles sound quaint, but these positions were vitally important in the colonial and early national period. When I was on Ashfield's select board, I expressed a desire to be the fence-viewer. I was teasing, but fences were no laughing matter in those early days. Hogs were essential to the eighteenth-century settlers of rural New England; they were marvelously fecund and easy to raise, and they could defend themselves against predators, like wolves and bears. If the owner marked their ears so they could be identified as his—the source of our word *earmark*—he could allow them to run wild, and they would feed themselves on anything in the forest. When he needed meat for his family, there they were. They did have some awkward qualities. They made an ugly mess of their surroundings. They frightened small children and elderly persons. And they had no respect for people's property. Unless restrained, they might eat a neighbor's carefully cultivated vegetables. The only way to prevent it was to build fences—to keep the pigs in, or to keep them out. But whose responsibility was that: the hog owner's, or the vegetable grower's? And how could anyone be sure whose pig did the damage, unless it happened to be caught *in flagrante?*

Colonists dealt with this problem in several ways: by declaring certain times when hogs were allowed to run free of confinement (usually during the winter months), and requiring that both hog-owners and vegetable-growers maintain good fences. This is where the fence-viewer came in. He inspected everyone's fences annually. If he certified that a farmer's fences were adequate, the farmer could recover costs against a hog-owner for his beast's depredations (assuming he could figure out whose animal did it).[27]

Another issue that agitated these early inhabitants concerned the boundaries of the plantation, particularly the line to the east, the border with Deerfield. The town boundary described in the original (1736) legislation was worse than ambiguous; it was physically impossible. It said that Deerfield's westward boundary lay nine miles west of the Connecticut River—but the Connecticut River meandered. Did the town's borderline meander with it? Furthermore, if you traced the town's boundaries from rock pile to maple tree and so on, in accordance with the legislation, you ended up not closing the figure, but a considerable distance from where you began.[28]

Clearly the matter needed to be readdressed. To clear up the mess, at a meeting in July 1762 the proprietors directed a committee of three men (Kellogg, Obadiah Dickinson, and Reuben Belding) to petition the General Court to confirm the existence of "the township of Huntstown so-called" and prepare for the legislature a clarification of the town's boundaries.[29] In January 1763 the committee submitted its petition to the General Court. It delineated a boundary with Deerfield that expanded Huntstown's area by moving the line one hundred rods (1,650 feet) to the east of the line contained in the act of 1736.[30]

In June 1765 the General Court accepted the survey presented by Kellogg and his associates.[31] Conway, at its centennial in 1867, heard a sour historical address by the Reverend Charles Rice, in which the learned divine asserted that "twice the Deerfield and Conway men got the worst of the matter in law and were compelled to draw in their lines." "Unquestionably," Rice concluded, "they were wronged." A few decades later, in his history of Ashfield, Howes coolly replies that a "disinterested committee appointed by the General Court," after thorough investigation, settled the matter in 1765, and writes that he could not see how "our good Conway neighbors can lay up anything against us for this."[32] It is hard to tell from the written record whether these disputants had tongue in cheek or still bore the ancient grudge.

Siting the meetinghouse

Another important matter left hanging during these early years was the location of the meetinghouse. The original 1736 grant from the General Court commanded the proprietors to build a "convenient Meeting House for the Publick worship of God." The proprietors resolved several times (in 1743, 1753, and May 1761) to satisfy this requirement, naming a succession of committees to oversee the project. Finally, at a meeting in Hatfield in December 1761 (the first meeting after the decision to move meetings there), they established a new committee and directed that the work proceed with dispatch, "to the best advantage of the proprietors." They also chose a new lot (lot 13, six acres) for the purpose, several rods south of the original lot designated for the meetinghouse.[33] In December 1765, meeting in Ashfield (after June 1765, we can finally use the town's modern name without anachronism), voters resolved not to revise the 1761 decision that the meetinghouse would be built on lot 13. In July 1766, the decision was again confirmed, and during the summer of 1767 the frame of the building was erected.

There was apparently still opposition to this site, however, and it was growing rapidly. The challenge stemmed from the fact that new settlers

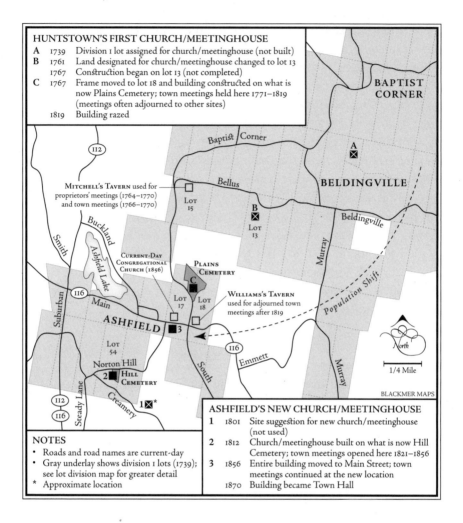

HUNTSTOWN'S FIRST CHURCH/MEETINGHOUSE

A 1739 Division 1 lot assigned for church/meetinghouse (not built)
B 1761 Land designated for church/meetinghouse changed to lot 13
       1767 Construction began on lot 13 (not completed)
C 1767 Frame moved to lot 18 and building constructed on what is
             now Plains Cemetery; town meetings held here 1771–1819
             (meetings often adjourned to other sites)
       1819 Building razed

BAPTIST
CORNER

Baptist Corner

112

MITCHELL'S TAVERN used for
proprietors' meetings (1764–1770)
and town meetings (1766–1770)

Bellus

BELDINGVILLE

LOT
15

Buckland

B

Beldingville

LOT
13

Smith

Ashfield Lake

CURRENT-DAY
CONGREGATIONAL
CHURCH (1856)

PLAINS
CEMETERY

Murray

116

Main

LOT
17

LOT
18

C

WILLIAMS'S TAVERN
used for adjourned town
meetings after 1819

Population Shift

Suburban

ASHFIELD 3

116

North

LOT
54

South

Emmett

Murray

1/4 Mile

Norton Hill

2 HILL
   CEMETERY

BLACKMER MAPS

112
116

Steady Lane

Creamery

1 *

NOTES
• Roads and road names are current-day
• Gray underlay shows division 1 lots (1739);
  see lot division map for greater detail
* Approximate location

ASHFIELD'S NEW CHURCH/MEETINGHOUSE

1 1801 Site suggestion for new church/meetinghouse
             (not used)
2 1812 Church/meetinghouse built on what is now Hill
             Cemetery; town meetings opened here 1821–1856
3 1856 Entire building moved to Main Street; town
             meetings continued at the new location
       1870 Building became Town Hall

were moving into the plains area (the geographical center of town, around the current Main Street) and to the south and west of it. Furthermore, by the 1765 act of incorporation, the inhabitants of the town had leverage over the absentee proprietors. Accordingly, on November 4, 1767, residents voted to meet the following morning at 8 a.m. at Samuel Lilly's house to inspect the site and then repair back to Joseph Mitchell's tavern at 11 o'clock to decide how to proceed. The next day voters rescinded the vote of 1761 and decided to move the frame from lot 13 to lot 18 and to build their meetinghouse there. A week later, the warrant for another town meeting (dated November 12, 1767) contained an article to "put a stop" to pulling down the frame "until further order of this town," but at the ensuing town meeting, the delaying article did not pass. Thus the building came to be set in what is now the Plains Cemetery.[34]

It had obviously not been easy for the town to decide on a site for its meetinghouse. Nor did the troubles end in 1767. Part of the difficulty was that the center of the town's population kept shifting to the south and west, and primitive transportation made it highly desirable for the meetinghouse to be located as near as possible to the center of the population. The other consideration was church politics. The meetinghouse by law served as the place of worship for the established (Congregational) church. As we will see in chapter 2, the town's Baptists resented having a new building erected for the Congregationalists. Chileab Smith, the Baptist leader, supported by his large extended family, was a formidable presence in Ashfield's politics throughout this founding period, and Chileab always welcomed an opportunity to keep the pot of religious controversy at a rapid boil.

The first town meeting after the town was incorporated in 1765 was held at Joseph Mitchell's tavern, on the east side of Bellows Hill (on what is now Bellus Road). Meetings continued there, in the tavern, until the new meetinghouse was partially finished, in January 1771. Thereafter meetings that began at the Plains meetinghouse would adjourn to a tavern, where a warm fire and spirits were available.[35] As it turned out, this building would serve as the town hall,[36] and the town would initiate its meetings there for at least fifty years (1771 to 1821), although the desire for better facilities was manifest continually, and with increasing intensity, from the turn of the century onward.

The center shifts

In 1801 the town established a committee to "fix a spot on which to set the new Meeting house." It was generally agreed that it should be placed as near as possible to the geographical center of the town, but where was that? Howes described the process for ascertaining it: "An inner circle was formed touching the outer lines of the town, and lines were drawn through the center of this circle to opposite sides." The exact center was

declared to be at the foot of a hill "just below the present creamery building," on what is now Creamery Road. That, however, was deemed not a
"favorable location," so the committee decided to place it on the "flat"
part of the plain, closer to what is now Main Street. But there was opposition to this location, too, so town meeting voted to leave it to a "disinterested committee of three persons" to decide the location. Men from
the neighboring towns of Hawley, Conway, and Plainfield were duly appointed. In a report dated February 20, 1812, they wrote, "Having closely
attended to the Business by viewing the various Roads and by hearing
various Pleas for and against the different contemplated Places," and
"viewing all matters on a fair and impartial scale," the committee chose
a spot that would "accommodate the various neighborhoods of town,
. . . should they exercise that Condescension Men and Christians ought
to do." The spot chosen was at what is now the cemetery on Norton
Hill, "near the Rev'd Mr. Porter's, where we have placed the stake." They
concluded their report prayerfully: "Wishing and hoping that all Party
Feeling may subside and that this Christian Society may be united in the
Bonds of Friendship, and love; and may live in peace; and that the God of
Peace may be with them here, and at last bring them to his holy Temple
in the Heavens."[37]

    If this report seems a bit pussy-footing (and note also the date of the
report, which indicates that it took over a decade to resolve the issue), it
must be remembered that the decision about the meetinghouse involved
many factors. The building would be used by a worshipping congregation; as the report of the "disinterested" committee put it, the building
was "for public worship." But it would be paid for substantially by town
appropriation.[38] Indeed, the meetinghouse that resulted from this report,
unlike many earlier meetinghouses in Massachusetts, would look like a
church. This architectural styling reflected a change in political culture
that was driven by religion: increasingly, parishioners wanted to banish
divisive political discourse from the place where they came together to
worship.[39]

    The contractor hired to build the new meetinghouse was Colonel John
Ames (sometimes spelled Eames), of neighboring Buckland, "a thorough
builder." He was already well known and admired for his church/town
halls in Marlboro and Northboro, Massachusetts, which were said to re-

flect the influence of churches built in London by Christopher Wren over one hundred years earlier.[40] High drama attended the Ashfield project throughout. Colonel Ames began work in 1812, before a "large concourse of people," but tragedy stalked this skilled craftsman. Four years earlier, in July 1808, he had witnessed the death of Horace Perkins, an eighteen-year-old Ashfield native who was working on the church at Northboro. Up on the bell tower, he lost his balance reaching for lumber being hoisted up to him on block and tackle. He fell headlong to the ground and died instantly. Ashfield's pastor at the time, the Reverend Alvan Sanderson, records in his diary that he "visited at Eliab Perkins', whose son Horace was last week killed . . . by a fall from a meeting house frame." In Ashfield, on September 13, 1813, Colonel Ames himself, "broken in health by hard labor, heavy responsibility and fear of [financial] loss," but with this project nearly finished, "committed suicide by cutting his [own] throat with a chisel in the back part of what is now the cemetery on the hill [now called the Hill Cemetery]."[41]

When it was done, the new building was truly magnificent. An anonymous woman's diary recorded her first impressions. "No meeting house in any of the surrounding towns could equal it in size or beauty. The beautiful and curious window at the west end, in back of the pulpit, was a marvel in our eyes. The height of the steeple—O, it was magnificent. The sweet tone of our bell—the sweetest ever heard by mortal ears. The man of iron at the highest point showing the direction of the wind, all, all ours."[42]

Hard quarreling

As if to mock such passionate delight, the handsome new church and meetinghouse soon became the locus of raucous conflicts.

In the early 1830s, Charles Knowlton, a recent graduate of Dartmouth's medical school, settled in town.[43] He was already notorious. In 1823 and again in 1824 he had been arrested for grave-robbing (he was digging up cadavers for medical research). He denied the first charge, but in the latter case, tried at Worcester, he was adjudged not guilty of robbing a grave, but convicted for illegal dissection and sentenced to two months in the county jail.[44] A few years later, while trying to set up a medical practice in North Adams, he had written a hefty tome titled *Elements of Modern Materialism*. It assailed what he saw as the humbuggery of prevailing Calvinist orthodoxy. He traveled to the eastern part of Massachusetts and as far west as Utica, New York, attempting to sell enough copies to cover the costs of printing his book. At Amherst, he was harassed by authorities for unlicensed peddling.[45]

In the early 1830s, as he began to establish a practice in Ashfield, he noticed that many young families needed sound information about human reproduction. To supplement his meager income (he had a growing family of his own), he wrote, self-published, and peddled in Ashfield and around New England and New York State a book called *Fruits of Philosophy*. Modern readers might regard such a title as disingenuous for a book about human reproduction and birth control, but it would not have surprised nineteenth-century readers, since the study of the physical sciences was still called "natural philosophy." Knowlton's purpose was the opposite of titillation. The subtitle of his book was "The Private Companion of Young Married People."[46] What he intended was to provide his patients and other readers with scientific information about a topic vital to their well-being. Nevertheless, his book aroused virulent opposition. In Needham, Massachusetts, he was arrested, tried, and sentenced to three months hard labor in East Cambridge prison for publishing and distributing immoral material. Despite such suppression, or perhaps in part because of it, his book sold three thousand copies in the first year and a half.[47]

In 1833, Ashfield's newly installed Congregational pastor, Mason Grosvenor, decried Knowlton's book as "injurious to the morals of the community."[48] From the pulpit, Grosvenor attacked the young doctor's "infidelity." The conflict between the two newcomers stirred passions to the point that another doctor in town, Jared Bement, a deacon of the church, exclaimed that there was not a person of calm nerves in the whole community. A large public meeting was called to air the controversy. When Knowlton rose to defend himself, he was shouted down and declared out of order. Pastor Grosvenor delivered a severe condemnation, whereupon another member, Nathaniel Clark, responded in Knowlton's defense. In the ensuing excitement, Clark and Knowlton were both expelled from the congregation. The matter was subsequently reviewed by a church council. It overruled the expulsions. Grosvenor left Ashfield two years later, and the controversy seems gradually to have blown over.[49]

Another sharp quarrel broke out among Ashfield's Congregationalists in 1840, this time over the choice of rival musicians to lead the choir. When no agreement could be reached, both leaders took up positions in the balcony and arrayed their supporters behind them. As the pastor called out the title of the first hymn, each leader chose a different tune, and both choirs began singing simultaneously. The resulting cacophony was so discordant that, after one verse, one choir left its seats. The conflict spilled over into the congregation, and for a time one faction seceded and held services elsewhere. Somehow a complete and lasting schism was averted at this stage.

In 1855, however, matters again came to a head, apparently over charges of irregularities in financial bookkeeping. An aged treasurer was accused of wrongdoing, and a deep rift developed between his accusers and defenders. The upshot was that a second congregation formed. In 1856 the new group built its own church on Main Street, in the center of town. (It is still there, as the Ashfield Congregational Church.) That same year, the board of the church on the hill decided to haul its magnificent building down to the village center, and to plant it on land sold to the church for a nominal sum by Knowlton's son, directly across the street from the rival Congregational Church.

To move such an enormous building across a hollow and down a long hill, perhaps a half-mile distant, was a project of almost unimaginable difficulty. Several contractors examined it but declined to bid on the job. Finally a man named Tubbs, from Springfield, accepted the challenge, for $700. He began work on May 15, 1856, following a late spring that year. He decided to move the whole building, without removing the spire. Logs fifty and seventy feet long and twelve inches thick were donated locally to serve as blocks and tracks. Tubbs underestimated the weight of the building; his apparatus broke several times and had to be rebuilt. As the building lurched down the hill, a heavy boat of stone was attached in the rear to keep the rig from moving too fast. Partway through the project Tubbs balked, refusing to continue unless the town obtained a pair of oxen for him to use. At first the committee refused, saying this was not part of the deal they had made, but finally they acquiesced, if Tubbs would supply the driver. At the bottom, Tubbs again suspended work and had to be paid an additional $80 to move the building onto its new foundation.[50]

When the move was finished, Ashfield found itself with two huge Congregational churches, directly across the street from one another. Ultimately the solution was to use the one on the south side of Main Street, the one newly moved there, for a new town hall. But the relocated building did not become Ashfield's town hall immediately.

In March 1858, two years after it came down the hill, town meeting appointed a committee to ascertain the expense of buying the basement of the relocated church for use as a town hall, and also to determine how much it would cost to build a new town hall from scratch. The committee soon reported: to purchase the basement of the relocated church would cost $500, plus $434.30 to prepare it for use as a town hall. A new building would cost an estimated $1,699.80. A motion to buy the basement failed, 134–142. Opposition came mainly from members of the breakaway Congregational church, who refused to support this windfall for the rival congregation.

Various other attempts ensued to purchase the relocated building, or some part of it, for a town hall. A major obstacle was removed when, in 1868, the two congregations were reunited. Still, it was not until 1870 that a deal could be put together. Nor was it accomplished easily even then. There is no record of the debate, but it is not hard to imagine how it went. On one side, people must have envisioned the glorious uses of the Wren-style building as a public facility; on the other side, people could not abide the thought that another congregation, their old rivals, might benefit from the transaction. The final vote in 1870 showed 94 in favor, 63 opposed. The resolution provided that the town purchase the whole of the old meetinghouse for $1,000, "provided that [the church] will throw in the bell and the four stoves connected with the building."[51]

Thus, deeply entangled strands of civic and church history, imperfectly separated, produced a pair of handsome buildings on Main Street, at the center of town. To this day, one of the finest features of annual town meeting is the luncheon served in the Congregational Church across the street from Town Hall. Its proceeds benefit the Hilltown Churches Food Pantry. Many people are happy to pay more than the stated price for a sandwich, hot soup, and a cup of coffee.

Where did the town meet?

There is one loose thread in this account of origins: where, between the Revolutionary War and the Civil War, did Ashfield hold its town meetings? The story is worth telling for the light it sheds on Ashfield's experience of the reform movements that swept America in the first half of the nineteenth century.

As I noted earlier, town meetings after 1771 usually began in the meetinghouse at the Plains Cemetery, although they soon adjourned to warmer, less austere quarters in a nearby tavern. So it continued for several decades. In 1820 town meeting asked innkeeper John Williams to furnish a place for the town to conduct its business.[52] He offered space in his tavern on Main Street, in rooms at the east end of his own dwelling place.[53] The rooms were spacious and the tavern centrally located. Town meetings in those days sometimes lasted for two or three days. Elections of town officers required a majority, and it often took several ballots to get one. Reports were not printed, but read. Discussions often "took a wide and sometimes unparliamentary latitude."[54] People who came from outlying areas sometimes needed to stay in town for the duration of the meeting, and the tavern offered a reasonably comfortable place to stay.

During the 1830s, however, a wave of agitation in support of the temperance movement swept over Ashfield. Dry versus wet supplanted Whig versus Democrat as the main source of division in town politics. In 1842 town meeting voted to direct the select board and constables not to allow the sale of liquor in town, and Ashfield became a dry town.[55] But in the preceding years, the intense feelings surrounding this issue surfaced in a series of maneuvers concerning the location and expense of town meetings. The temperance faction was strenuously opposed to holding town meetings in a tavern. Others resented the profits that Williams was making from the business that town meetings brought to his inn.

In 1837 Williams demanded to be paid for hosting the meetings. A report commissioned by town meeting concluded that he was not entitled to any payment. Williams renewed his demand. When a second committee recommended paying him, the report was accepted. At a subsequent town meeting, the order to pay him was rescinded. (There is no record that Williams ever recovered anything.) The outcome seemed to depend on which of these closely balanced factions rallied its forces to attend a particular meeting.

By the mid-1850s a consensus developed that the town needed a "new town house." In 1853, a committee was chosen to examine the possibility of using the local school, Sanderson Academy, which had been moved to the main street in 1817 (see chapter 9), for town meetings, but nothing came of that initiative. In 1856, as we have seen, the old Congregational Church was hauled from the cemetery on the hill down to the main street. Within two years (if not earlier in some minds), efforts began in earnest to purchase at least part of the newly relocated Congregational Church for use as a town hall. We have seen how those conversations, pursued in fits and starts over twelve years, made it possible, although just barely, for the town to purchase the whole building for its town hall. That marvelous building has served, from that day until now, as the locus of town meetings and government and generally as the heart of town life.

Where is the town common?

One enduring effect of these early conflicts between religious sects and maneuvers over where to locate the "publick meetinghouse" and how to pay for it is that Ashfield never developed a town common. Commons in many New England towns developed on the acres set aside for the meetinghouse. Because of the quarrels between the Baptists and the Congregationalists, and because the center of Ashfield's population shifted southward over the town's first three or four decades, there was no recognized and established town center until the middle of the nineteenth century. By then, there was no room on the main street for a common, no expanse of lawn or meadow beside the meetinghouse to set aside for grazing or public recreation. The breakaway congregation had built on the north side of the main street; Knowlton's gift was across the street. Neither site had room for a town common.

The problem was not addressed until the turn of the millennium. But that is another story. I will tell it in chapter 10, the last of our tales of modern governance.

2

Baptist Troubles

This book presents the governance of Ashfield as a significant example of democracy in action.[1] It should not come as a surprise, then, that a major episode from the founding period turned on a sharp clash between democracy and religious liberty.

Building a meetinghouse

The legislation that created the Huntstown plantation in 1736 directed that one six-acre lot be reserved as a home site for a "learned, orthodox" minister and another portion of the same size be dedicated to the support of his ministry.[2] It also required that the settlers build a meetinghouse to serve both as a place of worship and as the town's public meeting place. By law and custom, the siting of the meetinghouse was a matter for decision by the community at a town meeting, and its construction a public expense, paid for by taxes.

We've seen too that many early town meetings in Huntstown were devoted to the siting issue. The problem stemmed in part from shifting patterns of settlement, but at bottom it was a conflict between two religious communities, Baptists and Congregationalists. After several false starts, successive town meetings in July and August 1767 directed that the frame of the proposed meetinghouse, initially set up deep in what is now Baptist Corner, be picked up and moved to a new site in what is now the Plains Cemetery, nearer the center of town as it was developing. The building completed there remained the town hall, to the extent that Ashfield had one, until 1819. (See map, page 32.)

The question of taxes to finance the building of this "public meetinghouse" was complicated. It was not resolved until 1771, when King George III himself intervened against the town's majority and vetoed an act of the Massachusetts legislature. The drama pitted monarchical authority, defending religious liberty, against an act of the colonial legislature and the will of a majority of the people in Ashfield.

The story begins in 1740, when Chileab Smith, then in his early thirties and living with his mother in Hadley (his father had died when he was four years old), took the church establishment there severely to task for welcoming people into its congregation while they were still unconverted and living, as he put it, "under the power of a carnal mind." Appearing before the church council in Hadley, Smith railed that its members "were not living stones but dead in trespasses and sin." Such persons, he declared, did not belong in church; they were doomed to "perish eternally."[3]

Some who attended that meeting, he later recalled, "were for dealing with me" on the spot, but finally they let him go. He went to Huntstown, where he found his new neighbors as indifferent to religion as his old ones were. He began talking fervently to them about his religious convictions and inviting them to meetings in his home. By 1750, almost everyone then settled in Huntstown, about fifteen families, decided to organize themselves into a religious association, subscribing to the tenets of Anabaptism, that is, rededication and baptism of adult believers by immersion.

All eight of Chileab Smith's children and most of his new neighbors were of this persuasion. Chileab's son Ebenezer read the Bible enthusiastically, as well as other "good books," thereby acquiring, as his father put it, "head knowledge" to go with the passion in his heart for Jesus Christ. Soon Ebenezer began testifying at religious services. In 1761 the Baptists in Huntstown unanimously chose Ebenezer as their pastor.[4]

Most of Huntstown's earliest settlers, under Chileab Smith's energetic influence, were, or soon became, Baptists. They were also the first group in Huntstown to organize themselves into a congregation. By 1761 fourteen of the nineteen families in town belonged to or attended Smith's Baptist congregation.[5] It therefore seemed natural and right to them that the lots dedicated by the General Court's statutory grant to support religion should go to them. Operating on this assumption, town meetings held in Huntstown in 1760 and the spring of 1761 organized committees to build the meetinghouse and to levy taxes on the proprietors to pay for it.

In September 1761, the Hatfield faction reacted. As we saw in chapter 1, the proprietors' coup against the residents aimed at regaining control over the development of Huntstown. Stacking a meeting at Richard Ellis's house in Huntstown, they voted to hold future proprietors meetings in Hatfield. Given the distances involved (a full day's journey over primitive roads), this maneuver swung the balance of power from the Baptists in Huntstown to the so-called "Hatfield men," who were, not incidentally, predominantly Congregationalists. The consequences were immediate. In December 1761, in Hatfield, the proprietors voted to proceed with building a meetinghouse and named a committee, dominated by "Hatfield men," to oversee the project.

In 1762 a plaintiff (unnamed, but presumably not a Baptist) challenged the town's assessors for failing to impose taxes on the Reverend Ebenezer Smith, Chileab's son. (Legally recognized ministers were exempt from town taxes.) The case was tried in Springfield, where Israel Williams was chief judge.[6] Williams, who was also a member of the colonial legislature, was a hard-knuckle political boss. The Baptists had no chance in his court. Huntstown's assessors were found guilty, fined £40, and denied appeal to a higher court.[7]

Questions about tax exemption

To understand what was happening here, we must first look at a statute passed by the Massachusetts colonial legislature in 1720. It exempted Quakers, Anglicans, and Baptists from taxation by towns to support the established Congregational church. But so-called Separate Congregationalists (also known as Separatists) occupied a gray area. They dissented from mainstream Congregational doctrine about infant baptism. Nevertheless, authorities in the colony, tending to regard them as tax-dodgers, generally did not grant them tax exemption. In the late 1740s Baptists began to accept Separatists into their own flock. This was the background of the 1762 case in Williams's court, and it explains both his brusque dismissal of the Baptists' claim and their outrage at this treatment.

At this time new settler-families were steadily making their way to the hills.[8] In 1763 there was another sale of lots in Huntstown, the so-called second division. Included in the auction were lots that had been seized from Baptists for failure to pay taxes. Congregationalists, members of the established church of the colony, were increasing in numbers in Huntstown and beginning to get organized. In December 1762 the proprietors called a young man named Jacob Sherwin, who had graduated from Yale in 1759, to "settle with them in the work of the ministry." On February 22, 1763, a Congregational church was formed. The following day the church's elders ordained Sherwin and officially called him to be their pastor.[9]

When Huntstown became incorporated as the town of Ashfield in 1765, one might have assumed that people who regarded themselves as Baptists came under the 1720 statute that granted tax exemption to Quakers, Anglicans, and Baptists. Ashfield Congregationalists, however, took Judge Williams's position. Chileab Smith and his co-believers were seen as tax-dodgers. The legislature in Boston took a similar position. In 1768 it passed an amendment to the statute that incorporated Ashfield. It declared that Ashfield's Baptists were not exempt from taxes that supported the town's Congregational church and its minister.

Each church, Baptist and Congregational, now claimed that the lots set aside in the original grant for the town's minister rightfully belonged to its pastor, not the other fellow. By now, Congregationalists outnumbered Baptists, and they were strongly supported by the nonresident proprietors. From their standpoint, Ebenezer Smith was simply not qualified to be the "learned, orthodox minister" that the law required. They voted that the lots in question go to Sherwin, and they levied taxes on all property-owners to build the church he would serve and to pay his salary.

Chileab Smith was not a man to take such treatment lying down.[10] Frederick Howes would later glorify him by quoting a few lines from Gray's "Elegy Written in a Country Churchyard" about John Hampden, who, "with dauntless breast," gave his life fighting for the parliamentary cause against Charles I.[11] Polite opinion among the Congregationalists in the 1760s was less flattering. Many of his fellow townsmen viewed him as a quarrelsome old crank. As for Chileab, he had taken the measure of this gang of thieves while still a young man in Hadley. He had gotten to Huntstown first. He and his sons were not Yale graduates, but they knew their Scripture, and, unlike their Congregationalist antagonists, they strove to apply its precepts literally. They would be damned if they would pay for the upkeep of an establishment of unredeemed, unrepentant sinners.

This raucous dust-up between neighbors in a tiny town on the raw frontier of the colony soon caught the attention of the provincial legislature in far-off Boston.[12] For five years after Sherwin was hired, Baptists were dunned for taxes and their properties seized and sold at auction to pay his salary and build a meetinghouse that Congregationalists alone used as a house of worship. In May 1768 Smith and his fellow Baptists, furious about this treatment, petitioned the legislature for relief. Smith later claimed that, when the legislators heard his story, they asked why he had not complained long before. They sent him home to notify the town clerk in Ashfield that the proprietors must show cause why the Baptists' petition should not be granted, and that the collection of taxes and confiscation of property would be suspended until the controversy was resolved.

Before Smith could get back to town with his message, however, the colonial legislature, under Israel Williams's heavy influence, passed an amendment to the act of incorporation that empowered the proprietors to lay and collect such taxes as necessary to complete the building of the meetinghouse and for the settlement and support of the minister the proprietors had chosen. Men like Chileab Smith tend to hear people say what they wish they had said, and certainly there were men (like Joseph Hawley, of Northampton, Williams's bitter foe) who must have encouraged Smith's sense of outrage, which was easily kindled. In any case, by the time he got back to Ashfield, Smith believed that he had been double-crossed.

It became Smith's understandable obsession to get this new law repealed. Many pages of the pertinent volume and section of the Massachusetts Bay Province Laws are given over to recording petitions from Ashfield's Baptists and their sympathizers, and replies from the proprietors. The editor of these state documents loftily remarks that, although "repetitious, and, generally, written by illiterate persons in humble life," they deserve to be printed because of the significant part they played in securing "that religious liberty which, to-day, is the boast of our commonwealth."[13]

The authors may have used unorthodox spelling, but they were certainly not illiterate. The petitions from Ashfield clearly and powerfully express the grievances of Chileab and Ebenezer Smith, not to mention the disdain of the responding proprietors. The Smiths argue, in a petition dated 1769, that at the time their minister was ordained and called to be their pastor, in 1761, members of their congregation constituted "by far" a majority of the inhabitants of the town.[14] And so, they write, they set about building a meetinghouse on the lot designated for that purpose. They were forced to desist, they report, when a number of men of "contrary persuasion" (that is, Congregationalists) moved to town and, assisted by the nonresident proprietors, overpowered them in voting and raised large sums of money by taxation to build another meetinghouse and call and settle their own minister.[15] Though the 1765 charter of incorporation granted a considerable tract of land to the first minister to settle in town, the petitioners wrote, these new men and their allies among the nonresident proprietors seized the designated land and put their minister on it. Now they continued to levy taxes and to sell the Baptists' lands at auction, yet not one penny of the proceeds went for the meetinghouse of the aggrieved petitioners. Thus the Baptists were impoverished and their property seized to support a society they did not belong to.

The proprietors fired back. "Your excellency and honours," they wrote, "cannot rightly judge [this cause] unless the real character and true springs of action of the people professing themselves baptists in this part of the country in particular (we profess not to be acquainted with others) are fairly laid before you." These were the people originally called Separatists. The cause of their separation was, "with some . . . an unconquerable desire of being *teachers,* a privilege or indulgence which could be no otherwise insured to them, but by a disorderly separation from the churches to which they belonged and setting up a meeting of their own." Some had been forced to leave churches because they were guilty of offenses and refused to accept the punishment. Others "have had the effrontery to say, that the standing ministry is corrupt," that other ministers are unconverted, that other churches are impure and unholy, that they admit unconverted and unsanctified persons into their communion, and so forth. In short, these churches or meetings "or whatever else they might be called . . . have been a kind of receptacle for scandalous and disorderly christians" and may "with some degree of propriety, be considered as a sink for some of the filth of christianity in this part of the country." "Thus pride, vanity, prejudice, impurity and uncharitableness seem to have originated, and . . . supported a sect so pure that they cannot hold communion with ordinary christians." Surely everyone understood that government ought not to interfere with religion "farther than to *secure* the good and prevent the ill effects of it to the state." But whenever the actions of a religious community threaten mayhem, it becomes a proper object of the legislature's attention. "Of this kind, most evidently, is that religion which rejects men of learning and ability for teachers, and altogether chooses such as are illiterate and men of ordinary ability."[16]

Mercifully, another document in this collection shows that not everyone in Ashfield agreed with the authors of this broadside. A statement signed by twelve men declared that they had "no objection" to the Anabaptist society "being set free from paying to the maintenance of the other worship which they do not belong unto."[17]

The legislative committee that received these dueling documents recommended that the petition of the Baptists be dismissed. Affirming the freedom of every man to worship according to the dictates of his conscience, the committee nevertheless found no unfairness in the sale or disposition of Baptists' lands, nor in the community's levying taxes for the purposes in question. The full House of Representatives, however, did not concur with the committee's recommendation. It directed a new committee to prepare a bill to repeal the act of 1768 that directed action against the Baptists.

The final step in the legislative process belonged to the governor's council, a kind of upper house. The council ruled in favor of the proprietors, reaffirming the act of 1768. Thus, after a tortuous ordeal, the Baptists' quest to be rid of this burdensome tax seemed doomed. In the following year, 1770, the proprietors sold 398 acres of the Baptists' lands to cover delinquent taxes.[18]

But wait! This was the eve of the American Revolution, the kind of time when clever people delight to fish in troubled waters. Governor Thomas Hutchinson (a loyalist, appointed governor by King George III, and scourge of the Patriot faction in Boston) apparently sympathized with the rustic Chileab and Ebenezer Smith.[19] Or perhaps, besieged as he was by Sam Adams and his band of ruffians, Governor Hutchinson welcomed an opportunity to strike an ironic blow against his tormentors by rising in defense of religious liberty. Examining the legislation, he noticed that the original grant mentioned land for the establishment of Christian ministry, but nothing about ongoing support. He called this finding to the attention of a member of the legislative committee that had favored the Baptists' appeal and urged him to send the matter to a man in London who might be willing to present it to the king in council for review. Governor Hutchinson also promised to write a letter himself to Sir Francis Bernard, who, while serving as the royally appointed governor of Massachusetts from 1760 to 1769, had approved the 1768 act. In light of this new situation, Bernard might be willing to use his influence to have it vetoed by the king.[20]

In London, the Baptists' cause was taken up by Dr. Samuel Stennett. Educated in Scotland, Stennett was the poet of such hymns as "On Jordan's stormy banks I stand" and "Majestic sweetness sits enthroned upon the Saviour's brow." He was then pastor of a Baptist church in Little Wild Street, in London, and he seems to have had good access to the king's circle. His petition to the Privy Council recounted the controversy, with his own spin. The legislation creating the town of Ashfield, he wrote, had included the condition that the settlers must build a "meeting place and support an Indipendent [sic] minister." In 1765, he wrote, there were seventeen families living in Ashfield, twelve of them Baptist. The Baptists immediately established a church. Shortly thereafter, the "Indipendents" did, too, and began requiring the Baptists to support "*their* minister." This, he reported, was arguably agreeable to the original charter of 1765, but it was contrary to a "general law freeing Baptists and Quakers from taxation to support other churches." The act of 1768, he wrote, emphatically exhibited the grievance that Baptists were complaining of: it called for their property to be sold for delinquent taxes. The Baptists had petitioned the legislature for repeal of the 1768 act, but unsuccessfully. Stennett now called upon the king to veto the 1768 act, and speedily, because the time for disallowing it had nearly expired. On July 31, 1771, the king disallowed the 1768 act and ordered the "governor, lieutenant governor and commander in chief of his majesty's province of Massachusetts, and all others whom it may concern, to take notice and govern themselves accordingly."[21] In October 1771 the Baptists' confiscated lands were duly restored.[22]

Thus at the splendid Court of St. James's in London ended a quarrel between farmers in a frontier settlement in rural western Massachusetts. And thus was put in place an important milestone on the road to religious liberty.[23] The right not only of Baptists, but members of any religious denomination in the commonwealth (including Quakers), not to be taxed to support churches they did not belong to was strongly reaffirmed, and legislation to the contrary, including the act of 1768, was disallowed. Ebenezer Smith later claimed that only three persons in America (he does not say who they were) knew that there had been an appeal to London. The records of the Baptist church contain only a brief mention: "In October 1771, we were set at liberty by the King of Great Britain and our lands restored."

Did the Baptists in gratitude become loyalists, taking Britain's side in the coming Revolution? There is no evidence of that. On the contrary, in a town that was quick to sniff out sentiments hostile to the cause of the Revolution, Chileab Smith was never cited among the suspects, and several times thereafter he was elected to public office, including the select board.[24] Apparently this episode instead supports the observation that those who benefit from a political favor are rarely grateful to their benefactors. They believe they got only what was rightfully theirs.

How about the local Congregationalists? Was this episode a major grievance for them? Did it reinforce their resentment of distant, ignorant authority? Did the effort to force Ashfield's dissenting Christians to pay for the Congregational religious establishment end here? Unfortunately there is no evidence on these points, either.

The growth of liberty is often dependent on ironic triumphs. King John struggled to repudiate the promises wrung from him in Magna Carta. The triumph of Ashfield's Baptists was likewise full of ironies. Baptists were freed from paying for churches they refused to attend, but the majority in Ashfield was frustrated in its effort to build the community its own way. Ultimately, the triumph for liberty would contribute to the momentum that broke the hold of religious leadership and led eventually to a thoroughly secular community. From Chileab Smith's point of view, that may have been the crowning irony.

Those who disapproved of Chileab Smith and his family and friends— that is, the proprietors of Hadley and Huntstown/Ashfield—behaved badly. Several times in the course of their confrontations with him they sought to preserve their own power, choosing order and decorum over Christian charity. Having run him out of Hadley, they confronted him again in Ashfield. He taunted them, punctured their vanity, challenged their authority, showed them little respect and no deference, and they responded vengefully.

The town's records, and those of the Baptist congregation, afford several insights into the character of this man and the challenge he presented. In 1753, when he gathered the Baptists of Huntstown at his home and started a community of the converted, he was forty-five years old. His son Ebenezer was nineteen. Eight years later, the Baptists named Ebenezer Smith their pastor. The controversy with the proprietors took place in the 1760s, culminating in the king's veto in 1771. By now, Chileab was sixty-three. Along the way, he was elected to the select board in 1762, 1766, and 1767. Another of his sons, Chileab Smith Jr., was elected to the select board from 1784 to 1787, and again in 1789, 1791, 1792, 1800, and 1801.[25]

In 1785 Chileab and Ebenezer, father and son, fell to quarreling. The issue was whether Ebenezer should be paid for his work as pastor. The son insisted that he should have a fixed salary.[26] His father replied that ministers should not be hirelings; they should preach and minister out of love for God and His flock. The dispute was referred to neighboring Baptist congregations for advice. Finally an appeal was made to the regional association of Baptist churches in Worcester. After hearing both sides, the association ruled that Ebenezer was entitled to compensation and should be paid for his labors to date, and either be continued on the same basis or dismissed. The congregation in Ashfield refused to accept this ruling. On January 24, 1787, they "considered the result of the council before mentioned and found that it wanted the testimony of Scripture for its support" and concluded that the only way they could follow this ruling was if they were willing to ignore God's word. This they refused to do, "for many obvious and Scriptural reasons." An entry in the church's record for August 29, 1788, notes that, "Elder Smith and his party having taken from us our meetinghouse . . . and the Association, on hearing his story, having dropped us from that body," Chileab's group had no alternative but to find another place to meet.

Chileab set about organizing another church. On January 14, 1789, he and Enos, another of his sons, were ordained as elders and joined with other Baptists in neighboring Buckland to build a simple one-story church a few rods north of the Ashfield line. The two Baptist congregations remained separate for seven years. In 1796 Chileab's group removed its meetings to the Ashfield Baptist meetinghouse, and in 1798, the breech was apparently healed. Chileab Sr. died two years later, at ninety-two.[27] Ebenezer became an itinerant preacher and ended up in Stockton, New York, in 1816. His brother Enos continued as pastor of the Baptists in Ashfield until the 1820s, living to the end by his father's ideal of taking no regular pay for his service but accepting only voluntary contributions for his preaching.[28]

The conflict between denominations in Ashfield over support for the Protestant establishment raises hard questions about democracy, its origins, and the habits of mind that sustain it. We believe now that churches must not impose their will on the community; that was certainly Chileab Smith's conviction.[29] But it is sometimes at odds with majority rule, as it was here. King George III ruled in favor of liberty, against the democratic will of the people on the ground. Joy in Baptist Corner must have echoed the chortling at the Court of St. James's. But last laughs were still coming. King George would not be able much longer to impose his royal will on his subjects in Massachusetts. Baptists in Ashfield would find that Christ's kingdom of redeemed, converted Christians was an elusive goal as well. Events would spin on, out of the control of either of these triumphant celebrators in 1771.

From time to time the people of Ashfield have gained understanding of the requirements of democratic governance through trial and error. That is a major theme of this book, and this was such a moment. Here, by majority rule locally and with the support of legislative authority in Boston, they were trying to establish and defend their own power. Doing so required trampling on the rights of an obnoxious minority, which they were quite prepared to do. But if democracy was to endure, the majority's iron rule had to be broken. That it fell to a distant monarch to do it seems ironic, but elites have often played a key role in establishing the foundations of liberty and democratic government.

Can democracy establish a foothold, and can it endure, without certain "habits of the heart," values and institutions left as a legacy by Western culture? And what happens to democracy when those foundations erode? New England's ruling powers were often bigoted, imperious, patriarchal, and prone to abuses of liberty when protecting their own preeminence. They had to be monitored and countered. Sometimes it was bearers of more universal, secular, fair-minded values who opposed them. More often, tolerance came not from the desires or action of any particular group, but from the clash of competing groups.[30]

Eventually the hold of Puritanism was broken, but what cultural norms took its place? Are these new values altogether benign? And do they have any depth, any vitality? What further ironies, what unintended consequences, lie in wait for us on the road ahead?[31]

3

Governing through
a Revolution

War, particularly a civil war, presents a difficult set of challenges for democratic government. People must decide which side they are on, how far they are willing to push their convictions, and what to do with those who disagree. When the stakes are high—when the aim of war is a revolution in political allegiances—strains accumulate. The longer the war drags on, the harder it is for revolutionaries to maintain the necessary discipline.

Just one short decade after people of European background began to build houses in what became Ashfield, the people of this frontier settlement found themselves struggling for independence from the powerful, dangerously angry British empire. The looming clash had profound effects in the town: able-bodied men marching off down primitive roads to do battle in faraway places; deputations sent to distant armories to procure weapons and ammunition; town meeting levying steep taxes to support the town's soldiers and jailing neighbors suspected of disloyalty to the cause.

The people of Ashfield could have had only a dim understanding of the clash of sovereignties that engulfed them: the patronizing attitude of contemptuous British governors, the ambitions of the men in Boston, New York, Philadelphia, and Tidewater Virginia who led them, the opportunism of their French allies, and the shifting allegiances of their native neighbors. What they did deeply understand, however, was the political theory of republicanism. Ideology is sometimes a treacherous guide in international relations, but in this case republicanism served them pretty well. It was not the same as democracy, where voters themselves make the laws that bind them. The founding men of Ashfield knew democracy from personal experience. Republicanism was a theory. It rested on the notion (as James Madison once put it) that one was not obliged to obey laws if one had no part in their making, usually through accountable representatives. Eighteenth-century Anglo-Americans struggled over the meaning of that doctrine in practice; the American Revolution was one great testing ground. The formula "No taxation without representation" captures its meaning for colonial leaders. But the devil was in the details. Who was entitled to be represented? Could representation be virtual? What obligations did representatives owe to their constituents?

Ashfield's naming and incorporation as a town in June 1765 came in the aftermath of the conflict known in America as the French and Indian War, which ended in 1763. This war had clarified the burdens of Britain's empire in North America and brought an abrupt end to the imperial policy of "salutary neglect." British politicians, including King George III, his counselors, and his ministers in Parliament, were determined that their American colonies cover more of the costs of this empire. The infamous Stamp Act of 1765 reflected this new policy.

The records of life in colonial Ashfield during the decade between the Stamp Act and the outbreak of open warfare in the mid-1770s are not abundant. It is often difficult to tell how much they knew and exactly how they reacted to the events that led them to join in declaring independence. But there are, in Ashfield's case, clear public records that show they shared the general colonial fury over new British taxes and alarm over the heavy-handed enforcement of these levies, including the landing of British troops in Boston in 1768. The "massacre" of five civilians by British troops in Boston in March 1770 might have been far enough away that it did not frighten them much, but it surely made them furious. When a band of men in disguises dumped taxable tea into Boston harbor in December 1773, people of conservative temperament in the Connecticut River valley may have fretted about the spread of anarchy, but most people on the western frontier cheered the audacious prank.

The brutal and ignorant response of the authorities in London to these acts of resistance sealed the commitment to revolution on the

New England frontier. In March and May 1774, Parliament in an angry mood passed a set of measures known collectively as the Coercive Acts. In America they quickly gained the sobriquet Intolerable Acts. The acts closed the port of Boston and prohibited the loading or unloading of any ships, except those bearing military supplies for British forces, until the owners of the East India Company had been compensated for their losses at the Boston Tea Party. Undermining trials by jury, they authorized the governor (appointed by the crown) to remove to Britain any trial of a British military officer for acts committed in putting down a riot or collecting revenue. The governor had only to certify that the accused officer could not obtain a fair trial in the colony.

Most deeply resented and alarming was the Massachusetts Government Act, passed in May 1774. It virtually annulled the existing frame of government, based on the province's 1692 Second Charter. Henceforth the council (the upper house of the provincial legislature), previously chosen by the retiring members of the council and the newly elected House of Representatives, would be appointed by the king and hold office at royal pleasure. The governor, a royal appointee, would nominate the chief justice for appointment by the king. Juries were to be summoned by the sheriff, rather than elected by the towns. A final measure closed a forum so effectively exploited by the Adams cousins and their radical allies in Boston: it provided that no town meeting, other than the annual meeting to elect officers, could be held without prior written consent of the governor, and all town meetings had to be confined to the agenda he approved.

The Massachusetts Government Act struck at the heart of life in small towns like Ashfield. Hardly anyone in town, whatever he may have thought of some of the shenanigans in Boston, could have supported it. Nothing, not even the criminal acts of rebels in the colony's capital, could justify the suspension of the right to conduct essential communal business at a meeting called by the town's elected officials. What were those people in London thinking? While that law was on the books, practically everyone in Ashfield would have been ready to take up arms in support of resistance to British tyranny.[1]

In September 1774 the first Continental Congress assembled in Philadelphia. In that same month, the people of Ashfield took their own first, decisive step toward revolution. Sixty-five men put their names to a covenant that outlined the position of the revolutionaries. Basing their declaration on the dictates of self-preservation and "natural conscience" and on a sacred regard for the laws of "our country," they acknowledged themselves "subjects of our Sovereign Lord the King" (this from folks who had just had to restore land to the Baptists, by the personal order of George III!). Immediately, however, they qualified their fealty by proclaiming themselves "duty bound to yield obedience to all his good and wholesome laws."[2] Needless to say, such a guarded expression was completely unacceptable from the British point of view.

The assembly then proceeded to "bear testimony against" the oppressive laws of the British Parliament, whereby their chartered privileges were cashiered. Nor would they engage in any trade with Great Britain "until she withdraws her oppressive hand." Further, they would join neighboring towns and their sister colonies in America in contending for and defending their rights, "civil and religious," and would make preparation to equip themselves with "ammunition and other necessaries," at town cost.

The final clause of Ashfield's 1774 covenant was cryptic and, in the context, a bit anomalous. The signers pledged to do "all we can to suppress petty mobs, trifling and causeless."[3] It is not clear what this meant. Were there offending parties in Ashfield? Or was this a warning to rioters elsewhere, not to push their advantage or take the opportunity to settle private scores? Similar clauses were adopted by other western towns, reflecting the continuing weight of conservatives (sometimes known as "river gods," for the power they wielded in Springfield, Hatfield, Deerfield, and other towns along the Connecticut River) at town meetings.[4] There were no river gods in colonial Ashfield, but men like Samuel Belding, who held a royal commission as justice of the peace, and Lieutenant Phillip Phillips, who as an officer in the king's army had sworn to support the crown, might have shared the alarm felt by the river-bottom aristocrats at the radical turn that events had taken.

At any rate, what is notable is that the sixty-five Ashfield men who signed their names to this revolutionary act in 1774 committed a flagrant, public act of treason. If the Patriots had not won the war for independence, one wonders what might have happened to these brazen farmers. It was not a light thing they did. When Benjamin Franklin, America's most seasoned diplomat, remarked that if the American revolutionaries did not hang together, they would most assuredly hang separately, he was not kidding.

Toward Lexington and Concord

Over the ensuing winter of 1774–75, British authorities and provincial leaders moved by fits and starts, but with gathering momentum and inexorably, toward open hostilities. The preceding summer, General Thomas Gage had replaced Thomas Hutchinson as governor of Massachusetts Bay Colony. On the very day Gage arrived to take up his duties, May 13, 1774, a town meeting in Boston called for economic sanctions in an attempt to compel Parliament to repeal the Coercive Acts. On September 17, the First Continental Congress, meeting in Philadelphia, endorsed the Suffolk Resolves. Drafted by Joseph Warren and adopted a week earlier by a convention in Massachusetts, the resolves declared that the Coercive Acts were unconstitutional and as such null and void. They urged the people of Massachusetts to form a government to collect taxes and withhold the proceeds until the Coercive Acts were repealed, and they urged the people to take up arms and form their own militias.

These acts of open defiance and rebellion confronted Britain with a challenge to authority that could not be ignored. As the storm was gathering, British troops marched from Boston out to Charlestown and Cambridge and seized cannon and gun powder that belonged to the province. Thousands of militiamen swarmed to Cambridge, but the British were apparently not quite ready for open hostilities. General Gage expanded fortifications in the Boston harbor to enforce the British blockade, but he did not otherwise order a show of force.

On October 7 the Massachusetts House of Representatives met in Salem, constituted itself a Provincial Congress, and named John Hancock to head a committee of safety, with power to call out the militia. It directed that special groups within the militia be designated Minutemen and make ready for instant call. In mid-December, warned by Paul Revere of a British plan to seize military stores at Portsmouth, New Hampshire, militiamen overpowered a small garrison on guard and carried off arms and gunpowder. Rebellion was loose in New England; insurgents were arming themselves for deadly combat.

In February 1775 the British began to confront the uprising directly.
Parliament, formally declaring that Massachusetts was in a state of rebellion, forbade the colonies of New England to trade with any nation
but Great Britain and barred colonial mariners from the North Atlantic
fisheries. Meanwhile, a second Provincial Congress that had convened in
Cambridge on February 1 adopted measures to prepare for war. Later
that same wintry month, British troops marched to Salem, intending to
seize military supplies, but were turned back without violence.

Meanwhile, leaders to the south were taking notice of the fracas in
New England. On March 23, Patrick Henry gave his famous "liberty or
death" speech before the Virginia House of Burgesses meeting at St.
John's Church in Richmond. In it he prophetically declared that news of
the outbreak of open, widespread hostilities could be expected from New
England momentarily.

On April 14 General Gage received a pig-headed letter from Lord Dartmouth, secretary of state for the colonies, ordering him to use force, if
necessary, to carry out the Coercive Acts, and to strike quickly to quell the
disturbance before the insurgency could perfect its organization. Dartmouth's directive was both tardy and ill-advised. This was not the way
to meet the American emergency. A better approach might have been
based on an earlier resolution put forth on January 20 by William Pitt,
the Earl of Chatham, in the House of Lords. It called for negotiations,
following the immediate removal of the troops from Boston. Chatham's
motion was defeated by a 3-to-1 margin. Two weeks later, on February
1, Chatham gave additional details of the approach he favored. His plan
of reconciliation had four points: recognizing the Continental Congress;
pledging that no new revenues would be imposed without the consent
of provincial assemblies; recognizing the "supreme legislative authority
and superintending power" of Parliament; and requiring the Continental
Congress to adopt a plan providing revenue for the support of colonial
government in America. This proposal, too, was decisively rejected by the
House of Lords. When nations, especially imperial powers, are on a high
horse and bent on self-destruction, it is not easy, even for a politician as
astute as young Chatham, to call them to their senses.

The dangerous game of probe and response soon erupted into open
conflict on the outskirts of Boston. On April 18, a British officer was secretly ordered to proceed, with a detachment of seven hundred men, to

destroy the rebels' supply depot at Concord. At about 10 p.m., British troops gathered on the Boston Common and embarked in boats across the river to Cambridge. The Boston committee of safety, learning their destination, dispatched Paul Revere and William Dawes to sound the alarm. Revere reached Lexington, on the road to Concord, at midnight and alerted Sam Adams and John Hancock, who were staying there. At 1 a.m. on April 19, the two scouts left for Concord. On their way, they were surprised by a British mounted patrol. Revere was captured and brought back to Lexington before being released, but Dawes escaped and got through to Concord.

British troops, arriving in Lexington at dawn, found seventy armed Minutemen there. A British officer ordered the militiamen to disperse. Slowly the colonials began to file off, but without surrendering their weapons as commanded. A shot rang out. Without an order from the British side, volleys from that sector left eight militiamen dead and ten wounded. Sparks had finally touched tinder.

The British troops regrouped and marched on to Concord, where they destroyed gun carriages, trenching tools, flour, and a liberty pole—the symbol of colonial defiance. Later in the morning, the steadily swelling American forces attacked a British platoon at Concord's North Bridge. The British unit sped out of Concord shortly after noon, hell-bent for their base in Boston. But the countryside by now swarmed with militiamen, who assailed the British column from all sides. Only the arrival of reinforcements at Lexington saved the British from complete disaster. Relentless attacks continued until the expeditionary force reached Charlestown, where naval guns were able to cover the retreat, preventing a complete rout.

On this first Patriot's Day, British casualties amounted to 73 killed, 174 wounded, and 26 missing. Almost 4,000 American militiamen fought that day. Of them, 93 were dead, wounded, or missing when the day ended.

Ashfield responds

In mid-March 1775 a warrant, issued "in his Majesty's name" (as was customary and lawful at that time), called all freeholders and inhabitants qualified to vote to a meeting in Ashfield on April 3, 1775.[5] The warrant anticipated a vote on whether the town "will rase a some of money for to

Defray the necesse charg of the Minit Men During the time they are implied in the Sarvis." It further authorized the Meeting to enact "anything Reletive to the Minit Men as the Town shall think proper." (So much for Britain's Coercive Acts.) The warrant also anticipated a vote to see if the town would pay the charge "layed upon us by the late hous of Representitives." Clearly, the select board intended to call for a vote on requisitions enacted by the revolutionary state legislature.

Sadly, we have no record of the discussion at this revolutionary town meeting. It certainly produced dramatic results. Town meeting appointed a committee of five men (Reuben Ellis, Benjamin Phillips, Samuel Elmer, Chileab Smith, and Joshua Taylor) and directed them to raise "ten men for to be Minit Men." A second vote appropriated funds (£12 sterling, a considerable sum) to purchase a stock of "amunission" for the town.

Two weeks after this town meeting in Ashfield, as we have seen, imperial and patriot blood was shed on the road from Concord to Boston. The following day, April 20, 1775, a unit of militiamen from Ashfield marched east under the command of Captain Samuel Bartlett.[6] When they arrived at the front, the Ashfielders found the immediate crisis over. Some of them returned home directly and were paid by the town for five days' service. Considering the distance from Ashfield to Concord, about seventy miles, this was pretty scant pay. Among those who marched off to Concord, according to Ashfield's records, several enlisted "for the season," joining the forces gathering at Cambridge to lay siege to Boston.[7]

A few days after the battle at Lexington and Concord, on April 24, town meeting chose Elisha Cranson moderator (in July, he would represent Ashfield at a Revolutionary congress at Watertown). Voters also named a committee to "provide for" the troops "till further orders," and another to serve as a committee of correspondence. The latter committee—including Captains Phillips and Taylor, Samuel Belding, John Ellis, and Dr. Phineas Bartlett—turned out to be consequential. Not only would it maintain communication with other towns about the progress of the Revolution, it would decide, on June 1, 1775, to "take no notice" of charges that newcomer Ephraim Williams (we will hear more of him) was a "suspected Tory." The committee would further declare that, if "a complaint [were] laid before said committee against any person as being a Tory and not supported," the complainant would be "liable to pay the cost of the committee sitting."[8] Feelings about this struggle were heating up.

By August Ashfield was on a wartime footing. Voters agreed to "make the coats that are assinde to us" and to send a man (Lt. Phillip Phillips) to "Albenah [Albany, New York] to procure guns and amanison upon this town's credit."[9] (The word *ammunition* occasioned several delightful spellings by the scribes of Ashfield.)

In December the village of Ashfield crossed its Rubicon. Heretofore, as we have seen, warrants for town meetings had routinely been issued "in his Majesty's name." Even the warrant in late March, for a meeting to consider whether the town would raise and support a unit of Minutemen and pay the charges assessed by the Massachusetts House of Representatives to support the revolutionary Continental Congress, included that phrase. The warrant dated December 1, 1775, was different. Like its predecessors, it required the constable to notify voters about a town meeting scheduled for December 15, but it was signed by the selectmen and published on their authority alone. In this revolutionary situation, no higher authority was available, and none was deemed necessary. Here was an act for which these men would surely be called to account, if the Revolution failed to establish American independence.

Though the meeting in December 1775 did not deal directly with the war, it was of considerable consequence. Among the items listed in the warrant was raising the money to pay "the Rev Mr Porter's sallery for the year ensuing, according to contract." The meeting would also consider whether to direct anyone to complete work on the meetinghouse. And it would appoint a committee to work with the town clerk to put the town's records in order, that is, to decide which back records should be included and which parts of the minutes should be kept. This was not a small or routine task. Many legal matters—titles to land, delinquent taxes, and the like—depended on the town's records. For a jurisdiction cutting loose from British sovereignty, these records would become authoritative. Another consideration was that, if the war were lost, the town's records would contain evidence of treason.

The meeting did indeed take stern action. It appointed a committee to see that "the full five acres . . . on the ministerial lot" be cleared, as promised, by September 1, 1776, and "that [any] man that don't appear to work is chargable two shillings per day for two days to the Committee man that he is under." Five men were named to the committee made responsible for seeing that this work got done.[10] Meeting the charter's obligation to support the Congregational establishment had been stalled, owing to the controversy over the Baptists' refusal to pay taxes. The wording of the resolution of December 15, with fines for nonperformance, suggests some irritation with the delay.[11]

The same town meeting also named three of the town's most highly respected citizens (Phineas Bartlett, Aaron Lyon, and Nathaniel Sherwin) to assist the clerk in putting the town's official records in order.

Progress of the war

Let us return to Boston for an update on the progress of the larger war.

In the aftermath of the battle along the road from Concord to Boston, Patriot forces tightened the noose around Boston, laying a siege on the provincial capital that would last until March 1776. On April 23, 1775, while Ashfield was voting to supply the requisitioned troops, the Massachusetts Provincial Congress authorized raising 13,600 men, named a commander-in-chief (Artemas Ward), and appealed to other colonies to send help. By mid-May Rhode Island, Connecticut and New Hampshire had voted to send 9,500 men to Cambridge, and within a month, the Patriot forces around Boston numbered about 10,000 men.

On June 12 General Gage issued a proclamation imposing martial law. After a series of tactical moves and countermoves, the battle was finally joined on June 17, 1775, at Bunker Hill. The struggle for control over this critical vantage point overlooking Boston's harbor proved costly to both sides. A British assault force of 2,400 men under General Gage attacked a redoubt garrisoned by 1,600 Americans, commanded by Colonel William Prescott. When night fell, the British had won the field, but at a cost of 1,054 casualties, a high proportion of them officers. American losses numbered 100 dead, 267 wounded, and 30 taken prisoner.

Skirmishes continued during the winter of 1775–76. Patriot forces took control of Dorchester Heights, on the other side of Boston harbor, during the night of March 4–5, 1776. A British counterattack was prevented by foul weather. On March 7, the British decided to evacuate Boston, setting sail for Halifax, Nova Scotia. A series of pitched battles on Long Island, followed by the ouster of Washington's headquarters from Manhattan in late August, set up the second phase of the British plan to restore their authority in America: to use New York City as a base of operations for a campaign designed to split the American colonies in two along the Hudson River.

Military discipline and democratic culture

What kind of army were the Patriots able to put together at Cambridge in the spring and summer of 1775, after the success of their guerrilla-like tactics on the road from Concord to Boston? New Englanders, when they visited the encampment, were charmed by what they found. A letter from a chaplain to his wife commented cheerfully on the colorful variety of tent-making materials, bespeaking the various communities represented there.[12] Experienced, professional soldiers, however, had a decidedly different take. They shuddered when they considered that this raggedy band of turkey-shooters was preparing for set-piece battles against a well-equipped army of battle-tested veterans.[13]

The Continental Congress named George Washington commander of the Continental Army in June 1775, at about the time of the battle at Bunker Hill. Washington arrived in Cambridge on July 3 and began to take the measure of the forces under his command. His first reaction was disgust, coupled with deep apprehension. His troops, he said after meeting some of them and inspecting their lines, were "an exceedingly dirty & nasty people," utterly lacking in discipline, poorly equipped and insubordinate. Their officers, he thought, were worse. The mode of recruitment (leading troops they had raised themselves) and the terms of their service (short and ad hoc, often for a particular engagement) practically guaranteed that they would be weak and unfit for command.[14]

As the historian Fred Anderson has been at pains to point out, this early confrontation between the Virginian commander and his raw troops in Massachusetts was deeply significant.[15] Washington was not unsympathetic to New Englanders. He probably did not mean to be condescending when he ascribed their unfitness for combat partially to the fact that the province of Massachusetts has been "so long in a State of Anarchy, & the Yoke of ministerial Oppression has been laid so heavily on it." But he had been to war before. From his own grim experience during the French and Indian War in the mid-1760s and from his subsequent intensive studies of European military theory, he had become fervently devoted to notions of unified command, subordination, strict discipline, thorough training, and adequate supply. An Anglophile at heart and a slave-owner, he was by nature a severe disciplinarian, beginning with himself. He ordered long, hard floggings for careless soldiering, and he would inflict capital punishment fourteen times during the Revolutionary War, mostly for desertion.[16]

Washington appreciated that the men of New England had been the readiest among Americans to take up arms in defense of their liberties, but he thought the traditions of its militias threatened the viability of the Revolution itself, which would depend ultimately, he thought, on the availability and readiness of solid military forces. Like his British counterparts, Washington thought Yankee soldiers "resistant to discipline, averse to hardship, prone to desertion and mutiny, so faint of heart as to be incapable of fighting on an open field in the approved, manly, European style."[17]

For their part, the men of Massachusetts were eager to admire and respect their famed commander. Tempers flared briefly when word of his initial disdain got out, but Washington quickly apologized, and the troops seemed to realize that his anxieties were understandable. Nevertheless there was a deep and significant conflict here. New Englanders thought "standing armies" threatened liberty. Their culture was grounded on covenantal principles. This was an army of volunteers, of citizens, of equals. Their service was based not on obedience to a monarch but on a contractual relationship, a specific, voluntary agreement to serve under the officer who enrolled them. Jehovah was their commander-in-chief. They might not, many of them, have been devout, but they came from families and towns that thought it was a terrible mistake to risk God's wrath by cursing. The army at Cambridge and Roxbury was not an ignorant rabble, any more than any collection of American colonials in the late eighteenth century would have been. Indeed, such a force worked just as the government that organized it, the officers who commanded it, and the men who filled its ranks expected it to work. As an army, it was capable of remarkable feats of mobilization, courage, and passionate commitment, as it showed on the road back from Concord and Lexington in April. As for battle-readiness, it was ideally suited to warfare over a sprawling continent, primitively settled. But it was also vulnerable in set-piece battles, and this caused Washington deep concern, after his own mortifying, even dishonorable experience at Fort Necessity on the Pennsylvania frontier.[18]

Washington believed deeply in the strict subordination of military to civil authority, and in clear boundaries between them. New England's military culture depended on continuing political support and sympathy for the cause. Washington knew the value of these attitudes, but they were no substitute, in his eyes, for the virtues of military discipline.

Recruiting a continental army

From the beginning of the Revolutionary War to its end, town militias were the principal source of New England's contribution to the Continental Army. The Continental Congress, the government of the thirteen former colonies, established a quota for each state. In turn, state legislatures of New England assigned a quota to each town. But it fell to the towns to meet these quotas—or not. Largely they did not, especially after the initial enthusiasm for the struggle wore off. In fact, Massachusetts towns had a better record than communities in most other colonies. Militia service was well established in law and tradition in colonial Massachusetts. Able-bodied men between the ages of sixteen and fifty were required to serve in their town's militia. Militias were generally used defensively, mostly to protect towns against attacks by Native Americans, but the precedent was established early that men could be drafted into the militia, even to serve outside their home colony.[19]

The outbreak of war with England did bring changes. Before that, the annual mustering of militias had been great sport, affording a week-long bivouac out of town, good boisterous fun for the colonies' men. During wartime, however, service could be long, hard, and perilous. It was disruptive of family and farm life, sometimes at the least convenient seasons (planting season, harvest-time, winter). It might entail wounds that could become infected, as well as exposure to disease, and hospitals were awful. Desertions were frequent. Even good, brave men left the lines to relieve hard distress on their own farms: deathly ill wives or children, collapsing equipment, harvests urgently needing to be taken in, else starvation for their loved ones during the winter.[20]

Early in the war, from April 1775 to August 1777 or so, the Massa-chusetts legislature called on towns to fill up the ranks for the siege of Boston or for service in Vermont or on Long Island. In September 1776, for example, each town was directed to send one-fifth of its militia for ser-vice in New York and New Jersey, to thwart the British plan to cleave the rebellion down the middle, along the Hudson River. Ashfield men were there in force for that first great test of American resolve. Retreating to Manhattan Island and across the Hudson River into New Jersey, Washing-ton desperately needed additional troops to confront the massive forces Britain was bringing to bear (over 30,000 well-equipped, expertly led Brit-ish soldiers and sailors massed for the battle of Brooklyn). In November of that year, Massachusetts was finally forced to order that all able-bodied men be enrolled for service in the militia. The following year, 1777, Mas-sachusetts directed towns to resort to the draft, if necessary, to meet their commitments.[21]

The draft, when finally it came, varied in format. Sometimes, as in the winter of 1777–78, the commonwealth drafted men to serve for a particu-lar emergency. Soon, however, that would not do. The patriots' glorious victory at Bennington in August 1777 led to an unexpected crisis: the need to guard 5,700 British troops who surrendered there. Men from Ashfield arrived a day late to take part in the battle of Bennington, but they were there in plenty of time to participate in guard duty. By the terms of sur-render, the British agreed that their troops would be marched to Boston and shipped back to England, never again to serve in the war against the Americans. Someone had to see that this promise was carried out. For this purpose, the commonwealth ordered half of the militia from four counties to serve under General Horatio Gates for one month. The op-eration actually took a good deal longer than that. In January 1778, Mas-sachusetts had to draft an additional regiment of eight hundred men for three months to guard the prisoners until they could be dispatched from Boston harbor.[22]

Service in the military during wartime is almost always a miserable experience. This one certainly was. The rigors of farming made men physically strong, but it did not fit them for life in a military camp or on a battlefield. Men and boys who grew up on a farm tended to lack good habits of personal hygiene. Some of them knew little about how to feed themselves. Especially when they were lonely, they were prone to abuse alcohol. They did not exercise properly and got camp diseases, such as dysentery, that sometimes proved fatal.

Early in the war, fathers and older sons often served together. The Moses Smith family of Ashfield, for example, lost two members, father and son, at the battle of Long Island.[23] Later on, however, most recruits came from less affluent families, and a kind of primogeniture started to operate. Younger sons and brothers went to war, and many of them did not return home afterward, either because they were casualties or because they moved on to seek their fortunes elsewhere. In either case, the impact on the home community was often disruptive.[24]

Meanwhile, in Ashfield

How did Ashfield's self-government fare during the remainder of the Revolutionary War (that is, after the British abandoned their base in Boston and George Washington went south from New York)? As we have seen, prevailing opinion in Ashfield supported separation from Great Britain. A meeting in August 1775 voted to make uniforms and purchase guns and ammunition at town expense and to confer with counterparts in other towns about the progress of the war and determine what part Ashfield should be playing. This "committee of correspondence" was reappointed annually for the duration of the war. In addition, while Washington and his troops shivered at Valley Forge in the winter of 1777–78, the people of Ashfield voted to send blankets to the troops there.

Already by December 1776, however, the emotional and financial strains of the war were becoming evident. Town meeting directed its committee of safety to ask neighboring towns to join the call for a county convention so that the towns in Hampshire County, which then included Ashfield, could "get into regulation concerning prices of provisions, &c." At the same meeting, voters directed the committee to "put a stop to the carrying of grain out of town."[25] One senses a growing irritation with profiteering.

Ashfield contributed considerable manpower to the battle for independence. Citing official state records, the town's historian, Frederick G. Howes, lists, by name, 173 men from Ashfield who served as soldiers during the Revolutionary War, some for only a few days, most longer than that, and some for the duration. Of these, Howes lists six who died while serving.[26]

Howes comments that the town seems to have been more "embarrassed" by the financial burdens of war than by the obligation to raise troops. Having built a meetinghouse and settled a minister, and then, by the decision of King George III, having been denied the financial support of the Baptists for these mandated arrangements, the taxpayers of Ashfield were sorely stressed during this period. In February 1777 they appealed to the state for an abatement of the provincial tax and directed the town's assessors not to include that tax in their bills.[27] The record does not indicate exactly why this abatement was sought or granted, but it was.

But despite Howes's belief that financial woes were a particularly severe challenge during the Revolution, the raising of troops was also difficult for a frontier farming community. Men were sorely needed at home to clear meadows, build and repair homes and barns and roads, raise cattle, feed chickens, slaughter pigs, and build public spaces. The economic insecurity is reflected in the fact that, because of fluctuations in the value of currency, resolutions on taxes often gave the equivalent values in grain. A town meeting in June 1779 considered how to induce men to join the armed forces. After discussion, voters adopted a report that authorized men signing up for a nine-month tour in the war to be allowed, "in addition to the bounty allowed by the [state legislature], 40 shillings a month wages, stated upon Wheat at 4/6 per Bushel, Rie 3/4 and Indian corn at 2/6, and if any man have a Family which shall stand in Need of Bread corn it shall be provided at said prices at the cost of the town."[28]

Inflation was a constant and growing concern as the war dragged on. Howes cites John Fiske's famous book, *The American Revolution* (1891), as authority for the statement that "at the end of 1778 the paper dollar was worth sixteen cents, and before the end of the year it took ten paper dollars to make a cent." This explains why the town had to represent its obligations in grain equivalencies.[29]

By 1779 the challenge of raising troops and keeping them in the service had grown severe.[30] The legislature ordered that generals be dismissed if their battalions were undermanned. It was the towns, though, that bore the brunt of it. They had one month to fill their quotas, or else be fined

£350 for each man short. Selectmen could be fined as much as £10 per month for each man the town was short.

To fill the ranks, towns often resorted to the bounty system. In 1779, Ashfield added a bounty on top of the pay offered by the legislature to get men to obey the draft. A year later the town pledged twenty calves to each man who enlisted for three years, the animals to be purchased in May 1781 and kept at town expense for three years. Eight men enlisted under these terms.

Offering bounties was an imperfect remedy, however. Extra pay, whether in cash, clothing, foodstuffs, or livestock, had a corrupting influence. States began to compete with one another to fill quotas. Bounties offered by Massachusetts were relatively low at first, but soon they had to be raised. It was the towns that had to pay the bounties authorized by states—"unfunded mandates" are not an invention of modern legislatures. Poor towns, like Ashfield and Ashburnham, found themselves competing with rich ones, like Chelsea. And when rich towns offered bounties, some men deserted their original units. They became "bounty jumpers," joining the army several times in different places. By law, there were exemptions for vital trades, like millers, blacksmiths, iron workers, ferrymen, ship carpenters, and tailors.[31]

As the disruptions of war persisted, the legislature made various provisions allowing wealthier men to escape service. The penalty for failing to report was just £10 early in the war; later it was raised to £45. After 1778, a drafted man was allowed forty-eight hours (later shortened) to find a substitute. In Chelsea, in 1779, thirty-nine draftees paid £150 each to escape service. But there is no record of such substitution in Ashfield. No one had that kind of money. These exemptions, substitutes, and bounties made the American Revolution ultimately a "poor man's war." In Maryland, a letter-writer complained to the governor about "the Draught having fallen on many poor Men who have a number of children that depend solely on their Labour for a Subsistance." No doubt there were similar cases in Ashfield among the 173 men who served. By war's end, Massachusetts had only 4,370 men in the Continental Line; a full complement would have been 8,350.[32]

The war tore harshly at Ashfield's social fabric, still raw. (Recall that the first white settlers had come to Huntstown/Ashfield just twenty years before the skirmishes at Lexington and Concord.) On July 18, 1777, town meeting directed Aaron Lyon, chair of the select board, to gather evidence about "certain persons thought to be inimical to the American states."[33] A month later the board brought to town meeting a list of persons who "do appear unfriendly to the American states" and recommended that they "be brought to proper trial." The report named nine men, among them some of the most respectable citizens in town, including Samuel Belding, who had already been elected five times to the select board, and Lieutenant Phillip Phillips, son of the second settler in Huntstown.[34] Like Belding, Phillips was a justice of the peace (a position he held for many years, before, during, and after the war); he had accepted a commission from the king, and he deemed it his duty to remain faithful to his oath.[35] Hence his inclusion on this list.

Town meeting decreed that, while awaiting trial, these nine men were to "be committed to close confinement in this town." The place chosen was Captain Samuel Bartlett's house, near the center of town.[36] One of the charged men, Jesse Edson, pleaded sickness in his family and was exempted from confinement on condition of delivering up his arms and ammunition. The others, though, were held under armed guard, chosen and supported by the town.[37] The confinement of these men continued for seven days, over a weekend. Howes reports that many years later, a woman he identifies as "Aunt Betty Perkins" recalled seeing the prisoners marched down to church on a Sunday morning, under guard, to attend service, and that the guards took their muskets into church with them.[38]

Within a week, however, the determination to punish these neighbors for their loyalist sympathies collapsed. On August 29, 1777, town meeting met again and voted to "dismiss the guard and release the prisoners from close confinement."[39] It just did not make sense to spend public funds, raised by burdensome taxes, to impose house arrest on these men. Everyone knew them. Many may have been furious that they held back from the huge and dangerous effort to drive imperial rule from America, but it made no sense to keep them locked up. For security? Nonsense. For punishment? Certainly the offense of these men against public sentiment was serious. Families that would never again see fathers, sons, brothers, and cousins who had been lost on the battlefield or in horrible field hospitals found it hard to forgive those who held aloof, for whatever reason. So did those whose routines were interrupted by having their men drafted for service in far-flung theatres. The internal conflict was deep and real, as it often is in wartime. Ashfield tried dealing with it by imprisonment, but strict justice is hard to sustain in a face-to-face community. One wonders if anyone in Ashfield, that week in August 1777, knew to quote Shakespeare's great reflection on mercy: that it becomes a throned monarch better than his crown; that it is an "attribute of God himself; / And earthly power doth then show likest God's / When mercy seasons justice"; that, in the course of strict justice, none of us could expect salvation; and that, as we pray for mercy ourselves, we should be merciful to others. Whether anyone cited it or not, the spirit in these lines informed the town's approach to judging neighbors who showed signs of loyalist sympathies.

Ashfield was not alone in being torn apart by the intense pressures of war. Conflicts between Patriots and Tories raged up and down the Connecticut River valley. In Springfield and other valley towns in Massachusetts, in the early days of the war, the "river gods," led by Colonels Israel Williams and John Worthington, held sway, but popular leaders like Joseph Hawley and Caleb Strong of Northampton, fierce supporters of the war, fought back hard. They accused Williams and his political allies of trading with the enemy, being in the king's employ, and harboring loyalist sympathies. In 1777, a passel of letters written in 1771 by Williams was discovered near Albany and sent to the Patriot leaders. The correspondence, from Williams to Governor Hutchinson, was deemed treasonous in the radically changed atmosphere. The legislature ordered Williams and his son jailed in Northampton, where they were held until December 1777, when they were released into house arrest.[40]

The disruptions of the war were reflected in the life of Ashfield's local church as well. In June 1777 the town warrant included a proposed article that would have given the Reverend Nehemiah Porter leave to join the Continental Army. It failed to pass; town records do not indicate why. Apparently he went anyway, for in January 1778 the town voted "that we hire preaching while Mr. Porter is absent." The Reverend Jacob Sherwin (the same man who had earlier displaced Ebenezer Smith) was hired to preach in Porter's absence.[41]

Throughout the war, the community organized for prayer and fasting, to seek God's deliverance from the cruel hand of the British. In August 1777, the same town meeting that voted to arrest nine suspected loyalists also resolved that "this town will do all that lies in [its] power to suppress vice, and especially that they will use their endeavors to prevent profane cursing and swearing, that the name of God be not blasphemed among them."[42] How better to influence a conflict between infant colonies and the mighty British empire than to curry the favor of a jealous and wrathful God by righteous conduct? Many of these people might not have been fervent practitioners of the Christian faith, but in wartime, ancient beliefs and practices rise to the surface. New Englanders were a people of the Hebrew Bible, and chapter 20 of the book of Deuteronomy, for example, is clear about the fate of people who hang back during a holy war, as is the Book of Judges. God is not mocked. He punishes stiff-necked, willful people, but He does not abandon people who know where their blessings come from.[43] At town meeting in wartime, it was time to put this ancient faith into resolutions.

Framing a constitution for Massachusetts

While war continued, by now mostly well to the south of New England, Massachusetts moved to frame and ratify a state constitution. Towns were of course greatly concerned about this matter. Even in the brief history of the settlement of Huntstown/Ashfield, citizens had already been both beneficiary and victim of provincial legislation and decrees. They felt a vital stake in securing arrangements that would respect and protect their liberties.

As it turned out, Ashfield played a distinctive role in the framing and adoption of the Massachusetts Constitution of 1780. As part then of Hampshire County, a center of strenuous agitation on this point, it joined the push for a fresh, post-imperial constitution at a time when politicians in and near Boston were content to improvise with the government left behind by Great Britain. Further, as a town with influential Baptists in its midst, it was part of a growing resistance to the idea of an established church.[44]

Massachusetts was the last of the original thirteen states to adopt a written constitution during the American Revolution (except for Rhode Island and Connecticut, which merely modified their royal charters). Massachusetts had made a bad start as a constitution-maker in 1778, when the legislature prepared a draft that was promptly and decisively rejected by the towns, to which it had been sent for ratification. One of the principal objections to the 1778 project was that it had been framed by the legislature, rather than by a special convention. Constitutionalists in Massachusetts, some of the most fervent of whom lived in the two western counties of Hampshire and Berkshire, were among the first people in history to insist that the foundations of government must be laid not by the legislators who would wield its powers, but by a special convention consisting of delegates elected by the people, and that for ratification, the draft must be returned for consideration by the people assembled in their towns. This was no small matter. The constitutional historian Andrew C. McLaughlin, in a presidential address to the American Historical Association in 1914, said: "If I were called upon to select a single fact or enterprise which more nearly than any other single thing embraced the significance of the American Revolution, I should select—not Saratoga or the French alliance, or even the Declaration of Independence—I should choose the formation of the Massachusetts Constitution of 1780, and I should do so because that constitution rested upon the fully developed convention, the greatest institution of government which America has produced, the institution which answered, in itself, the problem of how men could make government of their own free will."[45]

One factor that contributed to the difficulty of constitution-making between 1776 and 1780 was that townspeople had to get used to the idea that throwing off Britain's yoke was just the first step. In the words of the Declaration of Independence, when a people is oppressed by an abusive and despotic government, "it is their right, it is their duty, to throw off such Government, and to provide new Guards for their future security." The state of nature without civil government is not an option. As James Madison wrote in the Federalist No. 10, if men were angels, no government would be necessary. Alas, they are not. When one government is overthrown, another must immediately take its place. It took some time to understand that the new government would have to be empowered to coerce its citizens. As Madison wrote in the Federalist No. 51, the government would have to be able to control the governed, even as the governed insisted on consenting to the men and measures that coerced them. These were complicated concepts. One can feel modern eyes glaze over as they are rehearsed. The truly remarkable thing about the founding period, in the United States, in Massachusetts, and in Ashfield, is that common people, farmers and mechanics, spent a lot of time and energy in meetings, working hard to develop a practical understanding of the principles of republican and democratic government and to build institutions founded on them.

At a town meeting in Ashfield on October 4, 1776, for example, during the first year of the Revolution, the townspeople enacted a set of resolutions on constitutional principles. In some ways the resolutions were naïve, but they were also deadly earnest. Their bedrock conviction was that government must be of and by the people. The spelling in this document, which I reproduce below, suggests that the men of Ashfield were not simply affirming ideas prepared by learned men elsewhere, but composing them for themselves.[46]

The resolutions adopted in October 1776 show that the men of Ashfield were ready in principle to cede some authority to a civil government located beyond the bounds of the forests they lived in. The first resolution affirms that Massachusetts needs a "forme of Sivil government Set up for the Good of this State." But immediately in the second resolution, they indicate that they will not allow the reins of government to slip completely from their hands. Constitutional drafts must be returned to the "Sevarale Towns for their Exceptanc Before the Ratifycation thairof." Ashfield, they said, would take "the Law of God for the foundation of the forme of our Goverment," inasmuch as the "Old Laws we have Ben Ruled by under the British Constitution have Proved Inefectual to Secuer us from the more than Savige Crualty of tiranical Opressars." They were bound in duty to "God and our Country to Oppose the Least Apearanc of them Old Tiranical Laws takeing Place again." There was no need to replace Britain with more heavy-handed authority. . . . We Do not want any Goviner but the Goviner of the universe, and under him a States Ginaral to Consult with the wrest of the united Stats for the Good of the whole."[47]

Home rule was their lodestar, and simplicity and thrift in government their compass. Each town, they declared, should be invested with authority to choose a committee or number of judges to hear and "Detarmin all cases betwixt Man and Man, Setel Intesttate Estates and Colect all Debts that have Ben Contracted . . . Exept in the Case of Murdor and then it will be Nesesary to call in Eleven men from Eleven Nabouring Towns that Shall be Cose for that Porpos Anuly to Joge and Condem Such Moderrers." As for the form of state government, they saw no need for the expense and humbuggery of a second chamber. A single legislative chamber would be enough. In the last of the ten resolutions, Ashfield declared it as "Ower Opinion that all acts Pased by the Ginaral Court of this State Respecting the Several Towns Be Sent to the Sevarals Towns for thair acceptants Before thay Shall be in force."[48]

Many other towns produced similar statements during the perilous summer and autumn of 1776. Taking this unruly bull by the horns, the state legislature prepared a draft constitution and submitted it to the towns for ratification in 1778. It was not received kindly; it was defeated by a margin of about five towns to one. Among the main objections were that race and wealth became qualifications for voting (Article V said that every male resident who paid taxes in a town, "excepting Negroes, Indians and molattoes," was entitled to vote for representative; and every male "worth sixty pounds" could "put in his vote" for governor, lieutenant governor, and state senator). Other respondents complained about the lack of a bill of rights, as well as the draft's provisions for control of the militias and its scheme for representation. Summing up the reactions of many citizens, a Newburyport lawyer, Theophilus Parsons, said that a state of nature was preferable to this hotchpotch. The farmers of Pittsfield came to the same conclusion.[49]

Their first attempt rudely rejected, the legislature set in train a process for correcting the mistakes of 1777–78. In February 1779 the House asked all persons qualified to vote for representatives to respond by the end of May, whether they wished to have a new "Constitution or Form of Government made," and if so, whether they would empower their representative to vote for calling a statewide convention for that sole purpose. Receiving a strong affirmative on both points from over two-thirds of the towns, the legislature called on them to elect delegates and promised that the draft produced by that convention would go into force if ratified by "at least two-thirds of those, who are free and twenty one years of age, belonging to this state, and present in the several meetings." There would be no property qualification, either in choosing delegates or in voting on ratification.[50]

On August 16 Ashfield elected two militia captains, Benjamin Phillips and Samuel Bartlett, to be its delegates to the constitutional convention.

Their instructions were clear, particularly on the matter of religious liberty. They were to "use their endeavors" to secure an article guaranteeing that "each Representative, previous to his belonging to [the legislature], shall be solemnly sworn not to pass any acts or laws where his constituents shall be in any sense, name or nature, oppressed or forced in matters of religion." Recent controversies between Congregationalists and Baptists were clearly on people's minds.[51]

Two weeks later, on September 18, 1779, 293 delegates from 190 towns across the commonwealth met at the First Church in Cambridge. It was a distinguished body of men that assembled, including John and Samuel Adams, John Hancock, James Bowdoin, Theophilus Parsons, and Caleb Strong of Northampton. The historian Samuel Eliot Morison, writing in 1955, commented that "almost every leading patriot of Massachusetts not then serving in the Army or Navy or in Congress was elected a delegate."[52]

The convention's leaders, mindful that the towns would have power of ratification, created a so-called Grand Committee to prepare a draft. It consisted of members from each county, with numbers weighted slightly, although far from proportionally, in favor of the more populous areas.[53] The Grand Committee named a steering group consisting of James Bowdoin, the convention president, and "a brace of Adamses," John and Samuel. That subcommittee delegated its functions to John Adams, "undoubtedly," says Morison, "the greatest expert on constitutions in America, if not in the world."[54] Adams prepared a draft in two parts, the first a "Declaration of the Rights of the Inhabitants of the Commonwealth of Massachusetts," this being the negative part, listing limitations on the powers of government;[55] and the second, "The Frame of Government," stating the powers of government, how they were distributed, and how officials were to be chosen.

Sessions of the convention to debate and amend the Adams draft were held in Cambridge during October and November 1779, and in Boston, by then reasonably safe from invasion, in January 1780. To underscore the commitment of the delegates, Morison describes the conditions of travel that winter: "The session opened three weeks late because of the hard winter. Many members from the interior could not get to Boston because the highways were completely snowed under. . . . But by 20 January the post road from Hartford to Boston was open for sleigh traffic, and if you could get to Hartford on snowshoes it was only a three-day sleigh ride thence to Boston."[56]

The convention worked on the Adams draft until March 2. It then forwarded its proposal to the towns for ratification. It asked selectmen in each town to call a special town meeting, where voters were to examine the draft, article by article, and vote whether to accept it. Selectmen were directed to report which articles, if any, failed to receive two-thirds affirmation from the town. The convention would then alter each of the disputed articles "in such manner as that it may be agreeable to the Sentiments of two thirds of the voters throughout the State."[57]

Oddly, there seems to have been no general debate across the state about the draft. Only two pamphlets were published, both opposed, both apparently written by a member of the convention, a Baptist minister named Noah Alden. He focused his objections on Article III, authorizing and requiring each town to provide at its own expense for the "public worship of God and for the support and maintenance of public protestant teachers of piety, religion and morality." The six weekly newspapers in Massachusetts (all but one published in Boston), although full of news about the war and foreign affairs, contained almost no reference to the debate on the constitution.[58]

Despite the relative quiet statewide, the return from Ashfield shows how closely the people of the town were engaged in this matter of a state constitution.[59] On May 16, 1780, a special town meeting gathered to consider the constitution. It chose a committee of seven to prepare recommendations. The town's delegate to the forthcoming ratifying convention, Captain Elisha Cranson, was appointed to this committee, as were the selectmen, Aaron Lyon, Chileab Smith Jr. (son of the town's vociferous Baptist), and Dr. Phineas Bartlett.

A week later, thirty-eight men gathered and proceeded to vote on each article. The first snag came over Article III of the Declaration of Rights. Chileab Smith was not the only one who objected to the establishment of the Congregational Church. The official report of the meeting shows a vote of 8 to 28 against this article and gives, as the reason for the rejection, that "it is unconstitutional to human Nature and no Precept in the word of God to support it." The town also voted against Article XXIX, which declared the right of all citizens to be tried by "judges as free, impartial and independent as the lot of humanity will admit," and stated that judges "should hold their offices as long as they behave themselves well." Ashfield, by a vote of 24 to 3, called for an amendment ordering that judges be chosen by the House of Representatives annually. By the same margin, the town voted to delete all provisions for a second legislative chamber. A senate, the report declared, is "unnecessary and Burdensom to the Commonwilth." Decisively (although in gradually diminishing numbers as the meeting wore on), the town voted to eliminate property qualifications for election to the House of Representatives and for voters to participate in the elections of state officials. Ashfield would have given the vote to "every Male person being 21 years of Age having the approbation of the Select Men and taken the Oath of Alligionc to the United States of America." Voters also objected to an article that invested judges of probate with the power to settle estates. Better, they thought, to give this power to the selectmen. Finally, concerning sworn oaths, some voters took offense that only Quakers were exempt from the obligation to swear to obey the laws "so help me God." If a mere affirmation, upon pain of perjury, was sufficient for "one denomination of Christian, then it is taking Gods name in vain to impose it upon any other denomination."[60]

On June 7, convention delegates reconvened at the Brattle Street Church in Boston to assess the returns from the towns. By now the convention was determined to put an end to its work and get a constitutional government up and running. It named a committee with one representative from each county to "arrange the returns." It was a daunting task. A modern computer would have been hard pressed to accomplish it. Towns had been instructed to respond article-by-article. Some voted up or down; others proposed alternatives—but no two towns adopted the same language for the substitute articles.

The main objections were to two articles. One called for a new vote in 1795 to determine if voters were satisfied with the 1780 constitution. Several towns wanted a more regular taking of sentiments on the subject. Most, though, like Ashfield, favored the draft as written, and the committee decided that it had been accepted. The other point of contention was Article III. It required the towns to provide for public worship and to support "public protestant teachers of piety, religion and morality."

Several towns, including Ashfield, strongly objected to this language.[61] Some thought it was too liberal, opening the door to public support for Roman Catholic churches. Ashfield's objection was that it gave the legislature power to collect taxes from everyone to support the ministry of the established Congregational church.

Morison, after "checking up on the committee's mathematics," concludes that, despite some "juggling of the returns" on the two disputed articles, the convention was justified in finding a two-thirds majority in favor of the constitution as submitted to the towns. He adds, "After all, many delegates were present from the dissident towns, and they had plenty of opportunity to check. They must have been persuaded that it was better to gloss over the two-thirds requirement for these two articles, in order to get the Constitution in force, since the process had already taken four years." One cannot help wondering what Ashfield's Baptists would have thought of such a rationale. It is true that the town's delegate, Captain Cranson, could have objected; perhaps he did. It is also likely that he might have accepted a rationale like Morison's. But the town had voted 28 to 8 to demand revision of Article III, and many other towns shared similar convictions. It is a good thing for those who were trying to slide by this awkward moment that Chileab Smith had not been chosen as Ashfield's delegate!

At any rate, the question was put to the convention on each article ("Is it your opinion that the people have accepted of this article?"), and the journal records that, on every article, "a very great majority" responded affirmatively. Accordingly the first governor was elected on September 4; representatives on October 15; and the new state constitution went into effect on October 25, 1780.[62] There is no evidence that anyone in Ashfield dissented from these actions.

What to do about "Mother Ann"

Toward the end of the Revolutionary War, Ashfield found itself embroiled in controversy with a band of "vagrant religious fanatics" called Shakers, or Tremblers. They were accused of "extravagance and disorder and indecency . . . especially in acts of worship." People living in the vicinity where they were encamped asked the select board to deal with what they viewed as a public nuisance.[63] On February 7, 1782, town meeting directed the selectmen and constables to "warn said straggling Tremblers now in town, and those that shall come in hereafter, to depart in 24 hours or expect trouble."

The Shakers' leader was a woman named Ann Lee, whose followers called her Mother Ann. She accepted homage as a divine person, believing herself to be a manifestation of the second coming of Christ. Her teachings were radical. She urged her followers to follow the example of Christ and to have nothing to do with the government of this world or with the increase of population. She regarded marriage as a compromise with carnality and urged converts to "shake off the flesh and take up the cross." The worship of her followers was ecstatic, involving exuberant dancing and clapping, and women and men participated equally.[64] Perhaps not surprisingly, many members of the mainline Protestant sects found these beliefs and practices outrageous.

Fleeing persecution in England, Mother Ann had come to America in 1774 with a number of followers. In 1776 they settled near Albany, New York, and established a small religious community. In May 1781 Mother Ann, along with two female and three male companions, embarked on a missionary tour to the east, stopping first in Mount Washington, Massachusetts, and soon passing over the Berkshire Hills to Enfield, Connecticut, and then on to Harvard and Shirley, both in central Massachusetts, where they spent the summer of 1781 evangelizing. They made converts as they went, but they provoked a good deal of opposition, too. Mobs attacked their meetings; they were whipped, and one of their men was beaten and suffered a broken arm. In January they fled from central Massachusetts and returned to Enfield, where mobs again roughed them up. Up the Connecticut River to West Springfield they went, and then on to Granby and Montague, and eventually to Ashfield, where they arrived in February 1782.[65]

The reception in Ashfield was not entirely friendly, as the warning of February 7 indicated, but the selectmen's notice was apparently not vigorously enforced. Shaker records show that the group did not leave town that spring until May 20. They spent the summer in Harvard, Massachusetts, where they met with more violence. Driven from that town in September, they again passed through various towns in Connecticut, where they encountered violent mobs. In November, they surfaced once more in Ashfield and "by invitation" built lodgings near the house of Asa Bacon, where they remained through the winter and into the following spring. According to a Shaker account, one meeting at Bacon's house that winter drew "sixty sleighs and six hundred people—counted by John Farrington, by Mother's order."[66]

In March 1783 a group of men, led by Revolutionary War veterans, came over the hill to Ashfield from the neighboring town of Shelburne. Their intent was to drive the "stragglers" out of the region once and for all.[67] According to Howes, they met first at the house of Chileab Smith Jr., and then proceeded to the home of Phillip Phillips, justice of the peace.[68] These were interesting venues. Smith was the son of the Baptist leader who had campaigned so vigorously in the early 1770s on behalf of Baptists against the established church. As for Phillips, we met him earlier as one of the nine men imprisoned by town meeting order in August 1777 for being "unfriendly" to American independence. (The Shakers' host in Ashfield, Asa Bacon, was another of the nine suspected loyalists.) At any rate, the group coming over the hill from Shelburne, bent on chasing the "Tremblers" out of town, was somehow persuaded instead to negotiate with Mother Ann. A Shaker account of this confrontation says that Mother Ann was subjected to the indignity of proving, to female investigators, that she was indeed a woman (rumor had it that she was a British spy in drag), but that she had the best of the argument, concluding the encounter with a sharp reprimand of her critics.[69]

From Ashfield's perspective, the outcome may have owed more to market factors than to religious doctrine or attitudes about public decorum. In the early 1780s, in the wake of the Revolutionary War, specie was hard to come by, taxes were exorbitant, poverty widespread, and social unrest on the rise due to rising personal and municipal debt. Yet in the course of a single year the town went from warning the Shakers out of town to tolerating hundreds and hundreds of visiting Shakers and even rising up to defend them from an out-of-town mob. Part of the reason may have been that, when these straggling Shakers came to town, they often came for weeks at a time, and they needed hay, milk, and food. They brought hard money and other commodities that were impossible to acquire in Ashfield. A booming trade developed between the Shakers and the townspeople, and it went on for months.

Of course, the same thing could have happened wherever these itinerant worshippers encamped, but it did not, or not to the same extent. Ashfield's diversity and nascent business acumen made it possible to glimpse opportunity where other communities felt only anger and contempt.

At the end of April 1783, after a relatively quiet winter sojourn, the Shakers left Ashfield bound for another town in central Massachusetts, where again they met violent interference. They eventually made their way back to New York State. Mother Ann died at their compound near Albany on September 8, 1784, at age forty-nine.

The town's history takes credit for Ashfield being "tolerant toward these people who were so sorely abused elsewhere."[70] The Shakers' own account confirms this assessment, recording that "the opposition to the work of God in Ashfield was never so great as it had been in most other places" and that "the inhabitants of the town of Ashfield were, generally speaking, very friendly."[71] No doubt Mother Ann and her followers tested the town's capacity for tolerance. By their faith, they outraged the religious establishment; by their practices, they irritated some of their neighbors. Yet the town, having been forced to cut some slack for the Baptists, may have drawn on that experience and on the presence of some veterans of that earlier struggle in its governing councils to deflect the threat of violence when the Shakers came to town.[72]

After Yorktown, the continuing revolution

In 1782, not long after the end of hostilities (following the battle of Yorktown in 1781), the Massachusetts state legislature levied a heavy tax to pay war expenses, provoking "murmurings and insubordination from every quarter" in Ashfield. The town voted not to collect the revenues and recommended to militia officers that they resign their commissions.[73] Many other towns took similar action. The network that rose up against England was still working, only now it was directed against the authorities that had replaced the despised Britons. County conventions were held to broadcast complaints and organize resistance. The uproar led, in the winter of 1786–87, to Shays' Rebellion. In Springfield, insurrectionists attempted (unsuccessfully) to raid an arsenal, and regular sessions of courts in Northampton, Worcester, and Taunton were obstructed by mobs protesting not only taxes but proceedings against debtors.

The turmoil caused considerable alarm to men like George Washington. They saw anarchy breaking out; they may also have recognized that the complaints had some merit. In Massachusetts, Shays' Rebellion was crushed by the state militia, led by General Benjamin Lincoln. Nationally, the faction that sought a stronger national government, led by the young constitutionalists Alexander Hamilton and James Madison, took advantage of unrest in New England to fuel the march toward the Annapolis Convention of 1786 and, during the summer of 1787, on to the convention that framed the federal constitution at Philadelphia.

Ashfield played a remarkably important part in these statewide and national maneuverings over a federal constitution. Many people in the town took sides with Daniel Shays and the insurgency he led. By consent of a majority of the selectmen in 1786, the town's arsenal was given to local militiamen who were joining Shays, and an officer and a company of soldiers volunteered and marched off to join the protest movement.[74] The rebellion was brutally crushed, but not before Ashfield had shown its sympathies.

In late 1787 the town chose Ephraim Williams as its representative to the convention called to decide whether Massachusetts would ratify the federal constitution. It instructed him to "use his influence that said constitution does not take place." The convention met in Boston in January 1788.[75] It was a critical moment for the nation. By then, a few states (Delaware, Pennsylvania, New Jersey, Georgia, and Connecticut) had voted to ratify the constitution drafted in Philadelphia, but several key ones had not yet done so—states without which the national government would not have been viable, including New York and Virginia. Thus the outcome of the convention in Massachusetts was critical.

It was by no means foregone. Massachusetts already had experience with rejecting one draft and sending the framers back for another go. Early tallies of the representatives sent to Boston from the towns showed 194 votes for the Anti-federalists (opponents of ratification) and 144 for the Federalists. The opponents had a good case against the draft prepared in Philadelphia. Among other grounds of objection, where was the bill of rights? Gradually it dawned on the proponents of ratification in Massachusetts that this was potentially a fatal flaw. Yet they dared not make ratification contingent, for fear of losing momentum. So they gave informal assurances that satisfied enough men—including Sam Adams of

Boston and Ephraim Williams of Ashfield—to make ratification possible. Williams (recall that he been accused of being a loyalist back in 1777) defied the clear instruction of voters back home and voted for ratification.[76] It passed on February 7, by a vote of 187 to 168. If Williams and ten others similarly instructed had not defied their constituents, ratification of the federal constitution would have failed in Boston. In that event, the whole project would have been in deep trouble in Virginia, where Madison's steady logic barely overcame Patrick Henry's fiery eloquence, leading to a 89–79 victory for ratification on June 25; and in New York, where Hamilton's ardent advocacy, leveraging the narrow successes in Massachusetts, Pennsylvania, and Virginia, won ratification on July 26, by a vote of just 30 to 27.

Thus, if the instructions voted in Ashfield had controlled Ephraim Williams's vote, the constitutional draft of 1787 might never have been ratified. Or, to look at it from the other side, it is not too much to say that Williams's decision to support the framers' draft helped materially to save the United States Constitution from being strangled in its crib.

Patterns set in infancy have enduring effects. The principal habit established at the birth of Ashfield (and of Huntstown before it) was independent self-government. No community, certainly not this one, is master of its own destiny. But from the first days of its founding, the people of Ashfield did not have much protection or support from beyond the bounds of their own community. They inherited habits of thought and practice (majority rule, elected officials, private property, gender roles, a common language), and they existed as a legal entity by virtue of their place in an established, legitimate order. When that order fell apart, old habits persisted for a decade or so until a new order could be constituted. Ultimately their local institutions survived the revolution, largely unchanged. The sojourn of the Shakers over the winter of 1782–83 tested the town's temper, but a violent confrontation was averted. The economic chaos of the "critical period" led to a readiness to take up arms, if necessary, to deal with unfair treatment, but also revealed a willingness to accommodate to arrangements that promised stability and respect for local independence.

Aaron Lyon was a member of the select board during the Revolutionary War. His granddaughter Mary Lyon, founder of the "female seminary" that became Mount Holyoke College, taught at Sanderson Academy during the 1820s. *Photograph by Dave Fessenden.*

Frederick G. Howes, author of a history of Ashfield from 1742 to 1910. *Courtesy Ashfield Historical Society.*

George William Curtis and Charles Eliot Norton, summer residents from the 1860s through the 1890s. *Courtesy Ashfield Historical Society.*

G. Stanley Hall, Ashfield native and president of Clark University in Worcester, Massachusetts, during Sigmund Freud's first visit, at Hall's invitation, to the United States in 1909. *Front row, left to right:* Freud, Hall, Carl Jung; *back row, left to right:* A. A. Brill, Ernest Jones, Sandór Ferenczi. *Courtesy Ashfield Historical Society.*

A view of Main Street, ca. 1895, with the old Sanderson Academy building in the left foreground. Ashfield Lake is in the background, and the newer Sanderson Academy, built in 1895, is visible at right. *Courtesy Ashfield Historical Society.*

Memorial at the Plain Cemetery to the men from Ashfield who died fighting for the Union in the Civil War. *Photograph by Dave Fessenden.*

Edwin Romanzo Elmer (1850–1923), *A Lady of Baptist Corner, Ashfield, Massachusetts (the Artist's Wife)*, 1892. *Courtesy Smith College Museum of Art, Northampton, Mass.*

In the early 1830s, Charles Knowlton, an Ashfield doctor, wrote, published, and peddled a book titled *Fruits of Philosophy.* It aimed to teach "Young Married People" how to practice contraception, "without requiring any diminution or sacrifice of that enjoyment which attends the gratification of the re-productive instinct." In 1832 he served three months in prison at hard labor for publishing and selling a salacious book. *Left:* A daguerreotype of Knowlton, ca. 1845. *Courtesy Pocumtuck Valley Memorial Association Library, Deerfield, Mass. Below:* Title-page of the third edition, 190 pages, shown actual pocket-size. *American Antiquarian Society, Worcester, Mass.*

FRUITS OF PHILOSOPHY,

OR

THE PRIVATE COMPANION

OF

YOUNG MARRIED PEOPLE.

———

BY CHARLES KNOWLTON, M. D.,
Author of "Modern Materialism."

———

"Knowledge is Wealth."
Old Saying.

———

THIRD EDITION, WITH ADDITIONS.

———

BOSTON:
1834.

INTERLUDE

4

Transformation

The prevailing culture of Ashfield changed relatively little from the town's founding in the last half of the eighteenth century to the mid-twentieth century. Historians of American development may be surprised by this statement; in the United States generally, this was a time of tremendous transformation: from agricultural to industrial, from rural to urban and suburban, from ethnic homogeneity[1] to great diversity, from isolation to integration in the worldwide system of nations. By comparison, Ashfield seemed caught in a time-warp. In the eighteenth century, it was a typical New England village: rural, agricultural, mostly Yankee, largely isolated from currents sweeping the rest of the continent and the world. By 1950, despite the mechanization of agriculture and the assimilation of radios, telephones, and motor vehicles, culturally and politically Ashfield was still pretty much the same rustic village it had been in the late eighteenth century.

Through the nineteenth century, Ashfield's population actually declined. From an all-time high of 1,809 people counted in the federal census of 1810, the population steadily decreased, to 1,180 by 1870, and to 955 at the turn to the twentieth century.[2] The principal occupations throughout the nineteenth century were agricultural, with the emphasis on producing milk, maple syrup, and apples. To be sure, there was also an entrepreneurial spirit, young men making money peddling things like peppermint extract and buttons.[3] But as they found better soil to the west, nearer to markets, many migrated toward upstate and western New York, western Pennsylvania, and Ohio. Those who remained behind were farmers and lumbermen, wringing a living from rocky soils and steep slopes, and tradesmen and shopkeepers who provided services.

There were, of course, periodic disturbances. The Civil War of the 1860s was the worst, tearing eighty-four men from their homes, transporting them to fight in Massachusetts regiments, mainly in Virginia and Louisiana. Twelve men from Ashfield lost their lives fighting in Lincoln's Union armies, more from disease and infections than from wounds. Many others came back suffering from permanent disabilities; others moved off to greener fields elsewhere.

Meanwhile, however, the industrialization and urbanization of America had little impact on those who remained in Ashfield. The biggest change after the Civil War was that Ashfield became a place of summer residence for wealthy families from Boston, Cambridge, Philadelphia, and New York City. Summer weather in Ashfield is heavenly, milder and less humid than in the cities along the coast and in the Connecticut River valley. The seasonal arrival of sojourners from less salubrious climes provided local families with work as maids and housekeepers, handymen and gardeners. It had remarkably little impact, however, on the prevailing culture of the town. Ashfield remained predominantly a farming community. For year-round residents, the delightful days of western New England summers offered relief from the rigors and dangers of winter, but they were hardly times of vacation. Farming families in summertime continued to do hard, back-wrenching work in fields, barns, and kitchens.

Some of the visitors made substantial contributions to the town. One of these was George William Curtis, an associate of Abraham Lincoln, later a Mugwump (the reforming faction of the national Republican Party), a founder of *The Nation* magazine, and the creator of the *Harper's Monthly* column "The Editor's Easy Chair." Another frequent visitor was Charles Eliot Norton, the famous Harvard professor, Dante scholar, art historian, international cultural entrepreneur, correspondent of Charles Dickens, executor of John Ruskin's will, intimate friend of James Russell Lowell and Edith Wharton, and a world-class name-dropper.[4] Curtis and Norton were major figures in the culture of late nineteenth-century America, and both were strongly devoted to Ashfield, although their image of it was strongly tainted by Victorian romanticism.

Together these two men staged a series of "Ashfield dinners," gatherings in August that brought famous people (Lowell, William Dean Howells, Booker T. Washington, Mark Twain, and George Cable, among many others) to their adopted New England village to lecture on the theme of "Democracy and Education." The dinners raised funds for the local public secondary school, Sanderson Academy (for more details, see chapter 9). Without this benefaction, the academy, founded in 1816, might well have disappeared.

Ashfield enjoyed real benefits from these summer visitors. Yet they had little impact on the internal life of the town. For the visitors, Ashfield stood as an exemplar of classic virtues, an America that was vanishing under waves of immigration, industrialization, and imperial ambition. The locals tolerated this romantic conception of their situation. Indeed, many of them were generous in expressing gratitude for the employment and philanthropy of their guests.

Tensions over this clash of attitudes—the condescending nostalgia of elite visitors versus hard wrestling with rural realities by the local people—were inevitable and occasionally broke through the surface, despite earnest efforts on both sides to suppress them. Granville Stanley Hall (1844–1924) stood where these forces—Yankee old-timers and cosmopolitan visitors—collided. Hall had multigenerational roots in Ashfield.[5] He grew up working a farm, an experience that taught him the habit of relying on empirical observation. In Ashfield's neighborhood schools, he was introduced to Latin, Greek, and algebra. At age sixteen, following an interview by the local school committee, he was hired to teach at a primary school in the town's Chapel Falls neighborhood. A year later, at his mother's gentle urging and undeterred by his father's skepticism (he thought the best way for his son to earn a living would be working a farm), Hall went for a preparatory year to Williston Academy in Easthampton, Massachusetts, and then on to Williams College to prepare for the ministry.

Hall's late teen years fell during the Civil War. He gained exemptions from the draft, first for a medical problem (a minor wound, attested by a doctor at his father's urging), and then by his father's payments for a substitute. All his life long, Hall was acutely ashamed of these deferments. He admitted he was terrified at the thought of battle, but his pals in Ashfield ridiculed "exempts," and he could not help feeling acutely embarrassed at their taunts.[6]

In his memoir, Hall carefully traced the trajectory of his higher education. From Williams College he proceeded to Union Theological Seminary in New York City (not yet the bastion of higher learning it later became, more of a training ground for Protestant ministers). Thence to Germany, where he discovered not only philosophy but also alcohol, women, and the pleasures of a non-Puritan weekend. Back home in the United States, he accepted a teaching appointment at Antioch College in Ohio. Soon thereafter Charles Eliot, the president of Harvard, invited him to give twelve lectures on pedagogy, which he agreed to do when Eliot allowed that he might also deliver twelve additional lectures (gratis) on contemporary German philosophy.[7] Attendance at the latter series was "small," Hall acknowledged, "as there was no examination at the end and the course did not count for any standing or toward any degree."[8] While at Harvard, he completed his doctorate.[9] Hall went on to teach psychology at Johns Hopkins, then at the height of its influence as the American exemplar of German theories of research and scholarship. As a vigorous champion of empirical methods in psychology, he endured a good deal of hostility from Cambridge worthies like William James.[10] Nevertheless, by the turn of the century he had emerged as a public intellectual of considerable renown.

In 1888 Hall had been invited to be the founding president of Clark University in Worcester, Massachusetts. Its benefactor, Jonas Gilman Clark, envisioned a great graduate university on the Johns Hopkins model, and Hall labored mightily to pull it off. But clashing interpretations of the concept led to disastrous quarrels, making Hall's early years there a nightmare.

It was during this hard period in Hall's life that he and Norton fell to quarreling in Ashfield. Earlier, Hall had enjoyed the patronage of Norton, who had been among the prime influences in quickening his intellectual aspirations. At an early Ashfield dinner, Norton cited young Hall as an example of what education might mean to the yeomen of his adopted town. Hall's neighborhood chums responded predictably, warning him not to become "stuck up." In his memoir, Hall tells of long conversations with Norton that opened dazzling vistas to the impressionable young man. "To him I owe a great debt," he acknowledged. But Hall also reports that Norton, for all his beneficence, often failed to connect with his rural neighbors. He introduced many of them to a wide world beyond the surrounding hills and showed them that "an aristocracy existed that was not at all dependent upon wealth." On the other hand, "there were local Philistines who flouted him and all his works and ways and some who even descended to insults and some degree of sabotage." For his part, Norton "may have sometimes lacked tact and patience, or overestimated the capacity of such a community for improvement. So at least I sometimes thought and even said."[11]

The climactic encounter between these rival roosters came in 1899, at one of the Ashfield dinners, in a quarrel over the Spanish-American War. Local opinion, strongly in support of the foreign policy of President William McKinley, clashed head-on with Norton's angry critique of imperialism. Whatever Hall himself may have thought about the war, he reacted sharply to Norton's condescending attitude toward his uneducated fellow townsmen.

The bitter clash over national policy created an atmosphere in which the warm glow surrounding the Ashfield dinners suddenly grew chilly. Curtis had died in 1892, and Norton continued on alone as organizer. When he devoted the dinners of 1898 and 1899 to a ferocious denunciation of Congress's rush to war against Spain, his conservative neighbors in Ashfield smelled treason. Norton allowed one apologist for imperialism, a clergyman from Roxbury, to speak in 1899, but when he finished, Charles Dudley Warner sprang to his feet and offered a resolution: "Resolved: That we postpone the Christian religion to a more convenient season."

It took several years for the furor to calm down. In 1901 Norton offered to resign as organizer of the dinners, but it was clear that no one else had his vision and special network of contacts. The 1903 dinner was a time of healing. Frederick G. Howes, Ashfield's sage historian, who had boycotted recent dinners, gave a reconciling speech. Hall also avoided controversy, confining himself to remarks about education. Mrs. Booker T. Washington (the only woman other than Elizabeth Curtis, daughter of George William Curtis, ever to address an Ashfield dinner) spoke about her efforts to organize meetings to uplift "colored women" in the South. Norton himself gave a moving valedictory, thanking his neighbors "for all that you have been to me and have done for me." The series ended with that dinner.[12]

Continuity

I have suggested that, through the first half of the twentieth century, Ashfield's culture changed very little from colonial times. To be sure, telephones were a wonderful invention, greatly facilitating contact, especially between women in town.[13] Radios brought real-time news of the region and the world, not to mention entertainers of national reputation, into local homes. Automobiles provided increased mobility, and gas- and electric-powered machines allowed farmers to produce more milk and, by refrigeration, to ship it further (although they did little to make farming less arduous).[14] Roads gradually improved, but not by much.

The amazing thing, however, is how little difference modern technology made in the culture of a town like Ashfield. At least until the last third of the twentieth century, Ashfield still fit the term used for it by U.S. Census demographers: it was a rural town, and predominantly agricultural. A typical male citizen of Ashfield in 1950 would have felt quite at home in the Ashfield of 1800. He would have delighted in introducing his ancestors to the new machinery, but there would have been a good deal of mutual understanding between these men. They would have been similarly educated, had similar occupations, interests and concerns, and occupied similar positions in their own households and communities.

Women join the democracy

In one respect, though, significant change was already under way by the middle of the twentieth century: the place and role of women. It would have a marked effect on the culture of Ashfield.

From a modern perspective, one of the most difficult things to understand is the role played by women in a frontier town like Ashfield at its founding. Historical research undertaken by feminist scholars is enormously helpful here.[15] It shows that women and men moved in distinct spheres in colonial America. Whereas men played public roles (voting and office-holding), women, with rare exceptions, acted in private, domestic spheres. Documents from that time (diaries, letters, and claims submitted in court by loyalist women) show that women typically had little or no knowledge of their families' property. Most of them could not put a market value on their own tools, land, grain, or livestock.

It is true that most of the records we have come from women in colonial cities, rather than rural areas. City women complained of "tiresome" lives, of drudgery and boredom, loneliness and depression. Unless they were wealthy (and few were), they had to spend a great deal of time spinning, making clothes and home furnishings. They also experienced multiple pregnancies and, for good and abundant reasons, lived in dread of the agonies of childbirth. Those who survived the ordeal of giving birth spent most of their adult lives rearing children. There was little time, energy, or inclination to get involved in public affairs.[16] A powerful ideology lent support to these necessities, extolling the virtues of women who devoted their lives to nurturance and homemaking.

Two qualifications should be noted about these generalizations as they might apply to a town like Ashfield. First, the lives of rural women were less rigidly restricted than those of their urban counterparts. Many women in the country joined in outdoor work, in the fields, planting and harvesting, and in barns, milking and mucking. Second, events often intervened to disrupt domestic routines. When men went off to fight with the militia, for example, women had to do it all, as best they could. But it is fruitless to look for women exercising direct personal influence on public affairs in a place like Ashfield during the colonial and early national periods. They may have done so indirectly, through their husbands, brothers, or sons, but I have found no evidence that they did so in public, or in their own names.

That is the first and most fundamental difference between Huntstown and modern Ashfield. Thus, the most striking change since colonial and early national days has been the emergence of women as active participants in local governance. Before this transformation took place, however, women had to overcome major obstacles to gain recognition as full citizens of the commonwealth. It did not happen overnight. It required steadfast pressure, and it encountered strong resistance.

Such an important struggle justifies a short digression. In the beginning, during the founding period, women were not constituents of towns in Massachusetts. The state constitution of 1780, confirming universal practice, explicitly limited the vote for state representative, senator, and governor to "males."[17] Apart from Abigail Adams's famous letter to her husband, John Adams, hardly anyone at the time seems to have taken offense at such provisions, at least not publicly.

During the nineteenth and early twentieth centuries, Massachusetts was home to some of the leading crusaders for woman suffrage, such as Elizabeth Cady Stanton, Lucretia Mott, Lucy Stone, and Julia Ward Howe, but it also harbored a strong contingent of women opposed to it.[18] In the period following the Civil War, women did begin to seek and gain election to local school boards. In 1868 Ashfield (along with the even tinier Franklin County town of Monroe) was among the first towns where women were elected to the local school board, followed shortly by Lynn, Worcester, and Boston.

Not everyone regarded this as a significant advance for the suffrage movement. Harriet H. Robinson, an activist and the author of a history of the women's suffrage movement in Massachusetts, called it a "palpable sham."[19] School committees did not control appropriations, the choice of supervisors, the building of school houses, or even the books children used. If they did, said Robinson, "the result [few women across the state exercising their right to vote for candidates for school board] might have been different." As it is, Robinson thought, the election of school committee members was "not a vital one with either male or female voters, and it is impossible to get up any enthusiasm on the subject."[20] A better indication of sentiment toward women voting was a nonbinding referendum in 1895 that would have allowed women to vote in municipal elections. Women were granted a special exemption that allowed them to vote on this question. Even so, it was rejected overwhelmingly. Ninety-six percent of the women who voted (23,000 of 24,000) voted in the affirmative, but only 32 percent of male voters (87,000 of 274,000). In 1915 voters statewide (this time only men) were polled on whether they favored a women's suffrage amendment to the national Constitution. The only community in the state that returned a positive vote was Tewksbury, where the tally was 149 to 148. Statewide only 35.5 percent voted yes.[21] By 1918 about half the states had granted women full or partial voting rights. In Massachusetts, however, it was not until 1920, with the passage of the Nineteenth Amendment, that women gained the vote. But even after that, for cultural reasons office-holding at the local level would not be open to women. It was not until the 1980s that a woman was elected to the select board in Ashfield.

By the end of the twentieth century, however, the revolution in women's public roles seemed complete and secure. Women were routinely serving in Ashfield's elected positions, including frequently as chair of the select board.

A cultural revolution

I turn now to the cultural revolution that occurred in Ashfield between mid-century and the mid-1980s. It is this we need to grasp, for it provides the context for the accounts of political life in Part II of this book.

In modern Ashfield there are several names that carry echoes of colonial and early national times: Howes, Sears, Craft, Williams, Gray, Pease, Cranson. Their forebears were among the early settlers; their surnames are on the Civil War monuments; some of them till land that was first cleared and cultivated by their direct ancestors.

The attitudes of these old-timers toward the transformation we are tracing vary across a wide spectrum. Some welcome it warmly. Craftsmen and farmers find a steadily renewing stream of discriminating new customers who admire and can afford their services. Some old-timers appreciate the willingness, the eagerness that newcomers show, to participate in local institutions, from churches to scout troops, from school boards to the planning board and water district.

Others, however, feel deep irritation at the invasion of people from alien cultures. One old-timer describes the influx, and the ensuing changes in Ashfield's culture, as a "bloodless coup." What maddens him most is that people who move into Ashfield, professing to love its rural character, set out immediately to change it. Asked for an example, he cited the creation in the mid-1990s of a youth commission.[22] Before the influx of newcomers, town families took care of one another's children, and it would not have occurred to anyone to ask the town for help, financial or otherwise, with this.[23] Another example he gave was the creation of a human rights commission, charged with forestalling expressions of prejudice by offering training in "sensitivity." Such programs, he said, are part and parcel of modern liberalism, which instinctively seeks a governmental solution to everything, including personal problems, but they are anathema from the standpoint of the town's ancient ideals.

The political dimension: "Steady habits" no longer

As it happens, this old-timer's politically oriented observations point to a change that can be measured quite precisely. One mark of Ashfield's transformation over the last quarter of the twentieth century is its abrupt about-face in partisan affiliation.

In 1970 the town was a Republican stronghold. By 2000 it routinely gave large majorities to Democratic candidates. We can pinpoint just when Democrats replaced Republicans as the dominant party in Ashfield by graphing voters who have enrolled with the two major parties since 1960.[24] The two lines intersect in the mid-1980s. Before that, there were as many as three times the number of Republicans as Democrats. The proportions gradually shifted until, by the turn of the millennium, there were nearly twice as many Democrats as Republicans, and the actual voting in elections shows an even more marked shift in partisan orientation.

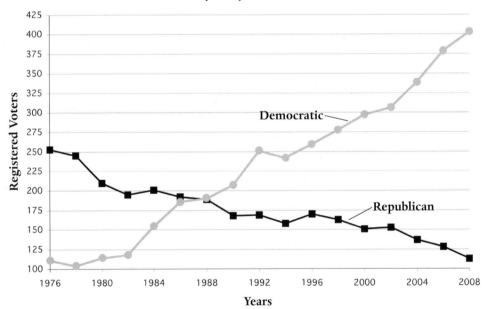

Enrollment by Party in Ashfield, 1976–2008

Statistics provided by the Department of the Massachusetts Secretary of State. Enrollment figures were not available for the years prior to 1976.

Such stark and persisting changes in a community's party affiliations do not occur easily. Usually it takes either a cataclysmic event (a war or a major economic depression) or a major migration of population to cause such a change. When changes like this do occur, they are usually accompanied by acute social tensions. We should not be surprised to find these things as we trace the profound shift that occurred in Ashfield on the eve of the second millennium.

Two factors contributed to the town's huge shift in partisan affiliation. One, undoubtedly, was migration. New people—a large cohort of young families—moved to Ashfield during the last quarter of the twentieth century. Most of them were Democrats. They came from cities, and often their households were headed by college graduates in their thirties and forties. They came to Ashfield not for a summer holiday but to make year-round homes and raise families. They were eager to engage in the life of the community, to be active in school politics, to join one or another of the town's many boards and commissions, both appointive and elective. Many of them worked at crafts (leather-working, glass-blowing, silversmithing), selling their products at shows in the area, at craft fairs around the country, and wholesale to major stores in New York, Boston, and Philadelphia. Many of them listened to National Public Radio while they worked. With the arrival of these newcomers in significant numbers, the population of Ashfield began to grow, and the culture of the town gradually changed.

But there was another factor at work here, too. Ronald Reagan used to say that he did not leave the Democratic Party; the party left him. That's how many of Ashfield's old timers feel about the post-Eisenhower Republican Party. As the GOP was taken over by radical reactionaries from the Southwest and, later, the South, many Yankees recoiled. Some found an outlet in maverick candidates, such as John Anderson in 1980 or Ross Perot in 1992; a few probably stayed home in disgust and did not vote; others gradually began to vote for Democrats for statewide and national offices. How many former Republicans actually switched party affiliation is difficult to determine, but anecdotal evidence suggests that over time many did.

Looking at actual voting, we can see how these shifts changed the political face of Ashfield over the last four decades of the twentieth century.

The presidential campaign of 1960 is a good place to begin. The Democratic candidate that year was Massachusetts' own junior senator, John F. Kennedy, and the Republican candidate was Vice President Richard Nixon.[25] Kennedy strongly carried his home state (roughly 60%, to 40% for Nixon)—but not Ashfield. Nixon won the town with 439 votes; Kennedy got just 115.

In 1962 George C. Lodge was the Republican nominee for the U.S. Senate, running against Edward M. Kennedy in a special election to fill the seat vacated when his brother was elected president two years earlier. Ted Kennedy won handsomely statewide (55%, to 41% for Lodge), but in Ashfield he lost badly, 385 to 60. In 1966 the Republican candidate for Senate, Edward Brooke, an African American, won in Ashfield over the Democratic nominee, former Governor Endicott Peabody, 383 to 45 (Brooke also won statewide by a lopsided margin, 61% to 39%). In those days, however they ran statewide, Republicans normally carried Ashfield by a wide margin.

There was one anomaly during those years, however, and it was significant. In 1964 Lyndon B. Johnson and Barry Goldwater finished dead-even in Ashfield, with 261 votes each.[26] This was truly a remarkable outcome at the time. What it showed was that many of Ashfield's Republicans were uncomfortable with Goldwater's red-meat, Southwest-style conservatism.

By 1968 partisan allegiance had reasserted itself in Ashfield. Most Republican candidates won easily. Nixon prevailed over Hubert Humphrey by 382 to 136. (George Wallace got just 12 votes here.) In 1970 Republican candidates for statewide office again did well in Ashfield. Josiah Spaulding topped Senator Ted Kennedy, 321 to 144; and for governor, Republican Francis Sargent beat Boston's mayor (and Williams College graduate), Kevin White, by 352 to 95. In the 1972 general election Ashfield voters were still strongly Republican for most races. Incumbent Senator Brooke beat his Democratic challenger, 515 to 86, and the incumbent Republican state senator won over his Democratic opponent, 440 to 197.[27] But the slim margin for President Nixon over George McGovern, just 372 to 258, hinted at a growing spirit of resistance to instinctive Republicanism.

A further glimpse of the growing difficulties for Ashfield Republicans came in the party's 1976 presidential primary. Gerald Ford, the incumbent, defeated Ronald Reagan, 88 to 23. President Ford, appearing steady and solid despite his pardon of Nixon, seemed just fine to most Ashfield Republicans. There was little support for a Western-style insurgency in these hills.

Despite the turmoil in the national party, the 1976 general elections revealed that local Republicans were still mostly dominant in Ashfield. Ford prevailed over Jimmy Carter, 415 to 293. Senator Ted Kennedy finally won the town, defeating a weak Republican candidate, 406 to 308. In other legislative contests in 1976 there was some pretty determined ticket-splitting. Ashfield voters supported Republican Silvio Conte for reelection to Congress over challenger Ed McColgan of Northampton, 537 to 210; and they emphatically returned Republican Jay Healy, from neighboring Charlemont, to the Massachusetts lower house, giving him 636 votes. In the state senate race, however, they supported the incumbent Democrat, John Olver, by roughly the same margin they had given to Senator Kennedy. This pattern—supporting incumbent liberal Republicans (Conte and Healy), but at the same time favoring Olver and Democratic candidates for the U.S. Senate (Ted Kennedy, Paul Tsongas, and John Kerry)—would hold until the end of the century.

A further indication of the character of Ashfield's Republicans came in the 1980 presidential primaries. John Anderson, a liberal Republican member of Congress from Illinois, was the clear winner in Ashfield, with 120 votes out of 244 cast by Republicans in that year's primary. The elder George Bush received 60 votes. Ronald Reagan, the eventual nominee that year, finished a distant third, with 42 votes. Ashfield's Democrats were also torn. Home-state Senator Ted Kennedy's insurgent campaign against a sitting president of his own party got 60 votes; the incumbent, President Carter, 59; and California's governor, Pat Brown, 11.

By 1982 a fundamental shift in Ashfield's politics was clearly setting in. In the gubernatorial race, Michael Dukakis prevailed over the Republican candidate by 357 to 288. Even so, two other races from that period showed that Republicans still had considerable weight. In 1984 President Reagan snatched a narrow victory over Walter Mondale, 414 to 406. And John Kerry, although a winner in Ashfield over the Republican nominee for the U.S. Senate, prevailed by the relatively narrow margin of 434 to 384.

It is at about this time that the lines indicating the proportion of registrants affiliating with each major party intersect. In 1986 Republicans made up 19.88 percent of Ashfield's enrolled voters; Democrats stood at

19.25 percent. Two years later, Democrats had increased to 19.98 percent; Republicans had fallen to 18.36 percent. From that point on, Democrats trended steadily upward, to about 27 percent by 2000; Republicans went in the other direction, to about 12 percent in 2000.

Moreover, judging by actual voting over the 1990s, it is clear that party enrollment figures substantially underestimated the degree of change in Ashfield's political culture. Many voters who registered to vote but enrolled with neither party apparently leaned in the Democratic direction. In the 1992 general elections, for example, Bill Clinton won in Ashfield, receiving 525 votes. Finishing second was the independent candidate, Ross Perot, with 230 votes. The elder George Bush, running for reelection, finished third, getting only 216.[28] In 1996 Clinton repeated his strong showing in Ashfield with 581 votes, to Robert Dole's 224. This time Perot trailed, with just 90 votes.

There was another revealing race just before the turn of the century. In 1998, Scott Harshbarger, the state's highly respected attorney general, gained the Democratic nomination for governor. Harshbarger's vigorous investigations of corruption had irritated urban Democratic officials across Massachusetts, and he lost the general election that year to the Republican nominee, Paul Celluci, 47 percent to 51 percent. Ashfield's Democrats apparently did not share the resentment against the crusading Harshbarger, however. He won in Ashfield decisively, 411 to 263.

The presidential election of 2000 affords a final glimpse of where Ashfield stood politically at the end of the twentieth century. Nationally George W. Bush lost the popular vote by a half-million votes and won the presidency only by prevailing in the Supreme Court in the contest for Florida's electoral votes. Students of that contest will recall that Florida's ballot invited confusion between votes for Al Gore, the Democratic candidate, and Pat Buchanan, a conservative running to Bush's right. Ashfield's voters had little difficulty making that choice. Buchanan got four votes out of about 1,000 cast. Gore won, receiving just over 50 percent (513). Ralph Nader, running on Gore's left, got 183 votes, about 20 percent. Only one-quarter of the town's voters (251) supported the eventual winner, George W. Bush.

Turning to referendums over the same four decades, we find a mixed picture, but also some revealing glimpses into Ashfield's political culture.

In 1970, as the nation agonized over President Nixon's "incursion" into Cambodia, Ashfield voters pondered a menu of options on that year's ballot. Should the United States press on for "victory" in Vietnam (70 voters chose that alternative), withdraw in accordance with President Nixon's policy (268 votes), or withdraw "immediately" (88 votes). Nearly as many of the town's voters favored stronger action in Vietnam as called for withdrawal. A decisive majority stood strongly with the Republican administration.

Curiously, amidst all the evidence of change in political attitudes in Ashfield, there have been a few constants. For example, the town's voters have always opposed a graduated state income tax. Massachusetts has a flat state income tax of around 5 percent. This is the bane of those who favor a progressive tax, and there have been repeated attempts (by referendums in 1972, 1976, and 1994) to build pressure for a graduated tax on income. The result in Ashfield has sometimes been fairly close (288–300, 315–419, and 368–396, respectively, in those three contests), but over the decades a slim majority has steadily opposed a progressive income tax.

There are other consistencies, too. Ashfield has a strong environmental sensitivity, and it lies about twenty-five miles from Rowe, Massachusetts, the site of a plant that used nuclear fuel to generate electricity from 1961 until it was shut down in 1992.[29] Nuclear wastes are still stored there. One might assume that townspeople would be easily frightened by warnings about the dangers posed by such plants. Yet support for nuclear power to generate electricity has been pretty steady over the years. In 1974, a referendum called for closing the nuclear-powered generator in Rowe and the Vermont Yankee nuclear plant in Vernon, Vermont. It was decisively defeated, 125 to 332. A 1980 referendum demanding a moratorium on building more nuclear-powered plants was nearly a draw (354 in favor, 343 opposed). Another referendum, in 1988, asked voters whether existing nuclear-powered plants should be closed; 499 voted no and only 410 yes.

On some issues Ashfield's libertarian streak has led it to take progressive positions, even when Republicans were normally prevailing in partisan contests. For example, in 1972, the town voted 513–74 in favor of making eighteen-year-olds eligible to vote. ("If they're old enough to fight in Vietnam, they're old enough to vote" seemed to be the sentiment that carried the day here, as it did elsewhere.) In 1976 Ashfield supported, by 497 to 241, the ERA, the proposed constitutional amendment to ensure equal rights for women.

Some results have been enigmatic. In 1972 Ashfield favored prayer in public schools by 473 to 130. A decade later, voters decisively rejected public aid to private schools, 133 to 503. It is not clear to what extent these results reflected a changing electorate, or just an enduring commitment to public schools.

On one topic Ashfield's response was as clear as it was predictable. In 1988 a statewide movement called for new rules regarding the treatment of domestic farm animals. It recommended the creation of a "scientific advisory board" to devise and implement new standards for the humane treatment of farm animals. Farmers and their many allies in Ashfield rose to meet this challenge. They prepared a resolution to present to annual town meeting. "The care of animals in a humane manner has been followed for generations on family farms in Ashfield," it declared. Livestock farming was "vital to the town's economic base and open space." The ill-informed drive to "protect" farm animals threatened livestock farming as a way of life.[30] The resolution passed town meeting unanimously. No one in Ashfield wanted counsel from the Boston suburbs about how to treat farm animals.

The state's animal-rights proponents put the question on the ballot in November 1988. Ashfield's voters welcomed another chance to register their disdain for suburban do-gooders, rejecting, by a whopping margin of 805 to 105, the proposal to develop new statewide regulations for the treatment of domestic farm animals. That dog simply would not hunt in Ashfield.[31]

The town's voters have typically shown strong resistance to well-financed campaigns by industrial lobbies. In 1976 a referendum developed by State Senator John Olver proposed to add a charge to the cost of drinks sold in bottles or cans, redeemable when the containers were returned. Despite heavy lobbying by bottlers, Olver's referendum carried in Ashfield by 454 to 302. It was on the ballot again in 1982. This time it carried by 471 to 154. Ashfield, generally a pretty conservative town in those days, was sensitive to environmental issues. Olver's bottle bill made sense to most of its voters.

By the end of the 1980s, votes on referendums showed that Ashfield was becoming a bastion of liberal causes. In 1988 a statewide effort to repeal the prevailing wage law was on the ballot. Strongly supported by unions but zealously opposed by most corporations, the concept of pre-vailing wage is pretty well understood by most voters in Massachusetts. It means higher pay for laborers, but higher costs for those who hire them, including towns. Everyone in town knew stories about how this law af-fected rural communities, driving up costs to urban standards. Neverthe-less, Ashfield's voters opposed repeal of the prevailing wage standard by 386 to 501.

Four years later, in 1992, Ashfield supported a question calling for a national health insurance program, 586 to 265; and public financing for political campaigns, 575 to 241. And in 1994 voters supported a referen-dum that would have made seat-belt use mandatory, 497 to 273. By the 1990s Ashfield had become a dependably progressive town.

Further evidence of the town's new political culture in the 1980s and 1990s emerged from a series of resolutions on foreign policy and national security. Many people in Ashfield ridicule these resolutions. They seem largely symbolic, and they have no measurable impact on national policy. On the other hand, town meeting is Ashfield's legislature, its main gov-erning body. Such resolutions give an opportunity not only to discuss the leading issues of the day, but also to take a collective stand on them.

In 1982 a resolution called for a freeze on the development of nuclear arms. It noted that there were no defenses against nuclear weapons and no winners in a nuclear exchange. It called on President Reagan to invite the Soviet Union to negotiate an immediate halt to the nuclear arms race, to transfer funds to domestic civilian uses, and to convert the nuclear arms industry to "civilian production, thus protecting jobs and strength-ening our national economy." The resolution passed at town meeting by majority vote (the specific tally was not recorded).[32]

Two years later town meeting declared Ashfield a Nuclear Free Zone. To promote the health and safety of residents and to advance global peace, the resolution said, no nuclear weapons were to be "produced, transported, stored, processed, or detonated within the borders of the Town."[33] In 1986 town meeting adopted a resolution with a little more bite; instead of sending messages to far-off officials, it added a directive to its own employees. The resolution noted that thousands of refugees were fleeing from violence and gross human rights violations in Central America, El Salvador, and Guatemala, and noted that the Immigration and Naturalization Service "rarely grants" political asylum to these refugees. It declared that Ashfield would be a Town of Sanctuary and Refuge for Central American refugees. Further, it directed that, to the extent legally possible, no employee of Ashfield should assist or voluntarily cooperate with any investigation or arresting procedures involving these refugees, and it invited other towns to join in making the United States "once more . . . a place of refuge for oppressed people."[34]

By 1990 the Soviet Union was collapsing, and national politics was full of talk about a "peace dividend." The town joined this debate, considering a resolution that directed the town clerk to notify President Bush that residents of Ashfield "feel compelled by conscience, civic responsibility and common sense to PROTEST the draining of our scarce financial resources for excessive military spending." While local government struggled to make ends meet, the resolution said, "approximately $1,880,000 from Ashfield's residents will be spent on the Pentagon's $300,000,000,000 budget." With the Cold War now "officially recognized as over," the resolution declared that national security depended, "not on missiles, bombers and overseas bases, but on such basic and fundamental necessities as a first-rate education for our children, affordable housing, low-cost medical care, and a clean environment." The resolution was adopted by a majority voice vote, making it clear that idealism (or was it utopian foolishness?) was at least momentarily ascendant in Ashfield.[35] An even more sweeping resolution was brought to town meeting two years later, calling on the national government to reduce defense spending by 50 percent each year for the next five years. It passed unanimously.

Such resolutions, on foreign and other national policies, tend to come up late on the agenda, and to judge by the dwindling attendance at the later stages of the meetings, most people in town do not give a hoot about them. One is almost embarrassed to read them fifteen years later. Their glibness contrasts so starkly with the careful wording and close attention paid to articles that deal with matters like zoning, schools, roads, police and fire department budgets, property taxes, and the like. On the other hand, in retrospect these resolutions seem no more foolish than the crackpot realism that passed for national policy in the wake of the attack on the World Trade Center and the Pentagon on September 11, 2001. Both reveal the hazards of unleashing ideology when prudence would serve us better—with this difference: in Ashfield's case, the consequences of unbridled principle did infinitely less damage than did the policies put in place by national-security elites.

A demographic portrait of modern Ashfield

Beneath these political shifts lay the changing demography of the town.

Ashfield's population grew steadily from 1960 to the end of the century. In 1960 the federal census showed just 1,131 people living in town. By 1970 the number had grown 12.6 percent, to 1,274. Growth gathered momentum over the next two decades: to 1,458 (an increase of 14.4 percent) in 1980 and 1,715 (an additional 17.6 percent) in 1990. By the turn of the century, it reached an even 1,800.[36] Thus over the last four decades of the twentieth century, Ashfield's population grew by nearly 60 percent.[37]

Prior to this time, Ashfield had been somewhat isolated from the forces that were causing population increases in various parts of Massachusetts. For example, the huge expansion of the University of Massachusetts in Amherst, beginning in the 1960s, led to substantial population increases in many Hampshire County towns and cities. A few employees and graduate students of the University lived in Ashfield, but not many. The twenty-five mile commute, particularly chancy in wintertime, prevented greater impact from this development.

Beginning around 1970, however, Ashfield began to attract a different kind of resident. Young families, many of them refugees from metropolitan areas, tired of commuting to suburbs, eager to live in a rural setting, began to put down roots here. Some, as I noted earlier, were craftspeople; others were writers and editors for major magazines and publishing houses, enabled by new technologies to work at a considerable distance from media centers in New York and Boston. Still others were professors and teachers, willing to drive as much as twenty or thirty miles each day to work in Northampton or Amherst in order to live in a rural community in the foothills of the Berkshires. They came with their families and immediately began to take an interest in local schools. (Later, as we will see in chapter 9, some of them, discouraged by the effects of the funding crisis that depressed the quality of local schools, began to establish charter schools, or to educate their children at home. Even then, one of these parents was elected to the school board and gave generously of her time to try to improve the local public schools.)

Others established farms in town, bringing a new kind of agriculture: organic.[38] At first there were tensions between practitioners of old and new techniques in farming, but gradually respect between them grew. They had, after all, much in common, especially the difficulty of wringing a living from New England's stingy soil and daunting climate.

With the influx of these young families, by the late 1970s one could begin to speak of a new Ashfield—so long as one was mindful of aspects that remain thoroughly traditional. In some ways, modern Ashfield is still a rural New England community. It is also relatively isolated. Residents must travel at least twenty miles (thirty minutes, on good roads) to reach a hospital, supermarkets, clothing stores, dry cleaning, movie theatres and classical music concerts, or a college or university.

Income

Ashfield is not an affluent community. At the time of the 2000 U.S. Census, the median household income of residents stood at $52,875.[39] This was half-again higher than the poorest of the neighboring towns (Hawley, Colrain, and Charlemont), and slightly higher than the statewide median, but far behind such affluent Boston-area suburbs as Lincoln and Wellesley, or even Longmeadow, a suburb of Springfield. The median value of homes sold in Ashfield in 2005 was $228,607; across Massachusetts that year it was $361,500.

There are certainly households in Ashfield that know the dull weight and painful sting of economic distress. The 2000 census found 7.6 percent of the town's population in poverty. (Conway, a comparable community contiguous to the east, had less than half that proportion: 3.5%.) Of children in Ashfield, 15.4 percent were being raised in poverty (compared with 41.9% in Holyoke and 34.3% in Springfield, but just 8.9% in Northampton and 2.9% in nearby Williamsburg). In addition, one out of four children under eighteen in Ashfield (25.9%) was being raised by a single parent.[40] Those children were not all poor, but given the strains of raising children alone, a proportion that high does serve as a reminder of the difficulties faced by many of the town's families.

Another way to measure the economic situation of Ashfield residents focuses on the relationship between housing and income. A group studying economic development in the Franklin County area developed a measure of the "affordability" of housing in various towns in both Franklin and Hampshire counties.[41] It related median household income to the median price of a single-family home. By this metric, remote and thoroughly rural Heath received the highest rating, an index number of 91.4—meaning that houses in Heath are very affordable or cheap in comparison with the median income of residents. Northampton and Amherst, the sites of Smith, Amherst, and Hampshire colleges and the University of Massachusetts, received scores of 24.5 and 21, respectively, on the affordability scale, reflecting the recent sharp rise in real estate prices in those communities. Thus, a person buying a house in Amherst would likely need to be wealthier than the person from whom she was buying it. Furthermore, inasmuch as tax rates tend to reflect property values, it was presumably becoming more difficult for homeowners of median income to pay property taxes in a town like Amherst. They would be under increasingly intense pressure to sell their homes to a wealthier family and find housing in a community where real estate values were lower.

On this affordability spectrum from Heath to Amherst, Ashfield stood at 40.5, in the top third of the communities measured, closer to Heath than to Amherst. Thus, while the pressure of property taxes is great for many Ashfield families, it is manageable by regional standards. If families of modest means living in Ashfield wished to reduce their property taxes, they would probably have to search for housing outside of Franklin County. And since Franklin County is the poorest county in Massachusetts, such families might have to look in Vermont's notoriously poor Northeast Kingdom, or down south—or move to Heath, which, by the way, is locally famous for its outstanding public primary school.

Occupations

According to the 2000 census, of Ashfield's employed people sixteen years old and older, about one-third (319) work in "educational, health and social services" and another hundred or so in a broad category that includes "professional, scientific, management, administrative and waste management services." Seventy-four people work in "arts, entertainment, recreation, accommodation and food services," 45 in "information," 39 in "public administration," and 29 in "finance, insurance, real estate, and rental and leasing" services. Adding up these numbers, we find almost two-thirds of employed people in Ashfield working in "services" of one kind or another. Of the remainder, just over a hundred work in "manufacturing," another hundred in "construction," a few less than a hundred in "wholesale trade" and "retail trade" combined.

That leaves just fifty-seven people in "agriculture, forestry, fishing and hunting, and mining." The number of people employed in agriculture has been declining in recent decades. In 1980 the census counted 84 persons employed in agriculture; in 1990, 79; and at the turn of the millennium, just 57. What was causing this precipitous decline? The principal factor was the disappearance of dairy farming. In 1950 there were fifteen or twenty dairy farms in Ashfield. Now there are three.

It is hard work making a living as a dairy farmer.[42] A typical day begins about 5 a.m. Morning chores include feeding, setting up to milk, cleaning the barn, milking, and feeding calves. Then a break for breakfast. Twice a week, the rest of the morning is spent hauling feed; every morning feed is mixed for the next day. In the afternoon, another feeding, then hauling manure—to his own field if the farmer grows his own hay; if not, to a neighbor's field. Then another round of cleaning the barn and milking. Work ends about 7:30 p.m. Next morning, the round begins again. There are no weekend breaks, no holidays, rain or shine, and no vacations, winter or summer.

Another factor is that dairy farmers depend on a support system: repair people, harder and harder to find, to fix cranky equipment, and large-animal veterinarians, also spread thin, who may be answering a call on the other side of the county when you need her or him most.

In light of the grueling work, slim profit margins, and dwindling support systems, it is remarkable that there is any dairy farming left in New England at all. Massachusetts produces about 300 million pounds of milk, an estimated 6–8 percent of the milk it uses. The rest comes mostly from large farms in New York State and the Midwest.

Considering that just 5 percent of Ashfield's workforce is employed in the census category that includes agriculture (along with forestry, fishing and hunting, and mining), the tenderness of local opinion toward farmers and farming is remarkable. In 2006 Ashfield's farmers pressed town meeting to establish a local commission on agriculture. It was readily accomplished. The commission has no real powers; its role is advisory, and it is unfunded. In fact, it is not clear whom the commission will advise, how, or about what. But farmers passionately wanted it, and it passed unopposed.

A more substantial indication of local sympathy for farmers is the absence of vocal opposition to a state program called APR, or Agricultural Preservation Restriction. It allows farmers to pay lower taxes on land used for farming. The program, designed to protect agricultural land from development, sets criteria that are not onerous. Parcels must be at least five acres in size, and they must have produced at least $500 in gross sales per year on the initial five acres plus $5 for each additional acre, or fifty cents per acre of woodland or wetland. Beyond these basic standards, in approving parcels for the program the state takes into account the likelihood that the land, if protected, will "remain in agriculture for the foreseeable future." Once a site is accepted, in exchange for giving up the right to use it for other purposes or sell it to a developer, a farmer pays sharply reduced property taxes. If he later changes his mind and takes his property out of the program, he must pay back taxes, and the town gets the right of first refusal if he decides to sell the land.[43]

Despite the fact that the APR program redistributes part of the tax burden away from farmers toward owners of other kinds of property, it generates virtually no controversy in Ashfield. No one resents this break for farmers. Everyone in the town values the rural landscape, and everyone knows that farming is hard. Those who grow a few vegetables themselves have at least a dim understanding of the vagaries of farming. Some amateurs even produce a little maple syrup or a few eggs. This experience helps to make us deeply grateful for those who supply our gross deficiencies and cover our inevitable failures. Living near them helps us to understand our dependence on them and on other farmers.

Education

Ashfield's population is relatively well educated. Of people over twenty-four, practically all (94.5%) are high school graduates (the figure for the United States is 80.4%). Almost half of Ashfield's adults (46.5%) are college graduates (compared with 24.4% in the United States).[44] Only a few other communities in western Massachusetts are comparable to Ashfield in this respect. Conway, with 46.9 percent who are college graduates, is slightly higher. Northampton and Williamsburg are close, with 46.1 percent and 39 percent, respectively. But the city of Springfield has 15.4 percent, Holyoke 16.9 percent; and many small towns in the area—Erving, Palmer, Ware—are below 15 percent.[45] A large proportion of Ashfield's residents are well educated—causing some of those without a college education to feel intimidated at town meetings, where people with verbal skills have an advantage in discussions and debates (although they do not always win the ensuing votes).

Race and other diversities

Another fact is worth noting. Ashfield likes to think of itself as diverse, by which people mean that our residents come from all over, with many different occupations and outlooks, a spectrum of attitudes toward culture and religion, a variety of family types. Contrary to this self-image, however, the class spectrum is not broad, by national standards, and there is practically no ethnic or racial diversity.

Blacks may actually have been proportionally as large among Ashfield's residents in the founding period as they are now. A black man named Heber Honestman participated in the 1739 drawing that distributed the original lots in Huntstown. (Unlike most who drew lots in the so-called "first division" of 1739, Heber, as he was universally called, eventually settled in Ashfield.)[46] A few decades later, a freedman named Peter Wells lived near the center of town, on what is still called Peter Hill. In 2000, according to the national census, in a population of eighteen hundred there were just eleven "black or African Americans," eight "Hispanic or Latino (of any race)," two "American Indians," six "Asians," and one person of "some other race." Twenty-eight people were listed as of "two or more races." That left more than 97 percent who were simply "white."

Two special town meetings

Our focus in this book is on town meetings—principally the annual meeting in May, but also special town meetings held throughout the year.[47]

Town meetings are the central arena of local politics and government. Here citizens elect town officials and establish a budget (appropriations and taxes) for the coming fiscal year. At each of these critical moments in the exercise of local democracy, citizens gauge and test their trust in one another and in their elected officials, and they set the boundaries of the public agenda.

Successive special town meetings in the spring of 2005, sandwiched around that year's annual meeting in May, dramatically revealed how this testing happens and to what effect. The first, in mid-April, focused on creating a town common (I will have more to say about that in chapter 10), but there were eleven other articles on the warrant that day, all relating to fiscal matters. Most were routine, dealing with expenditures for which there were not—indeed, could not have been—sufficient funds in the budget for the 2005 fiscal year, such as overtime pay for the highway crew to plow an unusual amount of snow that winter.

There were a couple of warrant articles, however, that were not routine, that might have caused trouble. One dealt with a medical bill, amounting to $167.50, for services rendered in the previous fiscal year. The bill had not been presented in a timely fashion. Under state law, paying such a bill after the books on a fiscal year are closed requires virtual unanimity (a 90 percent majority). When pressed for details, the select board said it was not free to speak candidly about this item. Many voters guessed that the circumstances related to a former police chief who resigned after suffering a job-related disability. To avoid litigation, the town had agreed to a settlement that seemed exorbitant to many voters. The select board pleaded with voters to pass this article without further questioning, and they did, with just a smattering of audible negative votes. When the moderator declared the required 90 percent majority, no one raised an objection.

Another article asked for $550 to cover the costs of mailing a request from the assessors for information about personal property. The mailing, consisting only of a long printed form, had mystified many recipients. When they went to Town Hall and asked for an explanation, they were told that a follow-up letter would soon be sent. It had still not come. This fiasco, an early warning of the episode involving Cranston and Perlman that I recounted in the introduction, could have raised a stink, but the questioning at the special town meeting was gentle and sympathetic. Thom Gray, a former member of the select board then serving on the finance committee, went so far as to thank the chair of the assessors board for alerting us to the need for an inventory of personal property for tax purposes. (Is that what was happening?) The money was voted, and once again, an awkward moment passed quietly, out of respect for those involved.

What (besides the lateness of the hour) accounted for the easy side-stepping of so many potential landmines? For one thing, Ashfield has become dependent on the "checks and balances" provided by the finance committee. Residents depend on the finance committee to examine the select board's requests carefully, even skeptically. In these cases, the committee supported the select board's requests, and if the committee was satisfied, voters were inclined to go along. Trust lubricates the wheels of government. It is easily lost, and once lost, it is hard to regain. But where and while it exists, democracy can be an efficient form of government. The danger, of course, is that voters may slumber and become pliant. Nothing on the agenda of this special town meeting roused the languid populace.

The select board called a second special town meeting that year for June 27, mainly for budgetary housekeeping—but also to consider an article presented by petition: whether to rescind a vote of the annual town meeting that called for an end to the deployment of Massachusetts National Guard troops in Iraq. The vote to recall the soldiers had passed in the waning moments of the annual meeting in May, by a vote of about 25–10. Though few had remained long enough to vote on the resolution, the result seemed not unrepresentative of prevailing opinion for a town that had favored John Kerry over George W. Bush by 839 votes to 236.

As it turned out, a small but intense group of citizens, feeling bruised when they heard later about the May proceedings, quietly organized to take counteraction. They gathered signatures on a petition to place an article on the warrant for the special meeting, "to see whether the Town would vote to rescind" the May vote. Close to one hundred voters turned out for this special town meeting, probably more than were in attendance at the annual town meeting in May at its midday height, and at least three or four times the number that had voted for the resolution when it was originally presented.

In an impressive demonstration of political mobilization and muscle, the petitioners seized control of the June meeting at the outset. First, someone moved to have the relevant article, which was listed last on the published warrant, moved forward to be considered first, presumably so that those who had come out to support the rescinding would not have to wait through the rest of the agenda. One of the petitioners immediately called the question on the proposed alteration in the agenda; this means that the moderator must immediately take a vote to see whether the proposal is to be voted on without any further debate. Such a motion requires a two-thirds majority to pass. The vote to cut off debate passed by 56 to 9 (raised hands, counted), and the motion to alter the agenda itself passed, by a decisive oral majority. The meeting proceeded immediately to Article 11, the motion to rescind the resolution calling for an end to the deployment of the state's National Guard troops in the Iraq conflict.

Another petitioner then made a brief speech in favor of rescinding, saying that, even though the May 7 resolution had contained several "whereases" that claimed support for American troops in Iraq, it was not convincing in that regard. It could only be interpreted as critical of the heroic efforts of these townspeople in defense of freedom. The speech was brief, reasonable, and respectful.

Next a speaker rose to oppose the motion to rescind. An elderly man, he had been a principal sponsor of the May resolution. He arrived a few minutes late for this meeting (his wife was hospitalized in Springfield, and he did not expect the meeting to get to Article 11 until later in the evening). He entered the hall as the previous speaker was finishing his remarks. When he was recognized, he spoke passionately about his own and his family's military service and about his respect for soldiers. But he deplored what he said were the president's lies that propelled us to war in Iraq and his administration's bungled policy during the occupation. He was sorry, he said, to see a recurrence of the spirit that had divided the town so bitterly a century earlier, over the war against Spain. At this point the moderator interrupted to urge him not to speak too long, and he readily complied, concluding directly with a call to stand by the earlier resolution. Immediately one of the petitioners called the question. The vote to end debate—again, with a two-thirds majority required—was 70–17. The meeting proceeded directly to a vote on Article 11, to rescind the vote taken in April. It passed by a decisive oral majority, almost unanimously.

It was over. It took about ten minutes.

Many at this June meeting, probably the majority, regretted that local men and women might feel undermined by criticism of a policy for which they were prepared to give their lives. But there was another concern here as well. Some voters in Ashfield believe that it is wrong to use town meeting to take a stand on national issues. People who care about such matters can write letters to the editor or to their representatives in Congress, or vote in presidential and congressional elections. Town meetings, they believe, are for local matters, things we know well. When we vote on local matters, our votes are decisive and have an immediate effect. In this view, it is foolish to divert attention into channels far from home.

In chapter 3, on Ashfield during the Revolutionary War, we saw that matters of foreign and security policy were vital concerns of local government during the founding period. The national government could not have functioned without the active support of town governments in New England. That is no longer true. Even so, town meetings sometimes serve as a forum for expressing feelings and convictions about matters that lie beyond our ability to regulate them effectively. Ashfield's town meetings have passed resolutions condemning domestic violence, for example. We've seen that they have enacted policies against transporting nuclear waste on highways through town. As a regulation of interstate commerce, the anti-nuclear resolution would probably not stand up in court. No matter. It expresses a wish to set limits on the impact of national policy in our small space. People speak of their frustration about a lack of effectiveness (what political scientists call a sense of efficacy) in national and global affairs. Some people in Ashfield treasure these opportunities to act as a community on such matters.

Still, one can understand the feeling, generally strongest among those whose families have multigenerational roots in Ashfield, that this kind of symbolic politics is a travesty, drawing time and attention away from local matters, where we must, and do, act with decisive effect.

With this much to provide context, we turn to accounts of modern Ashfield governing itself.

II

TALES OF MODERN GOVERNANCE

5

Town Hall and Town Meeting

At the beginning of the twenty-first century, there were 351 municipalities in Massachusetts, 312 of them incorporated as towns, 39 as cities. The cities and many of the larger towns no longer use the classical town-meeting form. Forty-two towns have representative town meetings; nine elect town councils. Five of those nine with town councils also have town managers; four elect a mayor to work with the town council. But of the 312 towns in the commonwealth, 261 of them, including Ashfield, still make laws and appropriate money at a meeting where all adult citizens legally resident in town are eligible voters, with an equal vote.[1]

Each small town in New England is unique.[2] Those that have preserved a town-meeting form of government practice it differently. In some towns, there is usually just one annual town meeting; others have special town meetings fairly frequently. Some places hold town meeting on a Saturday in the springtime; others do it on a weeknight in late winter or early summer. In some towns the annual meeting lasts one full day; in others it can go on for several evenings. Some town meetings are primarily run by a moderator, who exercises a great deal of discretion over the order of business and determines who may speak and for how long; for others the select board is the major player, preparing the articles on the warrant and setting the agenda, and participation in the meeting is governed by rules long established. In one town, voters may elect a long list of officials; in another, far fewer. Some towns vote for each line item in the budget (by a voice vote, a show of hands, or a written ballot, counted on the spot); others vote for budgets by secret ballot, on the day of town meeting but not at the meeting itself.[3] Indeed, in a given town, the practice may vary from one year to the next, depending on the issues that arise and the people who hold office.

Ashfield's basic structure and practices are fairly typical for a town of its size in New England. Its proceedings at town meeting are under the control of an elected town moderator, who has broad discretion over the conduct of the proceedings, subject to being overridden by a vote of the town meeting.[4] There have been a few significant changes in the structure of local government in Ashfield since the eighteenth century. One of the most important, which I will be discussing in chapter 6 along with other reforms instituted in Ashfield during the 1990s, was the addition of an independently elected finance committee to monitor the select board and provide town meeting with an alternative set of proposals for the annual budget (the select board prepares the budget in the warrant). There have been other innovations, too, but none of them fundamental. We have not departed far from the institutions and procedures established in the eighteenth century.

Governing arrangements

If we were to compare the government of Ashfield to the standard American model, we might say that town meeting is the legislature, the select board is the executive, and there is no local judiciary. But governments grow organically. Certainly those in New England did. For example, there is no branch of the state or county judiciary system in Ashfield. People must go to the courthouse in Greenfield, the county seat, for most civil and criminal trials. In fact, however, judicial powers are exercised in town by the locally appointed zoning board of appeals. The ZBA decides, after hearings, whether property owners may use their homes and land for certain purposes. Its decisions are based on law, and its rulings are subject to appeal, just like those of most courts.

The accounts that follow focus on town meeting and the select board, the town's appropriating and law-making body and its three-person executive. The claim that Ashfield's government is a direct democracy depends on the law-making and appropriating power of town meeting and the fact that the select board is elected and held accountable by the citizens, who can continuously monitor its operations.

The legislature in Ashfield (the law-making and appropriating organ) is town meeting. Here, as we've seen, every adult who legally resides in town has a vote; those who own property here but legally reside elsewhere do not. What we do at town meeting is limited by the federal and state constitutions, which reserve many matters to those higher jurisdictions. But at town meeting we adopt, and we may revise, zoning ordinances, we make regulations for town departments (such as the highway, police, and fire departments), we determine whether major officers (town clerk, treasurer, tax collector, assessors, planning board, and conservation commissioners) are elected or appointed, and we appropriate money to support local government. We adopt an annual budget (lately amounting to about $3 million), the burden of which is distributed among property owners according to the value of their property.[5] And on town meeting day, we elect a moderator, members of the select board, assessors, and other major officers of the town administration.

The power of the purse

Control over finances is the most important power that citizens in a democracy have over their government, and in Ashfield it is constantly in operation. The town's administrators and department chiefs have no money to spend until the town appropriates funds. There are only two important exceptions to this rule. One is for "winter roads." The highway department may exceed its appropriation to clear snow and ice, but a special town meeting must convene soon thereafter to pay for it. The other exception is a provision in state laws for declared emergencies. The head of government (the chair of the select board) declares a state of emergency and notifies the finance committee. For nonbudgeted expenditures, the emergency manager, appointed by the select board, must obtain a sign-off from the select board chair. Funds expended during an emergency must later be covered by state appropriation or by a special town meeting.[6]

Appropriations by town meeting may be categorical, or they may be closely detailed. The appropriate level of detail—in the police, fire, and highway department budgets, for example—is often a topic of discussion between the select board and the finance committee and at town meeting. Appropriations may also be conditional. For example, the highway or fire department may be authorized to purchase a truck for an amount not to exceed a certain sum, or funds may be appropriated with the stipulation that they be spent only if the department receives a matching grant.

The executive in Ashfield is plural. The select board has three elected members, each chosen for a three-year term, rotating so that normally one of them stands for election at each annual town meeting. In consequence, at no one time is the performance of the whole board up for review.[7] Voters weigh the performance of individual members of the board when they stand for reelection, but when the members stick together (which happens to have been the case for most of the 1990s, the period I am mainly discussing here), it is hard for voters to pass judgment on the performance of the executive branch, either to support it or to condemn it. This can be a flaw in the accountability of the town's executives. If the board collectively makes a major mistake, it could take three years to replace the offending members. On the other hand, replacing one member is sometimes enough to change the direction of the board.

In *The Federalist*, no. 70, Alexander Hamilton argues that a plural executive is a mistake. It leads not only to a want of "energy" but to obfuscation and irresponsibility, what Hamilton called "imbecile" government. He had a point. But he went on to list another consideration that tempers the enthusiasm of democrats for a unitary executive. He noted, approvingly, that a government with a single head can move secretly when necessary (in military planning, for example, or in dealing with criminal conspiracies). Those who created local governments in rural New England viewed the matter differently. Plural executives may be messier and less "energetic," but they are also less likely to march off on their own.

One new feature of modern governance at the local level—it is a fundamental innovation—is the commitment to open meetings. During my term on the select board, I was often uncertain about this. Was it a violation of the open-meeting law if I ran into a fellow board member at the post office and we, a majority of the board, discussed an appointment, or something we had heard about the police department? What if two of us were at a party and the conversation turned to a story in the paper about the sewer project? It was almost impossible to avoid such communications. The rule was to avoid any decisions or deliberations outside of an open meeting, but the line between unplanned conversation and effective deliberation was not easy to draw, even with a conscientious commitment to openness. The best safeguard was to elect candid people.

Our predecessors on the board had served when these new rules gradually came into being.[8] They found them genuinely bewildering. When someone's name came up for an appointment, were we really expected to speak in public, in front of the press, about her or his character?[9] Or, to take another example, as recently as the early 1960s the select board administered welfare funds. When I served, during the 1990s, we still had to administer trust funds that provided support for poor people. Were we expected to discuss the circumstances of our disadvantaged neighbors in public? Or were we to make the grants without considering the circumstances?

There were also conflict-of-interest laws. How could we staff the town's manifold boards and commissions without creating conflicts of interest? We needed people with knowledge in certain areas. How could we find someone with the requisite skills to serve on the conservation commission, for example, who would never do business on a matter that might come before that body? The law does provide for "special employee" status, allowing someone with a declared interest to serve. That was usually enough to clear the way for necessary accommodation. Often, though, it seemed to us that these rules were designed for urban environments. In a small town, we watch each other pretty closely. It is important that people not abuse their positions: that the police not treat elected officials differently from other townspeople, or that assessors not favor their own property or properties like their own. But we could not recruit perfectly objective people to do police work, or assessors who had no property. There are no saints in Ashfield. The best protections against abuse were checks and balances within government, a vigilant, balanced and merciless press keeping watch outside, and citizens with alert and well-informed consciences.

The administration of the town's civic affairs centers on the select board, but it has many other, independent elements as well. The trustees of our public library, for example, are separately elected, and they have trust funds to expend. The operation of the library depends on supplementary funds appropriated by the town, and state regulations require the trustees to spend a minimum portion of their budget each year on acquisitions for the library's collection. No one operates in perfect autonomy.

The select board hires and fires, within the carefully negotiated bounds of state law and regulation; it is not easy to fire a civil servant in Massachusetts, nor should it be. In Ashfield, there are three major departments: highway, police, and fire (listed in order of the size of their annual appropriation). The select board formally appoints employees of the highway department and reserve officers of the police force, although there is considerable deference to the department chiefs on these matters.

Town Hall hands

All of this was pretty stable, both in structure and personnel, while I served on the select board. When I took office in 1991, the secretary to the select board, Eleanor Ward, doubled as town clerk. We also had a town treasurer, a tax collector, and a three-person board of assessors, who were assisted by one experienced employee. The clerk, treasurer, tax collector, and assessors, being elected, were not answerable to the select board.

The treasurer, Janet Swem, was a smart woman, funny, patient and helpful, honest as an angel and with a character incapable of subterfuge. Occasionally we would approach her with an idea for bending a state regulation to our advantage. She would tell us if it might work and indicate whether or not she would be party to it. Her judgment was law to us.

The tax collector was another valuable official. Her job involved a good deal of discretion about arranging for gradual payment of delinquent accounts. We often counseled with her about how to encourage payment of these accounts. Should we publish a list of delinquents? Should we discuss the problem at a select board meeting, in front of the press? No one wanted to harass the delinquents. We knew them, knew in many cases what they were dealing with at home, knew that some of them made valuable contributions to the community in other ways. On the other hand, if some didn't pay taxes, others had to cover for it through higher rates, and that did not seem fair. It was a difficult problem. We also talked to the tax collector about whether to buy expensive new equipment to assist her in keeping accounts in her bailiwick. A farmer's wife with a heart of gold, she was very good at "making do"—probably too good, sometimes. Gradually she yielded to the idea of computerizing her office, but to the end, she kept her own records in a ledger with pen and ink.[10]

The highway department

The stories told in the succeeding chapters absorbed the most attention and energy of Ashfield's citizens during the 1990s. They cover the main functions of local government, with one major exception. There is no chapter dealing with the highway department. This department spends more money than any other function of local government except the schools, but it escapes close examination here because our town meetings rarely had to devote much time or emotional energy to it.[11]

When I joined the board in 1991, Les Ladd, a diligent, affable man, was the highway "super." He knew the routines of procurement; his crewmembers respected him. Ashfield has about eighty miles of town roads, most of them paved, some not. Each spring Les would present to the select board a list of his priorities for rebuilding and maintenance projects during the coming months. One might have expected a nightmarish struggle between neighborhoods, but somehow it never happened. He was a model of deference to the select board. Our discussions, which took place almost weekly, were mutually respectful. We recognized his intimate knowledge of conditions, but he never challenged our authority to set priorities.

Wintertime presented the department's supreme test. The men rose to it magnificently. The roads were kept passable, whatever challenges New England's winter threw at them. My wife and I have lived for a quarter-century in Ashfield, twenty miles from Northampton, where we worked and served in various volunteer capacities. In all those years, neither of us missed an appointment or a meeting due to weather. Given the severity of conditions during New England winters, that is a quite remarkable record. We owe it mainly to the highway crews.

In the chapters that follow, I explore several issues the town has faced in over the last few decades. I begin (chapter 6) with tales from Town Hall:

some of the people and interactions that gave Ashfield's political life its particular flavor during the 1990s, and our efforts to reform the organs of administration, to make them work better.

Next, in chapter 7, I address the major public project of the past half-century in Ashfield: building a system of sewers and a wastewater treatment plant to treat sewage. This project placed heavy demands on our little polity. We did not measure up very well—but then, neither did the state bureaucracy or our contractors, despite their professional training and vast experience.

Chapter 8, involving the management of the town's police force, treats one of the greatest challenges faced by democratic governments. Controlling the exercise of coercion often involves hard choices. Sometimes it requires finesse. As a town and as a select board, we stumbled repeatedly on this one. We still do.

Ashfield's residents over the past two and a half centuries have taken education seriously, seeing it as a vital part of our commitment to self-government. This story, told in chapter 9, begins with the history of the town's schools. I then recount how we lost control over what was taught in local schools (their soul), and fell to quarreling over the buildings (including a carcass). I conclude with notes on a growing number of citizens who express their determination to regain control over the education of their children by sending them to charter or private institutions or by schooling them at home.

Chapter 10, our last story, provides a happy ending. It tells how we belatedly created a town common.

6

Tinkering with the System

My wife, Molly, and I moved to Ashfield in 1983. Molly led a Girl Scout troop, and we occasionally attended a local church (we remained active members of a church in Northampton), but otherwise we were not much involved in town affairs. We lived just around the corner from Elmer's Country Store, then a grocery store and butcher shop located on Main Street (which is part of Route 116 as it passes through town). The proprietors, Jack and Lisa Mattis, became good friends and were an inexhaustible source of local lore and good-natured gossip. Jack's father, to hear Jack tell it, had been a legendary selectman in nearby Windsor, and it was obvious that he had inherited his father's keen interest in local politics. During his military service, Jack had been stationed on a base in Greenland, but apart from that his horizons had been bounded by the surrounding hills. I loved talking with him. I didn't realize it at the time, but I was going to school—and learning plenty.

During the 1980s, I observed Ashfield's civic life from a safe distance and noted that it generated a good deal of anguish. Sometimes I wondered why people couldn't just "get along," in Cyril King's memorable phrase. It seemed to me that the town's officials, the people at the head table during annual town meetings, were capable, well-meaning folk. The selectmen were downright admirable. Russ Fessenden, a retired foreign service officer, exuded wisdom, patience, and good manners. Dale Kirkpatrick was a cagey conservative with whom I disagreed about most things political, but I trusted his character and mastery of detail over local affairs. Tom Carter was best of all, a handsome, smart young guy about twenty-five years old when he first emerged in my consciousness. Soon after his election Tom was chosen chair of the select board by his fellow members. It was a good choice. He is a deep-dyed fiscal conservative, but clever and funny, able to diffuse conflict with a deft turn of phrase or an apt story. He never, ever used his wit to hurt anyone, but you were sorry whenever you found him opposing your side of an argument. He did not always win in Ashfield's increasingly liberal culture, but he was resolute and resourceful in debate. He did not have an enemy in town; everyone loved him.

The other person at the center in those days was Eleanor Ward, the town clerk and secretary to the select board. Eleanor was rail-thin and spoke through a firmly set jaw. She was a devout Roman Catholic and a devoted mother, and she had served in Town Hall forever. She knew where all the skeletons were buried, and she did not need James Madison or Francis Bacon to tell her that knowledge is power. You had to earn her trust, and she did not give it easily. When I first joined the select board, she several times put me in my place by withholding information. Gradually, though, we came to trust each other, and things became much easier for me.

Elect the finance committee?

Besides the festering conflict over the sewer, the other issue that drew my attention in the 1980s was the creation of a separately elected finance committee.[1] This was Jack Mattis's baby, and I strenuously opposed it. Mattis posed it in terms of checks and balances. As things stood, he argued, the selectmen brought a budget before town meeting having a virtual monopoly on information. An elected finance committee would be a watchdog, and the town could decide any issues between the select board and the finance committee.

For me, the issue was having enough people to fill these positions. I noted (it was, I think, my maiden speech at a town meeting) that many elective positions went uncontested. An elected finance committee would mean just another drain on available, capable people. As for checks and balances, I argued that Mattis was misusing the term. Town meeting was the legislature; the board of selectmen was the executive. Here were the checks and balances. A finance committee would mean a divided executive, and Alexander Hamilton told what to expect from a divided executive: weakness, "imbecile" government. (Did I actually cite *The Federalist*? What a smart-aleck I was! My neighbors showed a lot of patience with me.)

Happily for Ashfield, Mattis won that argument. The town went ahead and created a separately elected finance committee. Experience has shown that he was right on all counts. We saw in chapter 4 that the finance committee is positioned to provide a constructive balance to the power of the select board, allowing issues involving public funds to come before the town in the light of two independent, well-informed perspectives. As for finding enough people to serve, our most experienced citizens have readily agreed to serve on it: among others, wise old Tom Cranston, whom we met in the introduction, who chaired it during the first decade and a half of its existence; Eleanor Ward, after she retired as town clerk; and Tom Carter, after he left the select board. It has also given a perch at the head table to Dave Newell, curmudgeonly champion of fiscal conservatives; Phil Pless, dean of local realtors, who succeeded Cranston as chair of the finance committee; and Mary Link, a hard-working, articulate woman with broad experience in school issues. As the narratives about the new sewer system, the police department, and the disposition of the old Sanderson Academy building will show, the select board and the finance committee have not always seen eye to eye. Nor did their joint operation always expose serious errors in judgment. There is, after all, no magic in institutional arrangements. But the presence of two well-informed bodies, jockeying for influence, has contributed substantially to the town's enlightenment and to the engagement of its citizens.

The select board

I joined the select board in 1991, at the beginning of what turned out to be a decade of far-reaching change in Ashfield's governance. The next year Tom Carter decided not to stand for reelection; then Jack Mattis resigned after getting tangled up in an imbroglio over the appointment of a police chief. It was a pretty thorough changing of the guard.

Bill Perlman, whom we also met in the introduction, was elected to fill Tom's seat. It was a striking demonstration of Ashfield's openness to newcomers (not to mention the lack of natives willing to run). He had moved to town less than a year earlier and was then in his late forties. Perlman is a short, in-your-face kind of guy with an engaging manner—very clever, full of curiosity, but suspicious of being patronized and quick to take offense. He came from a family of distinguished radical lawyers in New York City. He had been deeply engaged in the civil rights movement in the South in the 1960s. His day job involved consulting in electronics. On one gig, he worked with companies seeking to develop devices that could screen out offensive television content for families with young children. He was full of schemes for making money—still is, bless him—although few of them seem to pan out very well. He brought real value to the select board. He had a degree in electrical engineering, which gave him a certain authority in dealing with the people who were designing and building our new wastewater treatment system. (He insisted on being the lead contact with those firms.) And he had time, apparently virtually endless amounts of it, which meant that, in dealing with contractors, we depended less on state bureaucrats and consultants than another town might have had to.

Dianne Muller replaced Mattis. Dianne was not a native, either, although she had far more experience in town, and was far better and more fondly known, than either Bill or I. She and her husband, Dick, had moved to town from a neighboring community about twenty years earlier. In a studio in their barn they made leather goods that sold countrywide in the finest stores (under the Cole Haan label, for example). By the time Dianne joined the select board, she and her husband were deeply knowledgeable about town affairs. Dianne had been elected several times to the regional school board; Dick was chair of the conservation commission. They knew practically everyone in town, and they were loved and admired by a wide circle of friends.

Town Hall staffing

The other major change at Town Hall in the early 1990s was that Eleanor Ward retired. She was replaced as town clerk (elected) by Lorraine Gordon and as secretary to the select board (appointive) by Priscilla Phelps. None of these replacements had a fraction of the local knowledge or experience in the public service that Ward did.

Priscilla had been an elementary school teacher in a suburb of Springfield. We chose her over another candidate because she lived in town. She was devoted to her work for the town, but she felt that Ward never quite trusted her, which complicated the transition. Soon after her appointment, Priscilla got tangled up in matters involving the police department—inevitably, perhaps, given her husband's service as a reserve officer and the fact that he was under consideration to be the new chief. When we chose a younger man as chief, Caesar's wife in Priscilla's position could not have avoided suspicion. Her office was across the hall from the police department, and her door was usually open. She watched the new chief's comings and goings—monitored them with a hostile eye, he felt, and not without some reason.

Another factor was Priscilla's work as the town's liaison with public officials and contractors. Here the problem was one of ill-defined boundaries. Bill Perlman and I, especially, liked to do our own networking. Bill had constant dealings with the sewer-project folks and resented any interference in this, whether by me or anyone else. I liked to exploit my friendships with Stan Rosenberg, our state senator, and John Olver, our representative in Congress. Stan, John, and I were old friends. We had been through various political wars together. They trusted me, and my good relationship with them was one thing I had to contribute to the town. Poor Priscilla! Bill and I asked her to help us sometimes with these contacts, but woe to her if she misstepped or went too far.

The town clerk for part of this time was also relatively new to town. As the single mom of a toddler, she had her hands full. She had difficulty keeping regular hours in Town Hall, being there when she said she would be. Phelps tried to cover for her; others tried to help. But it just wasn't working. One of the hardest things for town government is to nudge someone out of elective office.

Given the manifold difficulties swamping Town Hall, we decided—Perlman, Muller, and I—to initiate a thorough review of town governance. This was a weak and somewhat disingenuous way to deal with the town's personnel problems, but the difficulties we were encountering did have structural aspects as well, and there is something to be said for saving someone's face by dealing with such matters impersonally. The responsibilities and workload of town administrators have grown exponentially in recent years. This is a familiar and nearly universal story in modern governance: the proliferation of paperwork, the need to keep written records of everything and to touch base with everyone all the time. In the decades since Tracy Kidder explored "the soul of a new machine," computers have facilitated some tasks, as has the Internet, but they have greatly increased the demands on office workers. It is fun to noodle around with these things, but they exact a fierce toll on time and human souls.

No doubt we created some of our problems for ourselves. As a freelance engineer, Perlman could make time for what he wanted to do, and he loved being a political leader in a rural town. As a tenured academic, I too had a flexible schedule. Perlman and I, sometimes competing, may have goaded each other into spending more time at the job than was necessary, or good. At any rate, we both determined that Town Hall could use help, and Muller, observing us sympathetically and with more appreciation than we probably deserved, agreed to support a thorough study of the problem.

We created a task force on governance and asked Eleanor Ward, Susan Todd (whom we will meet again as a select-board member), Dave Newell, Janet Swem, and Tom Carter to serve on it. I agreed to act as convener, scheduling and chairing the meetings. We asked the group to study arrangements in comparable towns and to propose ways that Ashfield could improve efficiency and cope better with the demands on local government.

One thing we discovered early on in our research was that some towns had dispensed with electing their town clerks, tax collectors, and treasurers; the select board chose these officials and was responsible for their performance. The reasoning was that elections in small towns are not a very effective way to recruit and select the ablest people and assess their performance in office. Old Charley and Aunt Betsy might be honorable and pleasant folks and might at one time have been effective public servants. But if performance began to falter, no one wanted to say so out loud, and most people simply refused to run against an old friend. Many towns reported having been in the same fix, and several had dealt with it by having the select board appoint people to these positions.

There was, of course, a counterargument, and it was certainly heard during our debate over these reforms. Would it not give too much power to the select board? Consider the duties of these officers. Town clerks monitor elections. Was it not a potential conflict of interest to have members of the select board even indirectly oversee their own reelections? Town clerks also keep the town records. If a journalist or a citizen wanted to shed light on alleged abuses, shouldn't the officer in charge of town files be independent of local politicians? Treasurers make decisions about arrangements for loans and hire and interact with public accountants who certify the town's books. Tax collectors put the squeeze on delinquent tax payers and make arrangements for paying back taxes. Should those who exercise such powers answer to the select board?

These were good questions. But the arguments that prevailed in Ashfield were that voters could not directly monitor all of these functions, and personal relations in a small town interfered with objectivity. Town meeting would ultimately decide that the select board was in a better position to recruit, supervise and, if necessary, replace these officials than the electorate at large.

There was one major factor that swung opinion behind these proposals: the support of Janet Swem. The town clerk opposed the select board's recommendation (and was able to cite the state association of town clerks, and their solid arguments, on her side). The tax collector seemed ambivalent; she was about to retire anyway. But Swem, the elected town treasurer, was completely convinced that elections were the wrong way to fill these positions. They were not political. Relying on elections was too often a gamble. She thought it made sense to focus responsibility on the select board. That was no guarantee of effective, objective oversight, but at least one knew where to direct one's concern about poor performance. With Swem's support, town meeting overwhelmingly voted to accept the committee's package of reforms.

Moving to a town administrator

One major item in the select board's reform package was to hire a town administrator. The central notion here—to borrow a phrase from the report of the Brownlow Commission, which advised President Franklin D. Roosevelt in 1937 to beef up the White House staff—was that the select board "needs help." The commission advised the president to choose aides with "a passion for anonymity" to communicate his guidance to the bureaucracy and to monitor their compliance.[2] Ashfield had no single chief executive, and a bloated, freewheeling bureaucracy was not our problem. But it was clear that the administration needed help. The existing select board was willing and able to spend an inordinate amount of time on town business, but that situation was not necessarily good, and in any case it would have been foolish to expect it to continue indefinitely.

Where exactly did the town's administration need help? We needed someone to deal with the state bureaucracy, to understand what it required of the town and prepare options for complying. We had gotten into a quarter-century of trouble over our failure to comply with an order to clean up South River (see chapter 7). Some argued that the state's shifting mandates over those years were better ignored than obeyed. But we might have saved money by complying sooner, and we would surely have lessened the danger of a public health emergency. As for opportunities for grants from the state and federal government and from private foundations, Town Hall received mailings almost daily about grants we might apply for, but we had no time to scan the brochures, much less fill out the applications.

Another lost opportunity was regional cooperation. Small towns do not need to provide every service themselves, now that we have telephones, computers, and good roads. We share a public health worker and a manager of waste disposal, a building inspector and a facility for senior citizens. These work pretty well. If we had a town administrator, she or he might discover other economies.[3]

Coordination and control

We were also failing at the work of coordination. The conservation commission often did not know what the highway department and the park commission were planning. The police department and the human rights commission had little contact. Cooperation between the zoning and planning boards was intermittent at best, often depending on personal relations between the members and chance meetings at the post office or pizza parlor. No one was consistently making these connections.

Basically, by the mid-1990s we felt we were struggling just to keep our heads above water. The danger in hiring someone to help with these tasks was that the select board—and, more importantly, the people of the town—might lose control. Ashfield's best feature, along with its stunning physical beauty, is its lively civic life. People come to public meetings. They accept appointments to local boards. They recruit their friends to serve on committees. By one count in the late 1990s, over 250 different people, out of an adult population of 1,300 or so, served on at least one town committee or board.[4] Add in the churches and Scout troops, the volunteer fire department and ambulance service, the American Legion and the coaches and parents committee for youth baseball, and you've got pretty broad engagement. My fear was that if we professionalized the administration of Town Hall, it might dampen this engagement. Hardly anyone shared my concerns on this point. Most people believed that if things in Town Hall were efficiently managed, volunteers would enjoy their service on committees all the more. They would be less likely to feel frustrated or overburdened. That, of course, would depend on the person we chose as town administrator, and on her or his efficiency and willingness to serve quietly, from the shadows.

Once these principles (shifting the town clerk, tax collector, and treasurer to appointive positions and hiring a town administrator) were established, the question for the task force became how these functions would be shared in the new arrangement. Who would be secretary to the select board, take minutes, and handle correspondence? How would the town clerk and town administrator share their duties? Incumbents of the old order warned us that a great deal that happened in Town Hall was accomplished by accommodation, people picking up duties that were not in their job descriptions. No one doubted that. We knew there would be a bumpy transition; a lot would be left to personal adjustment. But the task force felt that the revised arrangements could work more efficiently, for the town's benefit.

The report, recommended unanimously by the members of the task force, went forward to the finance committee and then to the select board, and in May 2000 its main elements were decisively approved by town meeting. The board was fortunate to find good people to serve in the newly appointive positions. Most fortunate of all, Janet Swem continued as treasurer, now appointed rather than elected, for several more years.

There are a few points particularly worth remembering from these accounts:

Town-meeting democracy needs checks and balances. Ashfield was wise to adopt an independently elected finance committee. (Forget Hamilton's Federalist No. 70 and its argument for unity of administration. Madison's Federalist No. 51 provides better guidance. Power must be effectively checked.)

Reorganization is a disingenuous way to purge weak employees. On the other hand, it can help people save face, and that is an important value, too.

Appointing people can be a good way to get qualified people to serve in administrative positions. Electing them often is not. Keep responsibility focused. (Here Hamilton's *Federalist* no.70 does provide good guidance.)

A town administrator modeled on the Brownlow Committee's study of administrative management for the New Deal (aides with a "passion for anonymity") can provide vital assistance to volunteers who serve on boards and commissions. But beware of village peacocks, who preen, like Henry Kissinger, or operators, who pull strings from behind a curtain, like Dick Cheney.

7

Building a Sewer System

In 1962 Rachel Carson published *Silent Spring,* the call that quickened the modern environmental movement. Three years earlier, the Massachusetts Department of Public Health had taken some samples from the South River, a small stream that runs through the center of Ashfield and then through neighboring Conway, where it flows into the Deerfield River and on to the Connecticut River, one of New England's principal sources of fresh water. Analysis of the samples found a high coliform bacteria count—not surprising, considering that several houses and stores in the town center, not to mention the town's primary school, the fire and police stations, and Town Hall itself, were flushing untreated household sewage and other wastewater directly into the stream.[1] The authorities did not seem particularly exercised about the finding, though. More than a decade passed before Thomas MacMahon, director of the state's Water Resources Commission, sent a letter ordering the town to hire an engineer by April 1970 and to submit a preliminary plan for building a wastewater treatment facility by April 1971.

In the following pages, we will watch the citizens of Ashfield wrestling with the biggest public-works project in the town's history. We will see Yankee cunning dealing with faraway bureaucrats and their ever-changing demands, but we will also see pigheadedness that finally roused the state attorney general's office to call us to account. We will see the town caught in a vise, trapped between its own dueling ideologies and hesitat-

135

ing to use its powers of eminent domain. We will see people confused by conflicting scientific claims but failing to consult independent analysis. It is not a pretty picture. It demonstrates that democracy is not immune from the woes that plague all forms of human governance.

At its annual town meeting on March 7, 1970, Ashfield voters appropriated $10,000 to pay Weston & Sampson Engineers to prepare and submit the required plan to the Water Resources Commission. A year later, Weston & Sampson issued its preliminary report. It called for building an oxidation ditch, a conventional wastewater treatment plant, to render the untreated outflow fit to return to the state's waterways. Weston & Sampson estimated that the facility, with a daily capacity of 79,000 gallons, would cost $727,000. The town's share (after state and federal aid) would be $320,150. The report identified two possible sites for the treatment facility: a gravel bank on Baptist Corner Road, just north of the center of town, or a portion of a farm off Main Street, east of the center. Both properties were privately owned. (See map, page 141.)

On September 9, 1971, responding to the Weston & Sampson report, the state ordered the town to stop discharging untreated wastewater into the South River and to complete the construction of a treatment plant by November 1973. In those days, the select board sometimes responded to state mandates by quietly ignoring them, in the hope that they would go away. If it turned out that the bureaucrats in Boston were serious, presumably they would call again. Given the scale of this project, it seemed worthwhile to test their resolve.

An innovative system?

Around the mid-1970s a cloud no bigger than a man's hand appeared on the horizon. Members of the locally elected board of health began to take interest in an "innovative" system for treating wastewater.[2] What was it? Who was pushing it? We would soon learn.

In 1976 the town's voters unanimously appropriated $12,900 for an update of the 1971 Weston & Sampson report. The new report, published in April 1977, included, among alternative ways to treat sewage, an "innovative community septic system." At the next town meeting, in May, voters rejected the oxidation ditch. Instead they approved a "community septic system." In June 1977 the select board formally asked the state to approve a $500,000 community septic system.

At this point, attention turned to obtaining the necessary land. In the late 1970s two residents, Frank and Beverly Guditis, sold the town a 4.4-acre parcel on Route 116, just east and downhill from the center of town; this was one of the two sites recommended in the 1971 Weston & Sampson report. The cost was $18,500. In 1980 the select board arranged with an abutting property owner, Nat Smith, to exchange a small amount of the property obtained from the Guditises for adjacent land (less than one acre), to accommodate the requirements of the plan. On May 21, 1983, voters approved a $500,000 bond issue for the sewer system. The vote was 175–86, three more "yes" votes than the necessary two-thirds. So far, so good.

These actions came during a bitterly contentious time in the town. Russ Fessenden, who in his years with the foreign service had served with distinction during the reconstruction of Germany following World War II, had returned to the town where he had spent several youthful summers and had been elected to the select board. Some townspeople now accused him of seeking to steer the sewer project in the direction of property he owned, presumably so that he could reap a windfall. Fessenden was the son of a beloved local physician who had been a family practitioner to many of the town's older residents, and, to quote from the dedication of the 1994 Town Report, "We honor him not only for his professional achievements [as a foreign service officer] and civic service, but for his encyclopedic knowledge of the Town's history, his warm welcome to newcomers, his gentle wit and keen intelligence, his courage and, most of all, for the example he has provided all his life long of dedication to family and community." His accusers, many of them newcomers, were not intimidated by his towering reputation, however. They resented the men in power, whom they saw as a clique. Their assault on Fessenden was merciless. After repeated skirmishes, Fessenden concluded that the best way for the town to move forward was for him to resign from the select board, and he did so in June 1983. Marianne Hurley, the first woman ever to serve on the select board, replaced him, in an uncontested election. The town's leadership was further disrupted when Ed Scott, longtime chair of the select board, decided not to stand for reelection, citing poor health. Many in town suspected that Scott too had succumbed to the poisoned atmosphere.

The state intervenes, again

In the same year, 1983, another dramatic development tested the town's capacity to govern itself. The state's environmental regulations changed.[3] Henceforth, sewage treatment facilities would be required to have larger buffer zones. This meant that additional land adjacent to the Guditis property would have to be bought. The town arranged to have appraisals done for more of Nat Smith's land. As soon as they were completed, Smith declared that he was unwilling to sell his land at the appraised price.

This development led to an impasse. State authorities had begun to press the town to move ahead, but the only site the town and its engineers deemed feasible for a sewage plant could not be bought without an eminent-domain taking, and that required a two-thirds majority. Ashfield's voters were desperate to avoid such heavy-handed action, but there seemed to be no other solution. On May 4, 1985, the select board proposed to town meeting that a piece of Smith's land, a 22.5 acre parcel, be taken by eminent domain for the appraised price. A paper ballot produced 177 votes in favor of the taking, 193 opposed. It wasn't even a majority, let alone the necessary two-thirds.

Marianne Hurley, who had replaced Russ Fessenden, chose to regard this as a vote of no confidence and resigned. Her place was soon taken by Tom Carter, whom we met in chapter 6. Carter was a natural politician, well grounded in the town's cultures. He was in the agricultural supply business, and when he spoke, he had a knack for putting the feed down where the goats could reach it.

On September 28, 1985, after weeks of intense negotiation, voters at a special town meeting approved a proposed contract with Nat Smith. The town would take the "minimal acreage" required by the state, for a cost not to exceed $80,000. The parcel would include 1.05 acres by fee simple, plus groundwater and other necessary rights for the state-mandated buffer zone. Requiring a two-thirds vote, the article passed by a comfortable margin, 153–53. Some citizens dared to think that the worst might be over.

Alas, it was an illusion. Smith was not happy about the deal he had been offered. Another special town meeting at the end of October appropriated an additional $5,000 for engineering studies to determine whether the project could proceed with less land for the buffer zone. Eight months later, in June 1986, another special town meeting began by rescinding the arrangement voters had approved in September 1985. After further wrangling, the meeting adjourned for two hours while the select board negotiated modifications in the proposal with Nat Smith and his counsel. The new agreement was to pay Smith $10,000 for 1.05 acres of his land and place $70,000 in an escrow account to compensate him for development rights and an agricultural preservation restriction on 21.1 acres of land. The escrow money would be turned over to Smith as soon as the state approved plans for the facility, but he would receive the interest it earned until the transfer was completed. The select board, its own options severely restricted by the state mandate, had to swallow hard on that last provision, but voters, understanding the dilemma, approved the new deal.

Now the focus shifted to negotiations between the select board, Weston & Sampson, and the state's environmental authorities. Through late 1986 and 1987, town representatives met repeatedly with state agencies to seek approval for the town's preferred method of wastewater treatment and to ascertain how much land would be required to build the facility. During these discussions, we learned that the regulations governing groundwater discharge had changed yet again. Now even more land would be required for the facility before the state would approve Ashfield's plan.

In March 1988 the select board notified the state that new state regulations made the plan impossible. The town's voters simply would not approve a hostile taking of Smith's land by eminent domain. The board also declared that the mounting cost of the facility was beyond the town's capacity. This communiqué reflected a spirit of rebellion in town against the state's frequent and continuing modification of its requirements.

There ensued a further round of negotiations between the town and the commonwealth. This time the engineering firm played a central role. Weston & Sampson, presumably with the concurrence of state officials, issued an amended "Step 2 Design Report" in April 1988. It did not require groundwater or agricultural preservation rights on the pasture owned by Nat Smith, but it did require the acquisition, from Smith, of wetlands near the South River. This meant, of course, that the select board would have to go back to Smith, and to the town, to arrange for the purchase of this land.

It would take five years of intensive bargaining to arrange this purchase. The first step was consideration, on May 7, 1988, town meeting day, of a ballot question that would have exempted the sewer bond from the debt limit. It lost on a written ballot by a vote of 152 to 232. The effect was to nullify the deal struck at the special town meeting of June 1986. The aftermath was bitter on all sides. It took five months for the town's attorney to retrieve the money from Smith (the $10,000 purchase price, plus $70,000 held in escrow) in return for the deed and rights to the land that now reverted to him.

Solar aquatics

Meanwhile another major strand of this story began to gather momentum. Local environmentalists began talking about something called "solar aquatics."

The concept was simple. Sewers would collect water from sinks and disposals, showers and toilets in homes and other buildings and bring it by gravity to a site downhill. There the heaviest solids would be screened out and the liquid ("liquor," it was called) sent along to a secondary treatment in a large adjacent greenhouse. In the greenhouse would be sixty-four circular bins, each about six feet in diameter and eight feet high, lined with translucent plastic. The bins would be filled with live organisms: growing plants and small aquatic animals. The idea was to replicate, in the perpetual summer of a greenhouse, the process that cleans water outdoors. As the wastewater spilled through these bins in succession, it would be purified. In conventional systems, a machine had to churn microbes in the water up from the bottom; in a solar aquatic system, compressed air kept the remaining solids suspended in solution while the vegetation in the tanks provided a far more extensive surface for microbes digesting nitrogen. After spilling through the tanks, the liquid would pass into a clarifier, where the remaining solids settled and were removed. The water would then be subjected to further treatment in a second greenhouse, where it would meander through the roots of

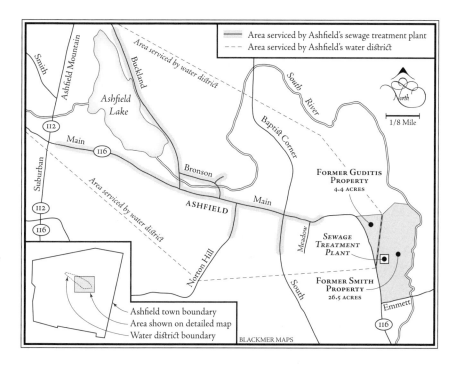

grasses, ferns, plants, and small trees growing in a bed of gravel. The greenhouses would re-create, in a concentrated form, the process by which water is purified in a natural environment. Having come through these various environments, the water would be sent along to a leach field outdoors. In Ashfield, this would be a large meadow on the eastern, downhill end of the site, and from there it would flow directly into the South River.

Advocates hailed this technology as a breakthrough that treated wastewater with nature's own methods. They told the town that it minimized the use of chemicals and grinding machines driven by electric power. A solar aquatic system would be gentle, quiet, and practically odor-free, and it would be cheaper to operate and maintain than a traditional system. It could be used to teach schoolchildren how to live in cooperation with nature, rather than imposing clunky machinery on it. (The facility, as originally designed, included a classroom for this purpose.) Screened-out wastes could be used as fertilizer or burned as fuel. It might even be possible to grow things in the bins, hydroponic lettuce, perhaps, or snails—escargot—and sell them to help defray the cost of the system.

The three members of the board of health began marshalling the case for a solar aquatic system. One of them, Tom Leue, was a passionate environmentalist who had worked as a consultant in Northampton, installing insulation and energy-efficient lighting in public buildings. He had also worked at Hampshire College in Amherst, helping to design and implement innovative ways to use energy more efficiently and instructing students how to save on electrical power. Another, Harry Dodson, was a Harvard-trained landscape architect with a strong and growing national reputation (he was helping to design sites in Boston's harbor and on the Buffalo Bayou in central Houston). The third member, Bruce Bennett, was a quiet man who had taken the trouble to visit sites where versions of the technology were already in use (on Cape Cod, in Providence, Rhode Island, and at a Ben and Jerry's ice-cream plant in Waterbury, Vermont).[4] These advocates were strongly abetted through this long struggle by Walt Cudnohufsky, founder of the Conway School of Landscape Design, who had taught landscape architecture and regional planning at the University of Massachusetts, and by Ken and Ethel Kipen, local artists with a well-informed and fervent commitment to environmental protection.

These respected people, Ashfield's "greens," viewed the town's need for a wastewater treatment facility as a great opportunity. They deployed their professional expertise and eloquence with evangelical zeal, in service of their vision of Ashfield in the vanguard of a movement to adopt technologies that used nature's own methods to meet the challenges of modernity. When their arguments were dismissed as wooly idealism, they shot back that their opponents must be either hidebound conservatives or people with a stake (not necessarily financial) in old-fashioned, discredited technologies. In these rhetorical wars, they found a sympathetic audience among Ashfield's increasingly well-educated and progressive populace, many of whom came to share their enthusiasm for positioning the town at the front of the movement for earth-friendly technology.

In October 1988 the board of health, in the midst of building its case for this new technology, learned that the federal government's Environmental Protection Agency (EPA) intended to begin closing out (that is, withdrawing) its 1977 grant of $743,106 in support of the sewer system unless the town moved directly to build it. This would, of course, have been a financial calamity for the town. But in light of the fact that state officials had first discovered that Ashfield was polluting public water almost thirty years previously, it was hard to argue that the feds were moving precipitously.

That same month the town voted $3,900 to survey alternative sewage disposal systems and prepare recommendations. Then, remarkably, nothing substantial happened for three years. Finally, in late 1991, Leue and Dodson from the town's board of health and Tom Carter from the select board, responding to a summons, went to Springfield and were told by the state's financial enforcer that in order to save the grant, the town would have to vote the money and move forward with final construction plans within ninety days. Otherwise Ashfield would lose the federal money.

This challenge provoked not immediate action, but an elaborate ballet. First, the commissioner of the Massachusetts Department of Environmental Protection (MassDEP) stated that he would "consider" asking the EPA to postpone the closeout until an evaluation of the solar aquatic technology was complete, but that the request had to come in writing from the chair of the select board. On February 5, 1992, the EPA accepted MassDEP's recommendation to delay closing out the grant, on the condition that the town notify state and federal authorities by May 30 (that is, following the annual town meeting) that it intended to proceed with the project. Construction would have to start by March 30, 1993, and the plant would have to be in operation by June 30, 1994.

Why, one wonders, were the authorities being so patient with Ashfield's desire to use solar aquatics? Was someone in the governor's office holding the bureaucrats at bay? In any case, there ensued in Ashfield a brief but intensive period of lobbying on behalf of building a solar aquatic facility. The select board suddenly found itself the object of attentions from the CEO of Ecological Engineering Associates (EEA), the company that owned the patent on solar aquatics. EEA, we were told, had comparable facilities in Halifax, Nova Scotia, and on Cape Cod, in Harwich, not to mention the Ben and Jerry's factory in Vermont and a mall in Weston, west of Boston.[5] EEA, promoting its green technology, had eager supporters in Ashfield. That these ideas met resistance from timid bureaucrats and the owners of old-style companies in the wastewater business only added to their appeal. It confirmed the sense that we were on the cutting edge of something fresh and bold. And it did not hurt that the CEO, a smooth-speaking gentleman with a soft Southern accent (was he from Kentucky?), was the entrepreneur. He reminded me of Harold Hill, who sold brass bands in the hit musical *The Music Man*. Our man's manner was more appropriate to his line: a gentle, green way to restore the purity of nature's water.

I had joined the select board in May 1991, so I was still feeling my way when, in mid-January 1993, Leue and I drove over to the impressive home office of Weston & Sampson, in a Boston suburb, for a meeting with MassDEP. Also represented at this meeting were EEA, gently but insistently pressing its case, and Weston & Sampson, the town's engineers, committed now, however reluctantly, by the town's strong vote for the new concept. The town's officials came away from the meeting with a promise from MassDEP that it would render its judgment about the acceptability of solar aquatics by the end of January.

That deadline came and went. On February 22 the select board contacted the town's state legislators, Senator Stan Rosenberg and Representative Jay Healy, to see if they could find out why MassDEP had not responded. On March 1 EEA reported that the state was requesting more data. Groans rose from their local champions; EEA's CEO, butter still firm in his mouth, counseled patience and cooperation. The state said it needed just two weeks more, maximum, and reported that it had contacted the EPA and received assurances that the federal government would not punish the town for the delay. We felt pretty special to be the object of such high-level attention, although we could not help wondering how these things happened.

Finally, on April 9, 1993, a letter from the state granted the town permission to use the solar aquatic treatment process, subject to various fail-safe (and ultimately very costly) provisions and conditions. The announcement produced euphoria among the progressive people of Ashfield, but for the voters and select board there were some bridges still to cross, and many costs to be financed.

Financing

The carrot was in place. Now we began to feel the stick.

Following hard on MassDEP's decision, an assistant attorney general for the commonwealth reminded the town's leaders and its attorney, at a meeting in the Springfield offices of MassDEP in May 1993, that it was still, after many decades, in violation of the Clean Waters Act. She offered an alternative to immediate fines: a consent decree, setting forth a judicially enforceable schedule for constructing a sewage treatment system. Sanctions, including daily fines of $10,000, would be imposed on the town if it failed to meet the deadlines outlined in the decree, which was signed by the select board on September 27, 1993. There was no wiggle room. It was apparent to everyone at the meeting, including all three members of the select board, that the game of ignoring the state's warnings and demands was over.

Following up quickly on the May conference with the assistant attorney general, the board convened a critical special town meeting on June 28, 1993. It was immediately clear that Ashfield, by the mysterious process that forms a consensus, was ready to get moving. The first article on the warrant called for the design and construction of a wastewater treatment facility using solar aquatic technology. It passed on an overwhelmingly affirmative voice vote. Only one or two voices were heard in dissent. (As troubles later mounted, many people claimed to have been those lonely dissenters.) The second article also passed practically unanimously. It appropriated an additional sum of $1,569,750 to cover the town's share of the cost of designing and building the system and authorized the treasurer to borrow $2 million (covering also the $430,250 that came out of the May 1983 bond-issue vote). A ballot vote two days later to authorize the bond to cover these costs passed handily, 312 to 18. Fidel Castro could hardly have hoped for a stronger mandate.

There was just one other little problem (besides building the system): acquiring Smith's land. First the town had to do hydrogeological testing, to determine how much land we needed. This required a temporary easement, and Smith was reluctant to grant it. The select board called a special town meeting for November 16, 1993, with just one article on the warrant: to take, by eminent domain, the necessary temporary easement. Under this gun, Smith agreed to the testing, and the call for the special meeting was withdrawn.

The testing, delayed for two weeks by the failure of the conservation commission to file the necessary papers on time, began in December and continued through a particularly cold and snowy winter. By the end of February the testing was completed. Negotiations with Smith resumed. By this time he had decided he had no alternative to selling the land, but he was understandably determined to get the best possible price. He was also seething with resentment over five years of haggling with the town (very difficult in such a small, tight community), leaving him thoroughly suspicious of the town's officers. Smith's initial asking price was $168,500 for thirty-nine acres of land. The town countered by trimming the site it wanted to twenty-four acres and hiring an appraiser, who valued the property at $60,000. Happily for everyone, Smith's new attorney, a quiet, steady man from Northampton, skillfully maneuvered both sides toward an agreement. The ultimate price, $95,000, conceded something to Smith for his suffering, but voters were eager to move on. At a special town meeting on April 28, 1994, the deal was approved by a vote of 134 to 2. We finally had the land the project required—assuming that the state would sit still on its requirements.

But if the select board expected easy sailing the rest of the way, it soon got a wake-up call. In October came two signals of the rising stakes of the project. The attorney general's office, fearing backsliding and determined to monitor progress toward the goals mandated in the consent decree, ordered weekly reports henceforth. And on October 24, a special town meeting authorized an additional $1.76 million in temporary borrowing, bringing the project's cost to $3.76 million. The select board assured the town that these funds would be covered by grants or loans from the state or federal governments, on very favorable terms. There was, in any case, no alternative but to ante up.

Then, in January 1995, came a real scare. The regional head of the federal Rural Development Agency (RDA) notified the select board that there might not be any more loan or grant money available for the town's wastewater treatment project. Funds were short, he explained, and there were many demands on them.

Thus do state bureaucrats blithely inform local politicians that their town is about to be garroted. The RDA was the principal hope for a favorable grant-and-loan package. Without it, the town would have to go shopping for a loan from a commercial bank, and commercial rates at that time were close to 9 percent, substantially higher than the RDA would likely offer. Cries for help went out to U.S. Representative John Olver, Senator Edward Kennedy, and State Senator Stan Rosenberg. Olver made a personal visit to the Department of Agriculture in Washington to intercede on the town's behalf—a truly extraordinary gesture.[6] The RDA official later admitted that he was impressed—"flabbergasted" was the word he used—by the pressure Ashfield was able to bring to bear as the RDA sorted through various applications for its funds. At a meeting a few weeks later in Senator Rosenberg's Northampton's office, an aide asked us how we would feel if the RDA picked up the whole remaining tab, almost $3 million at that point. At its meeting on February 13, 1995, the board, still stunned by the turn of events, voted to accept an RDA grant of $1.3 million and a loan of $1.65 million at 4.5 percent interest over forty years.

It is not clear what would have happened in the absence of the town's lobbying campaign. Would the state and federal governments have expected the town to pay the staggering bill alone? The state's demand that the town treat its wastewater was a classic example of an unfunded mandate. If the RDA didn't help, who would? Fortunately we never had to face that question.

Construction and crisis

Construction began in the spring of 1995. In April we awarded a contract to build the sewers to a firm called B & S Construction, of nearby Ludlow. The bid, for just under $1 million, was far below the competition, but our engineers and the state monitors advised us that the company had a good record.

Within a month, huge earth-moving equipment began to tear up Ashfield's Main Street and to install a collection system (that is, the sewers). It was noisy, slam-bang work—at one point, a B & S operator backed a loader into a police cruiser, earning his company the local nickname "Bash and Smash." But the disruption of this vital artery at the town's center was minimal. The highway was never impassable. Businesses and other establishments were never inaccessible. The plan was to build a

main sewer from the west end of Main Street, two miles east of the treatment plant site, with a spur north to pick up houses around the south end
of the lake, and two spurs south, to connect with houses on Norton Hill
Road and South Street. Work on the treatment plant itself was awarded
to Penta Corporation, of Moultonville, New Hampshire, which submitted the winning bid of $2,317,000. Here is where the "innovative" part of
the project would be concentrated: the translucent bins that would hold
the water-borne organisms while they treated our wastewater.

It all seemed to be going reasonably well. Bill Perlman enjoyed dealing with the engineers and contractors and devoted endless hours to it.
Inevitably, the drawings for the collection system had inaccuracies and
had to be adjusted. Often this had to be done practically on the fly, lest
we incur delays, run up the cost, and get into trouble with the attorney
general's monitors. That sometimes meant smoothing the feathers of
residents, some of whom had studied the drawings very carefully and
were ready to take alarm if the cost or convenience of their connections
went up. Perlman was very good at handling such potential conflicts. He
knew the system as a whole better than anybody, including the engineers
and contractors, and he could be glib when he needed to be. Over time
he gained the trust of his fellow board members. That was important,
since squabbling among board members would have opened the door
to trouble. Board members sometimes came perilously close to acqui-
escing on certain issues just to avoid a public fuss. There were some in
town who suspected that this, or worse, was going on. In fact, however,
the other two select-board members, Dianne Muller and I, were following Perlman's management of the project closely. If anyone was guilty
of ducking controversy, it was the town itself for failing to question the
advocates of the green technology more closely and failing to insist on
independent analysis of their proposal.

The last serious crisis of the construction phase came in the spring of
1995, when the engineers, Weston & Sampson, informed the select board
that an additional appropriation of $656,000 would be needed, bringing
the total cost of the project $4,419,200.[7] The board was stunned. The
idea of returning to the town's voters at this stage for another big pile of
money was almost unthinkable. The new demand would bring engineering costs alone to $814,700, over 18 percent of the total project. But the

vice president of Weston & Sampson was adamant. Part of his style was to present himself as the Good Cop, the town's champion in dealing with the state. In this case, he told the board that he was dealing with executives "upstairs" at his own firm; Weston & Sampson was a huge and very tough contractor that had many projects throughout New England. He told us they would not budge.

Among ourselves we fussed and fretted, but what choice did we have? The state would not allow the project to lose momentum. We could not hire new engineers; it was far too late for that. All we could do was say that this would be the last time that we, the present members of the select board, would approach the town for more money for this project. A very reluctant finance committee, including former select-board member Tom Carter, also swallowed hard and agreed unanimously to recommend the expenditure to the town meeting. The request aroused the expected anguish on the floor of the meeting, but it passed, nearly unanimously. What else could the town do?

That summer construction began at the treatment plant. Here there was genuine excitement, to see how it would look and how it would work. Despite some skepticism, most people at the time were thrilled that tiny Ashfield had positioned itself at the cutting edge of innovative, green technology.

Though it would be some months before the plant would commence operating, the select board in September hired Tom Leue (who had not run for reelection to the Board of Health) as operator. A year later, on September 9, 1996, the select board signed papers certifying "substantial completion" of the sewer system, and three weeks after that it did the same for the treatment plant. The town had missed the deadline set by the consent decree—May 1, 1996—by five months, but, as Tom Carter liked to say, it was "not bad for government work." Every indication from MassDEP and the attorney general's office was that the state was pleased.[8]

The town reacts

In September 1996, however, the chickens began to come home to roost. Property owners in the sewer district received their first bills: $59.50 per quarter, for debt service.[9] These fees were the first droplets of a flood that would soon engulf the owners of homes and rental apartments in the area served by the new system.

First, though, homeowners had to contract individually for hookups. Work began in October 1996; most of it was done by a local construction firm. Practically every morning, a fleet of equipment—huge trucks, bulldozers, and tractors—issued forth into the surrounding countryside for earth-moving and road-patching. Connecting the sewer to the public buildings and homes it served meant good business for the firm, but also many headaches. The drawings they had to work with were full of errors, and the overseer, a genial man working for Weston & Sampson, soon had his work compromised by a fatal illness. Perlman had to cover for that, too.

In October 1996 the select board, which had already devoted a stupefying amount of time to this project, decided to appoint a sewer commission to oversee the operation of the facility. (The board agreed to continue monitoring the completion of construction.) Accepting appointment to the new commission were three people with strong reputations in town: Tom Carter, who as select board chair had presided over the decisions that initiated the project; Mary Fitz-Gibbon, an editor and, like Carter, a homeowner in the new sewer district; and Bob Delaney, an optometrist who lived outside the district, to look after the interests of the town's general taxpayers.

It was Carter who devised and sold a scheme for distributing the costs of the sewer system among residents of Ashfield. His idea was that everyone in town had an interest in building the system, not only because everyone would have had to bear the fines for failing to build it, but also because people who did not live in the sewer district were beneficiaries of the system, too. Everyone who had a child in the school, or who used the post office, the library, or the stores and restaurants in the center of town, was served by the sewers.

But what about the heavy debt for the construction of the plant? How should that cost be distributed between the town's many voters and the relatively few residents served by the plant? Carter suggested a ratio of 70/30, which was roughly the ratio of the value of publicly owned property in the sewer district (the school, Town Hall, and so forth) to that of the privately owned houses and rental units. This meant that the larger, public share could be distributed thinly over the many voters, and the smaller share borne by the fewer private owners. Since Carter himself owned a home in the district, he might well have been criticized for acting in self-interest. After all, people outside the district still had to pay for their own septic systems, and no one was proposing that the town's taxpayers share that cost. But Carter's reputation prevented such accusations from even being voiced, much less becoming a factor in the debate. In part the easy acceptance of his formula owed something to relatively flush times, but it also reflected the town's confidence in Carter. When the select board and finance committee accepted his proposal, the deal was done. It was time to move on.

The saga continues

There ensued a period of calm, but it was short and deceptive. By the summer of 1998 the euphoria had begun to dissipate. The problems fell into two categories: operational (was the solar aquatic technology working, and if not, whose fault was it and how could its problems be corrected?) and financial (could users afford the bills, and if they were not paying them, how could the funds be collected?).

The technical problems came to official notice when the sewer commission told the select board on March 9, 1998, that the plant was not consistently meeting its discharge requirements. Did that mean that untreated water was being discharged into the stream? Or that it had to be treated in some other way at the end of the process? Was Tom Leue, the plant operator, tweaking it, adding chemicals (contrary to the promise of a greener technology) to make the effluent come out right? Perlman and the sewer commissioners suspected that he was, but others on the select board and in town were reluctant to jump to conclusions.

At the same select board meeting (covered as usual by the press), the commissioners reported that some users were not paying their bills, and it was the biggest users, the owners of apartment buildings, who were falling behind in their payments. The problem was serious, because the deficit caused by late or missed payments would have to be made up by raising the town's general property taxes in the next fiscal year. In other words, all of the town's taxpayers had to cover for delinquent property owners in the sewer district. Politically, that could not be tolerated.

The select board acknowledged its responsibility for both of these problems. It could not turn over a malfunctioning system to the commission. A letter to State Senator Stan Rosenberg initiated the search for remedies. Rosenberg was a rising star in the state legislature. His intelligence, energy, and candor made him a respected leader. His excellent staff, based in Northampton, reflected the same qualities. Most valuable for present purposes was Mary Jane Bacon, a no-nonsense woman who knew how to locate the levers of state government and wasted no one's time. When she read an early draft of the town's letter (it lacked the "music," the piteous pleas, but it clearly outlined the town's desperate financial situation over this project), it was all she needed. She contacted the financial person at MassDEP. Together they identified a fund—federal EPA money administered by MassDEP—that would enable the town to make alterations to the plant, to make its operation more efficient. First, though, the plant would have to be brought into compliance, since the fund was for improvements, not reconfigurations. Then Weston & Sampson, our engineers, could draw up the required corrective action plan, designed to correct the plant's deficiencies and make it cheaper to run. So long as the rationale was to make the "innovative technology" work, she thought, EPA would fund the changes.

There ensued a very hard struggle in Ashfield over the corrective action plan. Perlman had developed good relations with MassDEP monitors, who shared his deep skepticism about the new technology and were ready to abandon solar aquatics and replace it with something tried and true. By 1998 they were certainly not alone. Tom Carter had been skeptical from the start as well, and as operational costs mounted, his skepticism was hardening into a conviction that we had made a terrible mistake. The finance committee was also alarmed as the system's financial burden began to spill over onto the general tax rate.

On the other side, a group emerged that called itself the Solar Aquatics Interest Group. Its members were townspeople who had sponsored EEA and its technology in the first place. They suspected that Perlman's hostility, which they saw as partly personal, was subverting their dream of making Ashfield a harbinger of green technology.[10]

The split, as it gradually became public, drove a wedge deep into the town. The green group had a large following, mostly among newcomers. The skeptics found allies mainly among the old-timers, who had been passively acquiescent when the air was full of promise and high hopes. Now, with the promise tarnished and innovation beginning to look costly, opposition began to grow and harden.

What held the town behind the project at this stage was a firm reminder by MassDEP's representative, Joe McNeely, to Perlman and Carter, most pointedly, that the funds for "corrective action" would come only if the innovative character of the project was preserved. The EPA would not now share the town's costs for building a traditional system. He warned that not only would the town be stuck with what it had; EPA might try to recover funds already spent for the innovative technology. A calamity of that magnitude could not be countenanced.

Despite these constraints, Perlman and MassDEP were able to win an important concession at this juncture. As part of the testing process to determine where the faults lay, the EPA-funded corrective action plan could include experiments in which plants were gradually removed from the processing tanks, ostensibly to see how many plants were actually re-quired for the system to work. Experience, they argued, showed that the plants in the bins were causing expensive and time-consuming problems. If fewer plants, or plants of different types, would work, that might pro-duce substantial savings. Though they hated it, EEA's owner and designer could not resist this argument.

The struggle over operations

To Perlman, to the engineers at Weston & Sampson, and to the monitors of MassDEP, part of the problem was the plant's operator. They were convinced that Leue was constantly intervening in the process in an effort to make it come out right. It was therefore impossible to take an accurate reading of what was going on, to pinpoint the problem.

Indeed, the plant was a mess. Bins overflowed, spreading foul wastes on the floor. The plants in the bins needed constant attention, which they were not getting. Root systems grew dense and clotted, forming a solid mat of fetid material. Leue was also conducting his own experiments. At one point he brought birds into the greenhouse, to eat the aphids that covered the plants, perhaps at the same time increasing the similarity to a natural environment. What he hadn't anticipated was that bird droppings added to the elements that had to be purged from the water. Leue's zeal was commendable. He worked overtime and at odd hours, without complaint or billing for them. But even here there was a problem: it added to the difficulty of finding out exactly how much operating time the system required.

To those who were not experts (namely—to mention two categories of ignorant but responsible people—members of the select board and the town's voters), it was practically impossible to judge the matter fairly. Everyone knew that Perlman thought the head of EEA was a snake-oil salesman. Everyone knew that Leue was desperate to make the system work. You simply could not trust the data, much less the conflicting interpretations of it.

The matter came to a head in the winter of 1998–99. In December, Perlman met with Weston & Sampson engineers to prepare the corrective action plan. In January a deputation from the Solar Aquatics Interest Group came to a select board meeting and expressed deep concern about the proposed plan. The CEO of EEA had been reluctantly cooperating with MassDEP and Weston & Sampson at the meetings to discuss ways to evaluate the system's performance, but Perlman suspected that he was communicating behind the scenes with supporters in town, probably including Leue. He saw the local interest group as a stalking horse for EEA. (Actually there was little reason to distinguish between EEA and its local supporters. They had the same interest: to show that solar aquatics worked as they had promised it would and to rebut any evidence that it was not doing so.) At any rate, the January meeting was acrimonious. Despite attacks, Perlman remained steadfastly resolved to conduct the tests to determine exactly what solar aquatics was contributing to the treatment process, and at what cost. The other two select-board members stood firmly with him on this.

At about the same time the sewer commission filed a bluntly worded report detailing the plant operator's faulty performance. Leue filed a grievance and requested a public hearing in front of the select board. A large crowd, about seventy-five people, turned out at Town Hall on February 1. A local attorney noted for his judicial temperament and fairness agreed to moderate the meeting. He said he expected and would insist upon civility and mutual respect. Leue briefly presented his grievance, to the effect that the commission had not given a balanced picture of his performance. The burden of responding fell to Mary Fitz-Gibbon, a well-spoken, careful woman. Her indictment was gentle and respectful in tone, but devastating. She carefully detailed the problems at the plant, citing Leue for failure to carry out the commission's directives, inaccurate reporting, withholding timely information, and making unauthorized purchases. Leue's response to these charges was general: he insisted that he was doing everything in his power to make the system work (which no one disputed).

At the end of the hearing, Leue's mother, in a remarkable act that did not compromise her loyalty to her son or his (or her own) dogged commitment to green technology, commended the town for the fairness of the proceedings. Five days later, Leue resigned. A man who had had experience operating a similar plant at Disneyland in Florida was named to replace him.[11]

Corrective action

In the summer of 1999, the EPA approved a grant for corrective action. It provided $1.1 million in additional funds: $780,000 for testing and evaluation, $100,000 to design alterations to make the plant work more effectively and efficiently, and $230,000 for purchasing and installing the necessary changes. This grant brought the total cost of the project to $5.7 million, for a system that served 168 "dwelling units."

On October 18, MassDEP okayed the removal of plants from the tanks, one train (eight tanks) at a time, to test the importance of the plants to the system. This was a critical moment. Would the system operate as effectively without the plants? Certainly they were expensive and, MassDEP believed, potentially dangerous to maintain. The operator had to prune them and thin out their matting root systems. The bins were eight feet tall; the operator had to climb a ladder and balance over the water while treating the plants. Were these particular plants essential to the treatment process? Might it be possible to substitute other plants easier to maintain?

And what about the indoor leach field? It consisted of a greenhouse full of small trees (figs, mostly), ferns, and grasses, planted in gravel, all of it set on a concrete base. Partially treated water came in one side, flowed through this greenhouse and came out the other side, on its way to the outdoor leach field. As with the bins, this indoor leach field posed complicated problems of maintenance. It was nearly impossible to clean. Where could the effluent be sent while part of the indoor field was being cleaned? How long would it take? How could the growth of these living organisms be controlled? Was an indoor leach field necessary at all?

In the fall of 1999, while the scientists and engineers wrestled with these questions, local and state officials gathered at the plant to review the financing of the whole project. The men from the state reminded everyone, this time formally, that the succession of enormous grants we had received were all based on the notion that we were using an innovative technology. If we concluded that it was time to quit on solar aquatics and implement a more conventional system, we would be in jeopardy of losing our federal grants. But we would still be liable for the outstanding bills. In short, we had no alternative. We had to do our best to fix the solar aquatic system.

The financial man from MassDEP was a sympathetic figure. We had learned to trust him. Time and again, he had worked out ways to help us meet the spiraling costs of this project. No one doubted the force of his argument, however much it seemed contrary to basic principles of scientific analysis and good public administration. When he said that the plants and other organisms had to stay until the EPA signed off on the project, we had no choice but to accept his directive.

Fallout

By 2001, the membership of the select board had completely turned over. Dianne Muller chose not to run for reelection; she was replaced by the remarkable Susan Todd, a school principal in the nearby town of Heath. Bill Perlman resigned before completing his second term.[12] He had finally succumbed to the bitterness that surrounded his leadership on the sewer project, among other issues. He was replaced by Rick Chandler, an administrator of the state's agricultural extension service. I also declined to run for reelection, and I was replaced by Thom Gray, scion of one of the oldest and most distinguished families in town. The new board, as it took shape, was balanced, capable, and firmly rooted in the town's various cultures.

With the sewer project, however, it inherited a troubled legacy. It was pretty clear, not far into the new millennium, that solar aquatics, as deployed in Ashfield, was not working as advertised. The biggest problem was not what it cost to build it, although that was outrageous. Construction costs were substantially borne by federal and state agencies. The problem was the ongoing cost to operate it, and this had to be paid by the users. The problem was further complicated by the fact that we were not free to discuss it candidly and openly, because it might communicate to the EPA that we were not committed to the facility they had approved and funded, nor could we replace it with new, different equipment. As we've seen, our financial arrangements, a bewildering mix of grants and loans, were based on using an "innovative" technology. Nor could we expect any state or federal help to build a different system, and even a traditional, grind-'em-up system would cost more than a small town could afford on its own. (State and federal help had always been premised on what we were doing to the region's waterways. Heaven knows we had exhausted our appeals on that score!)

In 2003, Steve Tilley, a professor of biology at Smith College, undertook a study of Ashfield's wastewater treatment problem.[13] Tilley had once lived in Ashfield and had served for several years as a member of its school committee and conservation commission. He knew the town, and he had some interest in its politics, so he had several reasons for agreeing to spend some time studying its travails over solar aquatics.

Tilley's study, presented in 2004, focused particular attention on the claim that solar aquatics represented a significant technological breakthrough. He discovered that EEA, the firm that sold the treatment package to the town, based its system on a concept developed by John Todd, a biologist and inventor with an interest in ecological design.[14] Todd envisioned that municipal wastewater might be treated using a "green machine" built to mimic natural systems. Instead of building ditches and grinders that would churn the toxins out of sewage, it was possible, he argued, to create systems that would concentrate the process that nature itself used in streams. We could dispense with expensive machinery and the cost of maintaining it. We could save on the chemicals used in conventional plants. Instead, we would use green plants to assimilate the bad chemicals in the wastewater, as happens in streams outdoors. We could then harvest the plant products and sell them as food and fertilizer. Instead of unsightly, noisy, smelly, expensive machinery, we could treat our wastes in greenhouses. We could save money by not using chemicals and machinery. With many tanks, instead of one ditch, the system would be more resilient. We could generate revenue by selling the products of the process.

What was not to like?

As it turned out, Tilley contended, there were a few drawbacks. The technology, as applied to residential waste, was essentially untried. Hence it was understandable that the state's regulatory agencies would take a hypercautious approach, mandating costly redundancies in the system. Bureaucrats would certainly not be forgiven if the system caused a public health disaster. There were financial problems, too. A single company owned the patent; hence there could be no competitive bidding on the basic system. And the system's alleged economic benefits relied on marketing the plant products. No one knew whether state agencies would allow that. Given that this was a new technology, dealing with potentially hazardous wastes, it was reckless to assume that permission would be given.

Tilley described the process in considerable detail, showing by schematic drawings how it was meant to work and, by analysis of samples drawn downstream in the late 1990s, how in fact it did work. His conclusion was cloaked in scientific terms, but devastating. As designed by EEA and Weston & Sampson under the watchful eye of MassDEP, and as built by contractors closely supervised by Weston & Sampson and MassDEP, the solar aquatic system never worked as advertised.

Whose fault was it that we chose such a system? Here Tilley was more circumspect. At the end of his report, he summed up what he called "the roots of the difficulties." They were manifold. From outside the town, he spotlighted the pressure of time and funding constraints. Huge financial inducements were available for a novel and untested technology, presenting an enormous temptation. Yet its novelty meant that there were no independent studies of its practicality, or at least none that the town was aware of at the time. At the same time, both Weston & Sampson and on-site state regulators were deeply skeptical about the technology, which meant that they overdesigned and overengineered it.[15] Tensions between EEA and Weston & Sampson about the need for these enhancements were always resolved in favor of caution, resulting in a plant that cost far, far more than it needed to (sixty-four tanks, for example, when half that number and a substantially smaller greenhouse to contain them would have sufficed).

About failings inside the town, Tilley was equally clear-headed and candid. He cited four factors:

- Failure to address the wastewater treatment problem earlier
- Failure to put the design contract out to bid
- "Political and personality conflicts"
- Strong influence exerted by a small number of articulate, dedicated people, whose agenda went beyond building a cheap, efficient treatment plant and included exemplifying "John Todd's vision" and educating the public about it

Tilley's second point was particularly important. The failure to put the design contract out to bid was indeed an egregious mistake. Inexperienced greenhorns on the select board and in Town Hall simply assumed that Weston & Sampson would be our engineers for this project. We had hired them at the outset, and we could not imagine facing the future without them. Weston & Sampson of course was happy to encourage this attitude. We should at least have insisted on some sort of cap on project expenditures, without explicit renegotiation. Again, government-imposed deadlines had us over a barrel.

In retrospect, then, it seems clear that we should have put the design phase out to competitive bidding. But was that a real option? Would the attorney general's office have stood aside while we went through a full bidding process at this stage? The pressure to proceed expeditiously was ferocious throughout the consent-decree stage. It frankly did not occur to us to try the attorney general's patience on this one. The threat of imposing a $10,000-a-day fine on the town had us thoroughly frightened.

Tilley's gently scathing report concluded with a question about the whole enterprise: "If natural ecosystems owe their apparent stability to being huge, complex and open, and if [as experiments during the "corrective action" phase showed] green plants really contribute minimally to nutrient uptake in solar aquatic facilities, then just what real principles was the solar aquatic facility supposed to have demonstrated?"

If only we had consulted a biologist in the mid-1990s! But—after decades of stalling—would the state have waited while we did so?

I return, finally, to my central concern: what does this protracted episode reveal about the capacity of town-meeting democracy?

First, I must admit that this was not our town's finest hour. Ashfield was slow and reluctant to tackle the pollution of South River. We had to be forced to do it. When we did do it, a state agency put us in a vise, imposing a consent decree and threatening steep fines to hold our feet to the fire. The system, serving fewer than two hundred units, cost over $5.7 million to build. It took an amazing combination of state and federal grants to bail us out financially. It imposed staggering operational costs on users in perpetuity. The project was not a model of efficiency and careful expenditure of the public fisc.[16]

Was the project too big and too technical for town-meeting democracy, government by amateurs? There was perhaps more turnover than usual on the board in the early 1990s. Seven different people served on the three-member board during these years. Bill Perlman and I had to come to grips very quickly with this long-simmering project; Perlman had moved to town less than a year earlier, and I was a newcomer to the local political arena. Neither of us had much knowledge or understanding of what had gone before, and neither knew much about public-works projects. The other five who joined us on the board during this period were not much better prepared to lead the town through this process.

Was there too much acrimony over this project—or too little? Why did we not demand disputing testimony on the technology to begin with? Why did we allow it to become an ideological struggle?

Part of the problem was that the select board was trusted, on this enormously important project, probably more than it should have been. Various interested parties hounded us, but voters in general were too passive, too deferent.

It is hard to avoid the conclusion that democracy's performance was poor, just as Churchill said it would be[17]—but what were the alternatives?

We (voters, concerned citizens, elected officials) should have done this or that, for sure. But might not experts have made mistakes, too?

Coda: Success or failure?

By 2010, after over a decade of operation, it was possible to give an accounting of the performance of Ashfield's "innovative" wastewater treatment plant.

First, the plant's footprint is still as it was designed, engineered, and built to be. Inside two large glass greenhouses, wastewater is processed through a series of tanks and an indoor bed of stones, and the wastewater is still treated to a tertiary level, that is, suitable to be reintroduced directly into the state's waterways. Since 2000, there have been no violations of state regulations for effluent quality.

Functionally, however, the plant is not as innovative as originally intended. Commissioners (elected by Ashfield voters), in consultation with officials from MassDEP, determined that the plants in the tanks and in the marsh greenhouse made no contribution to the treatment process. By clogging the filters and drains, these plants caused tanks to overflow, spilling toxic wastes on the greenhouse floor and creating costly maintenance issues. Pursuant to this finding, the vegetation was gradually reduced and finally eliminated altogether, both from the processing tanks and from the marsh greenhouse.

As for the cost to taxpayers and users, it has stabilized. The debt for construction was retired in 2006. The cost of operation and maintenance was $132,000 in the year 2000; in 2010, it was $135,000. The plant operator spent fewer hours on site in 2010 than in 2000. The rate to users is slightly higher than average, compared to other municipalities in Massachusetts. Three factors account for this discrepancy: because the state insisted on fail-safe, redundant features due to the innovative nature of the technology, Ashfield's treatment plant has higher costs: it has fewer users than most, due to the town's small size; and because the effluent is discharged directly into the South River, wastewater must be treated to a tertiary level.

One of the dreams at the beginning of this project was that the facility might be used for demonstration purposes, to show schoolchildren, for example, this innovative way to treat a community's wastewater. That dream never materialized. At first there were occasional calls to arrange visits by school groups, but toxic waste spills made the plant an unsafe environment for visitors. By the time the fixes were made, its value as a demonstration project had withered.

What then are the lingering effects of the original concept? The project was overdesigned from the beginning. State officials did not want to be responsible for approving a project that collapsed or caused a public health emergency, so they made it fail-safe. State and federal money paid for the construction of these redundancies, but now Ashfield has a plant with a huge footprint, consisting of glass greenhouses that must be heated—an ironic consequence for a project designed to be ecologically sensitive.

Could it have been made to work? Not, I think, cost-effectively. Maintenance of the vegetation, within the state's guidelines for the treatment of toxic wastes, was bound to be expensive. Solar aquatics might have produced a lush garden, but it is not an efficient way to treat a community's sewage.

Townspeople are apparently satisfied with the way it came out. No one grumbles to commissioners about current operations or cost, though on both sides (advocates of this technology and skeptics), there is a feeling of having been abused by the process. No one seems ready to admit having made a mistake.

The Town Hall steeple renovation project was led by Stuart Harris, visible in the background directing the tower back onto its pedestal. Also visible are Ray Gray, right foreground, and Arnold Jones, with his back to the camera. *Photograph, titled* Guiding Hands *(August 5, 1986), by Ken Kipen.*

Town Meeting, May 2006. *Photograph by Dave Fessenden.*

Clark's (later Elmer's) Store, 1937.
Photograph by Bruce Fessenden.

Elmer's Store, 2008. *Photograph by Dave Fessenden.*

Ashfield's wastewater treatment plant shortly after its inauguration in 1996. *Photograph by Ken Kipen.*

The wastewater treatment plant, June 2010. Vegetation, originally the centerpiece of the innovative character of the project, has been removed from the bins. *Photograph by Dave Fessenden.*

Bill Perlman, Don Robinson, and Dianne Muller at play during a select board meeting, mid-1990s. *Photograph by Sally Straus for the* Ashfield News.

Croquet on Ashfield's new town common. *Photograph by Dave Fessenden.*

A view across the new town common toward Town Hall. *Photograph, titled* March Thaw *(March 6, 2004), by Ken Kipen.*

8

Controlling the Police

Max Weber defines a state as an organization that has a "monopoly of legitimate violence" over a particular territory.[1] Citizens of a democracy like to think of government in a softer way: we establish government to form a more perfect union, to provide for the common welfare. Weber, in his mordant way (like Thomas Hobbes), focuses hard on the first responsibility of any government: security. People's capacity for goodness makes compassionate government possible, but people's inclination to evil makes strong law enforcement necessary.[2] Democrats cannot escape the disagreeable truth: governments are necessarily coercive.

In larger polities, democracies deal with the problem of law enforcement by professionalizing it. Ideally, police officers are well trained and imbued with an ethic that treats people equally and fairly, without fear or favor. They are isolated from politics. However difficult to achieve in practice, such bureaucratic rationality makes sense as an ideal in a nation or large city. In a small town, however, it is at war with the spirit that quickens the community. Here, too, we expect police officers to be rational and impersonal, but we also expect neighbors to be friendly, forgiving, and flexible.

In this chapter, we will look at several episodes that highlight this tension. We will see police officers running afoul of communal mores as they attempt to implement a professional ethic. We will see officers who live in town (as many of them do) torn between active citizenship and an ethic that discourages members of the police force from direct involvement in local politics.[3] As for citizens, we will see them wrestling with the question of how much is enough. Acting in town meeting on that question requires police officers and citizens to summon mutual respect about matters that directly affect their livelihood and personal security.

My focus in this chapter will be on how force actually works in Ashfield. Police officers have the authority to compel people to act in certain ways and to desist from others. They can, and they often do, employ their powers to limit personal freedom, within a framework established by federal and state laws and local ordinances. In Weber's sense, Ashfield is a state.

The men and women who exercise police powers answer to the local executive, that is, the select board, and ultimately to the people of the town. During my nine years as a member of Ashfield's select board, conflicts over the use of police powers were recurrent. My first story tells of one particularly difficult episode, a clash that exposed the complicated way in which power works in our town.

The police infuriate a citizen

On a rainy night in late August, an Ashfield woman had dinner with a friend at a Mexican restaurant in nearby Northampton. Returning to Ashfield, she dropped her friend off and went back to her home on a rural road. As she was preparing for bed, she heard a crash. She put on her robe and walked out to the road to investigate. She found two teenage boys standing dazed near the car they had just driven into a tree. Determining they were not seriously hurt, she went inside to call 911 to report the accident. She returned to the boys to tell them that help was on the way. Seeing they were upset, she decided to stay with them until the police arrived.

The reserve officer on call that evening, a rookie in his early twenties, was on watch duty at Bill Cosby's estate in an adjacent town. He left as soon as he could, but he did not reach the scene of the accident until about thirty minutes after the call was placed.

When he arrived, he found a wrecked car, two teenagers, and an older woman. The woman by this time was a bit distraught herself, having waited in the rain for half an hour. The young officer, trying to determine what had happened, thought he noticed the smell of alcohol on her breath. He called for backup, and then began to follow the protocol for determining whether the woman was drunk. He asked her to walk a straight line and to perform other physical feats that are difficult for someone who has had too much to drink. She had a sore shoulder, and that and her growing irritation made these exercises difficult to perform. He asked her to recite the alphabet, which she was barely able to do through her sputtering rage. She angrily told him that she was "ABD" in English literature. (An ABD is someone who has finished all work toward a Ph.D. except the dissertation, but the young officer had no idea what she was talking about.) Besides, she said, she had nothing to do with the accident, apart from reporting it. She told the officer to take a report from the boys and let her go to bed.

By this time, Ashfield's police chief had arrived on the scene. Himself a young man, also in his early twenties, the chief moved with the confidence and command of an older man. The officer on the scene told him what he had found, that the woman had interfered with the investigation and appeared to be drunk. The chief agreed that they should take her to the state police barracks in nearby Shelburne and have her tested for alcohol. They handcuffed her, apparently exacerbating her old shoulder injury, placed her in the back of the cruiser, and took her to Shelburne. There a test determined that her alcohol levels were negligible. She was released and driven back to her home.

The next morning the village was full of gossip about what had happened. One center of such talk was Elmer's Country Store, then operating as a delicatessen. Elmer's was frequented by many women, including the two who had had dinner together on the night of the accident. The clientele at Elmer's was outraged at what the woman had suffered at the hands of the police.

Soon reports came to the attention of the select board. The chief insisted that the responding officer, being suspicious that the woman had been drinking, had followed the correct protocol. Despite our sympathy for the woman, we on the select board were inclined to agree with the chief. The young officer had jumped to conclusions (that the woman was somehow at fault and might be drunk), but given his suspicions he was within his protocols to administer the tests for drunkenness. The responding officer insisted that he had not acted disrespectfully, and we had no reason to suspect otherwise.

From the woman's standpoint, the matter looked very different. She had been a Good Samaritan. She had had to wait in the rain a long time for the police to respond to her call. She was not drunk; the breath-test in Shelburne showed no evidence that she was under the influence of alcohol. The police had handled her with unnecessary roughness. She felt sorely aggrieved, and the police and select board were offering no apologies. On the contrary, they were standing firm behind the officers and united against her.

To the woman and her friends, the obvious remedy was to take legal action. She filed suit against the police department; against both police officers personally, for their treatment of her that night; against the select board, for faulty training and supervision of the police department; and against two members of the select board personally (including me) for defamation of character. Citing an affidavit sworn by the owner of Elmer's, the suit alleged that one of us had described the woman as a drunk in a conversation at the store. Oddly, Bill Perlman, the third member of the board, a staunch defender of the police department and a personal friend of the chief, with whom he was in business at the time, was not named in the suit. It may not have been a coincidence that he and the woman's dinner companion that night were in the midst of a bitter struggle over terms of their divorce; the companion, a law student, was working as a paralegal assistant in the office of the attorney the aggrieved woman had retained to represent her.

The suit was ultimately settled by negotiation. The town's agencies and officers are insured against actions of this kind. The attorney for the insurance company informed us that, in her judgment, a jury might well decide in favor of the plaintiff and grant the damages she was demanding. She therefore counseled the company to settle for a payment of $25,000 to the plaintiff for her injuries, in return for a dismissal of all charges against individuals. The select board itself had no voice in determining whether to accept this settlement. It was done.[4]

Staffing and budget problems

The regulation of police power was one of our major concerns during my nine years on the select board. When I came to town in 1983, the chief was Walt Zalenski, a beloved figure in Ashfield. His wife, Barbara, a spry woman, was town librarian. Together they had raised a large family in Ashfield, but they had suffered a grievous tragedy. In 1963 a fire at their home killed three of their young children. How they had endured such a ghastly blow was more than most of us could fathom. As police chief, Zalenski could do no wrong. He performed as Santa at many local events. He also drove around town in the police cruiser, selling tickets for local Democratic Party fund-raisers and recruiting people to run for the town Democratic committee. Many people in town realized that such activities crossed the line, but no one objected, at least not publicly. He was in fact a superb police officer. His drug busts were legendary. He had no interest in people growing a little marijuana for personal use, but when dealers came through or began to set up operations in town, he struck quick and hard.

Zalenski's successor was also a superb chief, honest, hard-working, knowledgeable, approachable, a commanding figure. He personally recruited me to run for the select board in 1991.[5] But he was also a family man, and the salary in Ashfield was insufficient. When a nearby town offered him more money and command over a larger department, he resigned. Before replacing him with a permanent chief, we decided to conduct a thorough study of policing in town. A "police review group" was formed, and I agreed to chair it. We conducted hearings in neighborhoods around town. We listened to townspeople's assessment of police performance and asked specifically whether the current coverage was sufficient. We investigated how police departments in other towns were operating and how much support the state police were able and willing to provide. And we analyzed the budget of the police department, to look for cuts and efficiencies.

There was good turnout for these hearings, and the spirit was generally positive. People told many stories about effective policing: quick responses, sensitive handling of delicate situations. Many reported bad experiences with the state police and voiced strong preference for "local coverage."[6] We also administered a questionnaire, which drew responses from a far wider cross-section of citizens. It confirmed that people preferred local coverage, but it also made clear, far more than the hearings in people's homes did, that citizens did not want to pay for two full-time officers. Most thought we could get by with a full-time chief, supported by part-time reserve officers (men or women hired ad hoc, for service at particular times).

The departing chief, while he had served in Ashfield (and afterward, via the grapevine), campaigned hard for a second full-time officer. Bill Perlman, who strongly agreed with the town's consensus critical of the state police (indeed, he had done a good deal to shape that consensus), also wanted a second full-time officer on the local force, but Dianne Muller and I were skeptical, as was the finance committee. The issue stayed alive for several years, roiling relations between the police department and members of the finance committee, who suspected the department of "cooking the books" to support its case.

While this inquiry was in progress, we named a new chief. Like his predecessor, this chief soon left to take a better-paying position in a nearby town. We quickly decided to name, as acting chief, a twenty-two-year-old local man. Despite his youth, he was well trained and looked fully up to the job—big and strong and well-spoken. He worked very, very hard at giving the "local protection" the town so strongly desired, around the clock. He also tried to be frugal and responsible with the town's funds, obtaining a number of grants that enabled him to provide expanded services without increasing his budget. He reveled in being a model for young people in town, riding the department bicycle around the lake and guiding young people out of trouble and toward constructive alternatives.

It looked like a brilliant appointment, but it was also risky, as we learned soon enough. For some reason, the knives were out for this young man. For some people, including members of the finance committee, the opposition was open, honorable, and policy-related. Other opponents, however, were anonymous and more dangerous, dealing in rumor and innuendo. We were putting a young man in a very hot seat, one for which he was emotionally unprepared, and we were ultimately unsuccessful, despite considerable effort, in protecting him while he matured.

The conflict between the chief and the finance committee at first centered on budgetary issues, but over time it too became personal and destructive to the individuals involved and to the town. One critic was a fiscal hawk on the finance committee. He had formerly been a fiscal agent for the local school district and gained a reputation throughout the region for sharp dealings and fierce bureaucratic infighting in his effort to save money for the district. As he studied the police department books, he found questionable practices and suspected some padding. The chief was salaried. Why was he getting paid overtime, and why was he accepting work on "detail"—traffic duty at road construction and repair sites? This was indeed a corrupting practice throughout the commonwealth, an irresistible, recurring target for investigative reporters at the *Boston Globe*. State law gave strong preference to local police officers to direct traffic at roadwork sites. They did it off-duty, in their uniforms, at a premium hourly rate, paid by construction companies, who of course passed the cost along to their clients—often, that is, to taxpayers.[7] You could argue that police officers were underpaid and needed this work to make ends meet. But you could not convincingly argue that the duties they were performing required a police officer's skills. They spent most of the day staring down into a hole, interrupting their languid daydreams only to give hand signals to drivers who did not need them. Citizens observing this practice could not help feeling disgust. And in Ashfield, the chief had the exclusive power to name officers to work construction detail within the town.[8] Whoever made the appointments, it was a way to keep discipline and control, but it certainly invited abuse.

At any rate, the finance-committee hawk went after the police department like a yellow-jacket at a picnic. A salaried person, he argued, owes everything he's got to his job. There is no "overtime." If he had time to spare, then we needed to adjust the expectation, and the salary. As for construction detail—well, the critic might as well have been reading from an oft-published script.

Then there was the business of a second full-time officer. In the mid-1990s we began hearing about a new federal program called "Cops Fast," which encouraged police departments to hire additional officers, paying their full wages for the first year or two and then gradually shifting the financial burden to the local government.[9] The idea was of course irresistible to those who wanted a second full-time officer in Ashfield. Why couldn't we just take this federal money and then, if we decided after two years that we didn't need the second officer, drop the program? Could we do that? Sure. Why not? Someone mentioned some fine print in the application, but advocates were eager to accept the chief's reassurance that there was no binding obligation to continue if we found we did not need the officer. It looked like a flimflam to some of us, but who knew for sure? We got the money, and we hired the second officer, but it felt fishy. Responders to our police-review questionnaire had urged us to be frugal with the police budget, and we were being profligate. Never mind that it was federal money. It was unnecessary, a waste.

Throughout these controversies the select board stood staunchly by the young man they had appointed to the chief's position. The detail program, while questionable, was lawful, and our chief was handling his responsibilities under it openly and honorably. Ditto the Cops Fast program. For the select board, Dianne Muller asked state authorities to check into allegations that the police department had made inappropriate billings against this grant. After careful review, state officials confirmed that nothing was amiss in the department's filings. The board finally submitted the matter of police oversight to the finance committee as a matter of confidence in its administrative responsibility. They had no alternative but to give us a unanimous vote of confidence.

Not long thereafter, however, our young chief resigned. It was a sad denouement. He had been subjected to cruel pressures, at too early an age. Perhaps we were wrong to appoint him. We were certainly unsuccessful in protecting him from his enemies.

By the way, before he left, this chief was able to extricate us from the Cops Fast program, although not without considerable difficulty. Under the program's regulations, with each annual budget cycle we became responsible for a greater proportion of the second full-time officer's salary. After three years of this growing aggravation, voters dug in their heels. Officials in the justice department in Washington kept citing language in the contract, but the chief told them that we had bought into the program under false pretenses. Rather than take us to court, the feds finally relented. In this case, as in many others, the young chief effectively carried the town's water.

Coming to grips with anti-Semitism

The police department was involved in one other nasty bit of business during my tenure. Back in 1993, when our chief resigned, we searched for someone to serve as a temporary replacement while we conducted the search for a permanent chief. The not unreasonable expectation was that the temporary person might eventually become the permanent, full-time chief.

There were several candidates, including the husband of the select board's administrative assistant. He had reportedly been a police officer near Springfield before he and his wife moved to Ashfield a few years earlier. He already served part-time as a reserve officer in our police department. Many people in town liked him a lot, finding him a steadying influence in an otherwise young, inexperienced department. On the other hand, the resigning chief, feeling sorry that he had left town rather suddenly, mentioned that he had a friend in Florida, an experienced and capable guy. Trusting our ex-chief and eager to avoid a hiatus in the department, we sent for his friend.

With the heat off, we placed ads, collected applications, and set up an interviewing schedule. We concluded fairly early that the local applicant was not our man, partly because the other reserve officers seemed not to welcome the idea of having him for their chief. The departing chief, still respected in town, was lobbying pretty hard for his friend from Florida. But tensions began to develop in Town Hall, and soon a smoldering conflict developed between our administrative assistant and the new man. Finally an angry outburst between them brought charges of harassment and angry denials and countercharges from the acting chief.

At this point, things took a vicious turn. Bill Perlman reported that he had received an anonymous, blatantly anti-Semitic telephone call in the middle of the night, warning against appointing the man from Florida (who was apparently Jewish, although most of us had not been aware of that); he later told us that there had been a second call. Perlman was not one to take such a thing lightly. He fired back with angry fury and began to carry a pistol to select board meetings. Nor was he alone in his rage. Noah Gordon, a local man whose novels enjoyed great fame in Europe, denounced the phone call and demanded public expressions of outrage. The district attorney's office promised a full investigation. Reporters from the Associated Press and several television stations came to town to do stories.

We had no mechanism in place for dealing with such a situation, although it was evident to members of the select board that the town needed one. We needed to do something dramatic and public. We began by calling a meeting in the school cafeteria and urging everyone to attend. A huge throng turned out. Many people gave eloquent expressions of outrage and of solidarity with Perlman and with anyone else in town who might be the object of insults and intimidation. At that meeting, there were calls for the creation of a local human rights commission, whose job would be to educate us all about the baneful effects of prejudice and discrimination, through frequent programs, teach-ins, and, where necessary, investigations of threatening acts. The select board readily accepted that suggestion, and we created a human rights commission as quickly as we could.

We never did find out who made the phone calls, but the public hearing showed that, whoever the person was, he or she was isolated in Ashfield. The act was roundly condemned by everyone in town who had the guts to make a public statement about it.

Controlling the application of force is a particularly tough test for democratic government. It must show firmness and strength in regulating illegal behavior; it must at the same time control its own passions.[10]

The clash between the aggrieved Good Samaritan and Ashfield's young police force put the town between a rock and a hard place. The woman felt abused, and her supporters shared her sense of victimization. The offense of the police, if offense it was, was understandable. Police need some discretion to protect us from the ravages of drunk driving. Legal processes exacted a pound of flesh from the town as compensation, allowing everyone to walk away with a sense of vindication. The settlement, however, was not democratic; it was not based on a decision of the people of Ashfield.

Nor did the selection of a series of police chiefs cast local democracy in a favorable light. The town's administrative officials made some weak choices, and the town was unable to provide an environment that allowed the men chosen to mature in service. Moreover, the elimination of personal factors from the bureaucratic exercise of force was never perfect. Police officers regularly leaned in the direction of citizens they knew or who had influence in the community, and members of the select board not only allowed it to go on, they encouraged it, perhaps even in some cases allowing themselves to be beneficiaries of it.

Most important, in deciding whether to add a second full-time officer to the force, the democratic process faltered. In anonymous question-naires, citizens clearly indicated that they preferred a force consisting of a chief as the sole full-time officer, supplemented as needed by reserve officers. But when it came time in a public meeting to cast a vote (by raised hand, or even by voice) in favor of a budget tailored to support reserves but not a second full-time officer, majorities could not be found for the lesser amount. Was it because people did not want, in front of the police officers in attendance at the meeting, to seem ungrateful for past services, or were they reluctant to offend the department for fear of being slighted in a future emergency? It is hard enough in a budget vote to stand up against one's friends who teach school or serve on the library board or the parks commission. When you compound personal relationships with concern for your own safety, resistance to unnecessary spending is even more difficult.

Note also the disruptive effect of pressure by higher authority—in this case, a financial carrot offered by the federal government. In considering whether we wanted to employ a second full-time officer, the fact that the feds would pay for it, at least initially, weighed heavily. Once the connection between benefits and costs was broken, it was hard for the town's voters to think clearly about it. Thus the people of Ashfield were diminished as citizens.

On the plus side of the ledger, although not strictly a police matter, in its confrontation with anti-Semitism Ashfield showed commendable vigor and firmness.

Control over the application of coercion is explosive business. It is a test for government at all levels. It is especially difficult for a democracy. Despite frequent stumbling over these matters (the select board's and the town's), however, few in Ashfield would favor handing control over the police department to expert administrators or external authority.

Coda: Democracy takes charge

In the summer of 2009, Ashfield experienced a rude awakening, disturbing several years of apparent tranquility surrounding its police department.

It began when complaints about an incident at the Ashfield House, an apartment building on Main Street, were presented to the select board. The board quietly investigated the incident and on June 4 decided that there were no grounds to discipline anyone in the department.

Four days later, four reserve officers submitted to the board a "vote of no confidence" in the chief of police, and on June 19, a female officer presented to the board a memorandum charging the chief with acts of sexual harassment and racial and sexual discrimination dating back to 2005.

As word of the controversy leaked out, rumors began to circulate and residents started to take an intense interest. On June 22, the weekly select board meeting had to be moved upstairs from its usual location in a small room in the basement. The atmosphere was tense. One resident, who called on the female officer to spell out her complaints in public, was called to account by another who said he was ashamed to hear such a challenge voiced at a public meeting in Ashfield.

On July 1, the board convened an executive session to review the female officer's complaint and listen to witnesses. It lasted for nine hours. At its conclusion, the board appeared on the steps of Town Hall and announced that the chief would be suspended for ninety days and required to submit a letter of apology and to attend training on sexual harassment. He would then be allowed to return to the department on probation for an additional period of ninety days, whereupon the board would decide whether to rehire him. The chief replied that he was satisfied that he had gotten a fair hearing and would comply with the board's sanctions.

At this point, all hell broke loose. Three citizens circulated a statement asserting that the select board had repeatedly violated the state's open-meeting law and questioning whether the chief had been treated fairly. As evidence they presented an e-mail exchange between members of the select board. The header on the first message indicated that it had been sent at 3 a.m. following the June 22 confrontation at Town Hall. In this e-mail one select-board member vented to his colleagues. He was inclined, he wrote, to recuse himself from consideration of the matter, not because he was bending to the will of the ignorant and malicious, but "to lessen the prospect of a successful appeal of [the chief's] termination." The chief, he said, "had transformed himself from an annoyance to a dangerous person, and a real liability to the town." He was not concerned that the female officer had overstated her case; he was mostly surprised that she had suffered this long "without putting a bullet in [the chief's] head." He went on to assail those who had attended the board's meeting earlier that evening. "If anyone wondered how people were dragged from jail and lynched in the old west," he wrote, "you need look no further than tonight's meeting. The pathetic gullibility of an ignorant crowd was displayed in spades tonight." He knew there would be a "political backlash" if the board moved against the chief, but he could not worry about that. "It comes with the territory, and to allow ourselves to be swayed by that possibility illustrates one of the problems with a democracy. In order to do a good job, you sometimes have to risk defeat in the service of the citizenry, whether they deserve it or not." In a replying e-mail, another board member seemed to endorse the suggestion that the author of the first e-mail recuse himself, lest his personal relationship with the chief be invoked later to challenge the chief's dismissal.

It looked as if the distribution of this exchange would cook the board's goose. But wait! The swirl of dueling documents was only beginning.[11] Over the weekend, copies of the female officer's affidavit accusing the chief of harassment began to circulate, unedited except that the names of witnesses were blacked out. Apparently she had authorized that it be released. It was a brutal document, six pages long, single-spaced, plus three pages of addenda, copying e-mails full of vulgar language exchanged between the chief of police and his officers. The affidavit itself was full of vivid details about verbal harassment (no mention of physical harassment), allegedly occurring over a span of four years. According to the officer, the chief had teased her about her ethnic background, accused her of being a lesbian and a virgin, and made crude remarks about other women who worked in Town Hall. Why hadn't someone complained before? The officer claimed she had done so, confronting the chief several times, demanding that he cease. Lending credence to the accusations, she cited the names of people—other officers, other employees in Town Hall, residents—who had allegedly witnessed these outrages.

As the town struggled to come to terms with these charges, the local press began to report specific details of the officer's allegations. In a story published under a banner headline in the county's daily newspaper, we learned that the charges included an allegation that the chief, at a department meeting, had in jest waved a loaded pistol in the face of one of the officers.[12] To some, this was a more serious charge than those involving sexual harassment. How could we be safe in a town where the police chief had no better sense than to engage in "gun play" (as the newspaper's headline put it) with his officers?

The following day, Ashfield's affairs were again spread across the front page of the county newspaper under a banner headline, and it was, if anything, even more sensational. The chair of Ashfield's select board had suddenly resigned. His presence had become a distraction, he wrote in a letter to the town clerk. Saying that he left "with head held high," he deplored the failure of the board to dismiss the chief, who "clearly should have been fired based on the charges leveled against him."[13]

These cascading revelations threw Ashfield into turmoil. The newspaper's website received a heavy volume of postings aimed at the town's travails, most anonymous, many downright vicious. In town, an epidemic of public meetings broke out. Some people focused on the select board's failures and abuses, including poor supervision of the police department and careless behavior in violation of open-meeting statutes. Others focused on attitudes toward the police department, some residents attesting to the chief's vigorous, even-handed, and effective enforcement of the law and his fairness toward all residents, others deploring his verbal assaults on women and his immature leadership of the department.

Police work often requires secrecy. Officers must respond to calls involving domestic disputes or the abuse of children. Good police work is sometimes able to resolve these situations without public disclosure. Accepting the mystique that surrounds police work, most residents at first were prepared to live with limited information and closed-door meetings. The remaining members of the select board, Ashfield's executive, tried to handle the matter confidentially, away from public view and clamor. Several factors disrupted this strategy. Some people, trusting the complainants, saw grounds for immediate dismissal; others, more skeptical, hoped to find a less drastic remedy: a reprimand, some training for the chief, and a fresh start. Members of the board themselves could not agree about the gravity of the charges, and as more charges were published, opinion in town came to reflect the board's ambivalence.

Then another factor kicked in: some people in town sensed an opportunity to settle old scores. Soon we found ourselves discussing how the select board was conducting its business and the strained relations between employees in Town Hall that had apparently been festering, mostly out of public view, for many months.

As of this writing, the deepest issues raised by this episode remain to be addressed. How do people in a democracy control those who apply coercion in their name? Normally, the executive—in this case, the select board—acts for the people. If these officials act badly, voters may replace them at the next election. For this to work, however, voters must know what is happening in their name, not necessarily the details, but enough to judge whether or not the matter was handled fairly and effectively. Citizens of a democracy must demand to know what is going on; if they are frustrated, rumors have the field to themselves, and that is not a healthy situation. Ashfield would not tolerate it. Democratic government must be transparent. As the historian Henry Steele Commager once wrote, "The generation that made the nation thought secrecy in government one of the instruments of Old World tyranny and committed itself to the principle that a democracy cannot function unless the people are permitted to know what their government is up to."[14] Many of the routines of government are necessarily handled by officials. But if constituents are to control their government, they need to be able to examine the actions and deliberations of those who act on their behalf. Ashfield's summer scandals of 2009 highlighted the difficulty of applying these standards to the control of police work.

9

Educating Children

The purpose of this book is to assess the performance of a small town in the pursuit and exercise of democracy. Most of the book supports the argument that local people, operating through democratic assemblies, are capable of self-government. Education is at least a partial exception—no small concession.

The education of its children is the most important thing a community does together. It is certainly the most expensive. School budgets consume over half of the money the voters of Ashfield appropriate at each annual meeting. In 2005, for example, citizens voted to spend nearly $2 million to pay for schooling, part of a total town budget of just over $3.5 million.[1] Why is it so difficult to use the leverage from this appropriation to exert control over the regional school district that educates the town's children?

Local schools have always performed minor miracles. They teach literacy to virtually all the children who attend them. They inculcate patriotism. They orient children to the town they live in and make them aware, in at least a sketchy way, of the world and universe. They care for children while their parents are at work and notify community care providers of problems in troubled families. Nevertheless, in the context of the concerns of this book (how the town, through its governing assembly, exercises control over public affairs), the field of public education must be deemed a significant failure.

I begin with a brief account of how the citizens of Ashfield educated their children from the Revolution to the Civil War, and then tell how, for a time, philanthropic summer residents helped the town to meet the increasing costs of schooling.[2] Against this historical background, I describe the outside pressures that overwhelmed local resources in modern times, forcing the town to accept absorption into a regional school system and its citizens to choose between radically altered public elementary and secondary schools and the alternatives of private, parochial, or home schooling.

Schooling in nineteenth-century Ashfield

In the nineteenth century, primary education in a rural community like Ashfield took place in one-room schoolhouses.[3] Parents gathered in neighborhoods (in Ashfield, there were sometimes as many as a dozen or more "districts" operating on an ad hoc basis from one year to the next) and made plans to erect or repair school buildings and hire teachers. These teachers—at first mostly young men, but increasingly, as the century wore on, young women—served for a term or a year, but rarely for more than a year or two in a given district. Male teachers soon went on to other careers. For the women, teaching school was more dignified than doing domestic work for a living, but the circumstances of their lives typically changed so rapidly that few of them stuck to the work for more than a few years. One Ashfield native remembered having twenty different teachers over his ten years in Ashfield's primary and secondary schools.[4]

After 1816, besides these neighborhood elementary schools, there was also a secondary school in Ashfield. It came to be called Sanderson Academy, for its founder, the Reverend Alvan Sanderson. After serving as pastor of the Congregational Church for eight years, Sanderson resigned for reasons of health and founded the school. He died a year later, at the age of thirty-six, and left $1,500 to support the school that would bear his name. A board of trustees was organized shortly after his death and incorporated in 1821 as the Trustees of the Sanderson Academy and School Fund. The academy flourished for a decade and educated over one thousand students from Ashfield and surrounding towns. By 1832, however, interest had waned. The funds Sanderson left were exhausted, and the trustees apparently ceased meeting regularly. The school opened for one or two terms a year, "usually as a private enterprise."[5]

The curriculum for Ashfield's children was simple and straightforward. All students, from the youngest primary students to the oldest (from ages about five to twelve), were educated together. They were arranged around the room, with the teacher in the middle. In these circumstances,

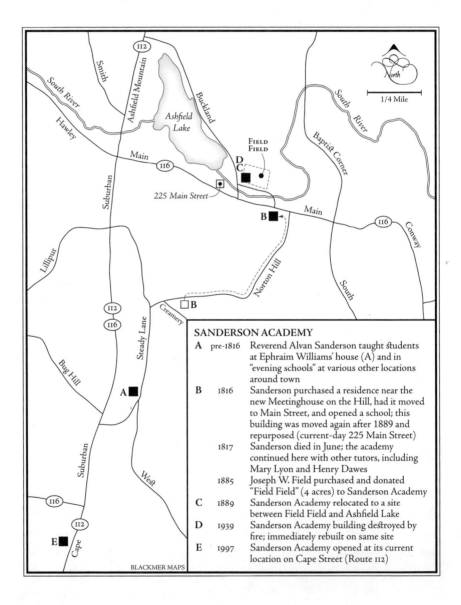

SANDERSON ACADEMY

A pre-1816   Reverend Alvan Sanderson taught students at Ephraim Williams' house (A) and in "evening schools" at various other locations around town

B 1816   Sanderson purchased a residence near the new Meetinghouse on the Hill, had it moved to Main Street, and opened a school; this building was moved again after 1889 and repurposed (current-day 225 Main Street)

1817   Sanderson died in June; the academy continued here with other tutors, including Mary Lyon and Henry Dawes

1885   Joseph W. Field purchased and donated "Field Field" (4 acres) to Sanderson Academy

C 1889   Sanderson Academy relocated to a site between Field Field and Ashfield Lake

D 1939   Sanderson Academy building destroyed by fire; immediately rebuilt on same site

E 1997   Sanderson Academy opened at its current location on Cape Street (Route 112)

BLACKMER MAPS

maintaining order was a constant challenge, and it is not surprising that some teachers were remembered primarily for the discipline they meted out. The day began, after roll call, with a recitation from the Bible, which ended with each pupil reciting a verse from memory.[6] Then came reading, with the lowest primary students performing first. Next geography, arithmetic, writing (including grammar with parsing), and spelling. Afternoon exercises repeated this pattern.

One ambitious boy who grew up in Ashfield remembers the terror and thrill of learning to write orations. In 1859, at age fifteen, he walked eighteen miles to Greenfield, the county seat, to hear U.S. senator Charles Sumner give a speech.[7] Measuring himself against one of the great orators of the nineteenth century, the young Ashfielder reported that he found it easier to copy the dramatic gestures than the learned allusions and fiery passion.[8]

At the secondary level, Ashfield's academy introduced students to Latin, Greek, and algebra and instructed them in parsing such classics as Milton's *Paradise Lost* and Pope's "Essay on Man." Worcester's *Universal History* was another staple. Ambitious students were even encouraged to "dabble" in Plutarch's *Lives* and historical works by George Bancroft, David Hume, Thomas Babington Macaulay, "and even Gibbon."[9] This was not a bad precollegiate education, although only one graduate of Sanderson Academy from the decade before the Civil War went on to college. Most became farmers or tradesmen; some went into business, a field in which several of them were quite successful.

A single schoolmaster in those days taught many subjects to students at various grade levels. Instructors depended on the hospitality (including bed and meals) afforded them in the homes of students' families. Most of them were quite young, at the beginning of careers that sometimes took them to great heights. Notable among Ashfield's early schoolmasters were Mary Lyon and Henry Dawes. Lyon, the founder of Mount Holyoke College, was born in 1797 in the neighboring town of Buckland. She attended Sanderson Academy and was hired by the academy as a preceptress in 1822. "It is doubtful if any teacher in Sanderson ever created such a moral and intellectual awakening as Miss Lyon," writes the town's chronicler, Frederick Howes. Other teachers in the area came to Ashfield to observe her methods; Lyon herself noted that there were visitors in her classroom almost daily.

From the outset, Lyon was especially interested in the education of girls. On October 24, 1827, an advertisement appeared in the *Hampshire Gazette* of Northampton, announcing that the winter term at Sanderson Academy would be "devoted exclusively to the instruction of FEMALES, under the care of Miss Mary Lyon." "The course of instruction will be essentially the same as was pursued the last winter, with the addition of Chirography [penmanship]. The price of board, including fuel and lights, from $1.17 to $1.25. Tuition for the whole term of fourteen weeks, $3.50, to be paid at entrance. As the course of instruction, though short, will be systematic, it is important that the pupils enter at the commencement."[10] In 1828 Lyon left Ashfield to join the staff of Ipswich Female Seminary. In 1834 she began raising funds for an institution of higher education of women, and three years later she opened Mount Holyoke Female Seminary, the forerunner of Mount Holyoke College, in South Hadley, about twenty-five miles from Ashfield.

Henry Dawes, a native of neighboring Cummington, taught for a year at Sanderson Academy following his graduation from Yale. He too was twenty-five years old when he was hired in 1841.[11] Dawes later served in the state legislature and the U.S. House of Representatives, as U.S. attorney for the western district of Massachusetts, and ultimately as U.S. senator from Massachusetts from 1875 to 1893. He is best remembered nationally for the Dawes Act of 1887, which provided for the dissolution of Native American tribes as legal entities and the distribution of tribal lands among individual members.[12]

Norton and Curtis get involved

So it continued until the 1870s, when Charles Eliot Norton and George William Curtis, famous summer residents, began to take an interest in the education of the yeomen of their adopted village, so warmly romanticized in their imaginations. We met both men in chapter 4; Norton was a professor at Harvard who owned a summer home in Ashfield from 1865 until his death in 1908, and his friend Curtis was a prominent journalist. Both saw Ashfield, at least potentially, as the epitome of American culture, self-reliant, unsophisticated, unspoiled by modernity. Education they saw as essential to preserve and develop the raw virtues of republican citizenship. They took a special interest in Sanderson Academy, and they were determined to revive it and place it on a firm and durable footing.

To restore the old, dilapidated building seemed a priority, and so they left a subscription list in a local store to solicit contributions. After several weeks only a few dollars had been pledged. Howes writes that the two summer residents decided to pony up "a liberal sum," which he recalled as $300 apiece, provided that an equal sum could be raised in town within two weeks. Thus challenged, the local trustees quickly raised the matching sum from townspeople, and the building was renovated.[13]

The next step in the revival was the institution of the Ashfield dinners.[14] As we saw in chapter 4, these dinners, intended as fund-raisers for Sanderson Academy, gained a considerable reputation, both locally, as a celebration of the Ashfield community, and nationally, as an important cultural event. Curtis saw to the latter, mentioning them in his "Easy Chair" essays in *Harper's Monthly*. Held generally in late August from 1879 until 1903, the dinners included a day of oratory capped by a glorious feast at Town Hall. Speakers addressed the theme "Democracy and Education." Besides Norton and Curtis, who spoke every year, some of the leading public intellectuals of the day strutted their stuff: G. Stanley Hall, himself an alumnus of Sanderson and founding president of Clark University in Worcester; William Dean Howells, novelist and editor of the *Atlantic Monthly* for a decade; Charles Dudley Warner, editor of the *Hartford Courant* and author of travel books; James Russell Lowell, poet, essayist, critic, and ambassador to Great Britain; L. Clark Seelye, the first president of Smith College; novelist George W. Cable; famed attorney Joseph H. Choate; educator Booker T. Washington, founder of Tuskegee Institute in Alabama, and his wife (one of two women to speak at the dinners, the other being Elizabeth Curtis, the only daughter of George William Curtis); philosopher Josiah Royce; novelist Richard Henry Dana; and British jurist Sir Frederick Pollock, not to mention various governors and legislators of the commonwealth. You could get a good meal at one of these dinners—chicken and biscuits, apple pie—for one dollar. Net proceeds for the academy from the twenty-five dinners and triennial fairs came to about $7,400, a tidy sum in those days.[15]

The academy building was located on Main Street, in the town's center. As more houses were built on the street, residents began to complain about the noise and disturbance caused by pupils at play. "At times," Howes writes, "the selectmen were called upon to prohibit ball playing and other games in the street fronting the Academy."[16]

In 1885 another summer resident, John W. Field of Philadelphia, investigated the matter and bought a lot, three and a half acres, near the center, across the main street. He presented it to the academy's trustees as a playing field (it is now known as Field Field). Two years later, when Field died, his remains were buried in the town he had grown to love. The following summer Eliza Field, his widow, gave the trustees a fund to build a memorial hall dedicated to her husband's memory. She originally intended it to house the academy's library and a museum, and she told the trustees that she intended eventually to contribute to the library a collection of books that belonged to her husband and herself, as well as a "large collection of photographs, many interesting oil paintings and our collection of bronzes." Gradually the conception changed, however, until 1889, when the building was designed and constructed as a new school, just off the main street, with its own abundant playing fields.[17]

Mrs. Field's philanthropy continued. She regretted that students had to pay for education at the academy; she wished it could be free for all children of the town. To that end, she contributed $500 annually for two years, provided that the town raise a like sum. It would be enough, she thought, to make the school free for all town children. Afterward she created a trust for that purpose, the income of which was intended to yield an amount similar to what she had been contributing annually. Calling the Fields "the greatest pecuniary benefactors of the Academy," Howes writes that "the grounds should still bear the name of 'Field of Sanderson Academy' and the upper assembly room should never lose the name of 'Field Memorial Hall of Sanderson Academy.'"[18] We will see, later in this chapter, what became of that sentiment.

Strong currents in the twentieth century

By 1910, nine district schools provided elementary education in Ashfield. Over the ensuing years, town meeting closed some of these schools for lack of students (one they closed had just seven). In the mid-1920s town meeting established a committee to consider consolidation, but its recommendation was rejected.

In February 1939 fire destroyed the Sanderson Academy building. Almost immediately the town, implementing the earlier recommendation, accepted a plan to construct a new building (on the same land, given in 1889 by the Field family) to house both elementary and secondary education. Remarkably, just eight months later, on October 4, 1939, the new Sanderson Academy was dedicated. The principal speaker at the ceremony was U.S. senator Styles Bridges of New Hampshire, who in 1918 had begun his career as an instructor at the academy.[19] Classes were held in the new building starting in January 1940.

Losing local control

In education as in other endeavors, Ashfield has never operated in a vacuum. Efforts to reform education across the commonwealth had a strong impact on the town.

During the antebellum period, Massachusetts was the primary arena of Horace Mann's pioneering campaign for the "common school." In the late 1830s Mann was appointed secretary of the newly created Massachusetts Department of Education. His annual reports laid out a vision of elementary and secondary schools that were free, universal, and supported by local property taxes. Mann also encouraged the development of "normal schools," where teachers could be exposed to the latest pedagogical theories, including the gentle, student-friendly visions of the Swiss educator Johann Heinrich Pestalozzi (1746–1827). Mann's pedagogical vision conformed nicely with the feminization of school-teaching, although it brought him into conflict with schoolmasters in Boston, who favored a sterner approach to discipline.[20] One effect of Mann's strong leadership was to spur the centralization and bureaucratization of public education in Massachusetts. Increasingly the state's department of education took charge over the certification of teachers, setting standards and developing curricula.

Over time, these developments had a tremendous effect on schooling in Ashfield, as is apparent in accounts of developments in Ashfield's schools during the first half of the twentieth century.[21] In a 1910 report that reflected the thinking that governed enlightened educational policy, Sanderson's principal issued a clarion call for change. Ashfield's academy would abandon the conventional pattern of high school education. "The educational ideas of the last generation have been weighed and found wanting," he declared. Sanderson's course of study needed to be "completely revised."[22]

The following year, Sanderson's administrators made several changes, partly to meet state requirements. To stimulate training in "vocational" agriculture, the state legislature offered to pay two-thirds of the salary of a special instructor in that field. Taking the bait, in 1913 Sanderson organized an agriculture department, which drew an initial enrollment of fifteen boys. One consequence was that Sanderson was obliged to restrict the teaching of some academic courses to alternate years. New courses in agriculture and domestic science were added[23] and the curriculum reorganized into three new programs: college preparation, agricultural science, and home science. The timidity of these mostly cosmetic reforms caused one leading local observer, looking back from the vantage point of the 1960s, to question whether the ideals of the pre-1910 generation were really wanting and whether the "complete revisions" promised in principal's recommendations were the "correct solution for whatever problems the machine age even then was posing for education."[24]

As the Great Depression clamped down on Ashfield, the school committee and Sanderson administration were forced to make additional adjustments. In 1933 four students transferred from Sanderson to the Smith Vocational School in Northampton, where they could obtain strong training in a variety of fields. Even after these transfers, Ashfield's superintendent observed in his 1934 annual report that probably only 25 percent of high school students in town were "college material." The rest, he counseled, needed "something besides the traditional courses." The following year Sanderson inaugurated three new courses: the first, called Business Practices, replaced Ancient History; another, Problems of Democracy, replaced Modern European History; the third was a special course in English for non-college-bound students. The latter offering omitted some reading found in the standard course and substituted drill and practice in letter writing, composition, and spoken English.[25] After World War II, other innovations quickly followed: in 1949, IQ tests; in 1951, physical education; in 1952, courses in typewriting and bookkeeping; and in 1957, public speaking became mandatory for all eleventh- and twelfth-graders.[26] These attempts to keep pace with the complex demands of modern society put a tremendous strain on local educators.

The trustees of Sanderson Academy

The continuing role played by a body called the Trustees of Sanderson Academy is a unique feature of public education in Ashfield. Earlier I recounted its origins as an entity to administer the bequest left by Alvan Sanderson in 1817. After ups and downs, it was reborn late in the nineteenth century to administer funds raised by the Ashfield dinners and to manage the property bequeathed by the Field family in the 1880s. The trustees rented the Field property to the town for a nominal sum, and it became the site of Sanderson Academy. In 1911 and again in 1938 the trustees paid for substantial renovations and remodeling of the academy building—the one that burned down in 1939.

The building erected to replace it was built by the town. At that time, consideration was given to disbanding the trustees, but when lawyers pointed out that the property in that case would revert to the Fields' descendents, the trustees decided to carry on. They gave the town a deed for the land on which the new academy was built, plus $10,000 in insurance money, on condition that the name of the school be kept. Since then, the trustees have used income from the trust to maintain the athletic fields behind the school and to provide scholarships for Sanderson alumni pursuing higher education.[27]

Rising costs

During these years the cost of education rose dramatically. In 1910 the town appropriated $6,200 to educate 214 students, about $29 per pupil. Other expenses were $24,400 that year, meaning that school costs were about 20 percent of the total town budget. By 1940 the cost to educate the town's 180 students had risen to $22,300, $124 per pupil, but still just over one-quarter of the town's total annual budget.[28] In 1960 the cost to educate 261 students was $98,700, or $378 per pupil. By the mid-twentieth century school costs had risen from one-fifth to over one-third of the town's total budget.[29]

Meanwhile, at the state and national levels, efforts to improve public education were intensifying. Feeling threatened by the Soviet Union, Congress called for a stronger, more sophisticated curriculum, especially in mathematics and natural sciences. A new awareness of world affairs also led to demands for teaching foreign languages.

In Ashfield these currents, both financial and global, stimulated an effort to form a regional school district. Fearing a loss of control and mounting expenses, Ashfield strongly resisted this movement. In 1954 voters at town meeting overwhelmingly rejected a proposal to join several other towns in building a regional high school. Instead the town voted to spend $45,000 to add a new wing to Sanderson, for additional classroom space.

By the mid-1960s, however, incentives offered by the state to enter into a regional school district proved irresistible. Town meeting voted to join seven other towns in western Franklin County, plus Plainfield in Hampshire County, to form the Mohawk Trail Regional School District. The new district incorporated various arrangements for primary education (Ashfield shared Sanderson Academy with Plainfield), but it projected just one secondary school, to be built in Buckland (adjacent to Ashfield).

The district agreement

Thus, however reluctantly, Ashfield became part of a multitown regional school system. The district's organic law was a pact, comparable in complexity to the pact that regulates the use, by contending denominations, of the Holy Sepulcher in Jerusalem. The regional agreement gives each town representation on the school committee, but weights each representative's vote according to the town's population, calculated in fractions.[30] These fractions are adjusted from time to time to reflect shifts in population. Thus, in 1994, Ashfield elected three of the regional school committee's twenty-one members; each of the town's representatives had a vote weighted at 5.6 percent of the total. After the 2004 election each town elected two members, a total of sixteen members. Again, discrepancies in population among the constituent towns were reflected in the vote of each member. Each of Ashfield's two members had votes worth 8.5 percent of the total. Each of (slightly larger) Shelburne's two representatives cast votes weighted at 9.5 percent; tiny Hawley's two members cast votes worth 1.5 percent.

The agreement, a kind of treaty between sovereign powers, explicitly provides that no town will be deprived, without its consent, of an existing local elementary school. During the past decade, two towns (Heath and Ashfield), relying on faulty population projections, built new elementary schools. The district now maintains more capacity—more schoolrooms, more teachers, more administrators—than it needs. If fiscal considerations dictate that it needs to close one of them, which shall it be: the lovely little one in remotest Heath; the relatively new one in Ashfield; or the one in Shelburne, the largest town in the district, the one that might most easily find alternative uses? Whichever way you lean, you confront local pride, made obdurate by the agreement.

What does any of this have to do with the power of town meeting over the education of Ashfield's children? The regional school committee has spent much of its time and attention during the past few years not reviewing textbooks and lesson plans and graduation requirements, but trying to decide which school or schools to close.

The cumulative outcome of these developments is that the people of Ashfield have almost no control these days over the education of their children. We vote an appropriation annually to support the regional school district, including our local elementary school and the regional high school in Buckland, five miles north of town. We also pay the tuition for students who choose to attend a vocational high school, in Turner's Falls or Northampton. About ten local youngsters take advantage of this option each year. We elect our two representatives to the regional school committee. A member each from our select board and finance committee serve on an informal regional group that counsels with administrators and the regional school committee about how large an appropriation the towns can bear in the coming cycle. In the spring of each year, the hilltowns ring with the sound of verbal combat over the school budget, which now consumes well over half of each town's annual budget and usually at least half of the morning session of the annual town meeting. In the 2005 fiscal year, Ashfield's voters appropriated $1,907,483 for public education, nearly 60 percent of the grand total of $3,237,032.

In fact, it is impossible to tell who, if anyone, does exert effective control over local public education. The nine-town system has a district superintendent who, with his small staff, negotiates with the state education bureaucracy and legislators, with principals, teachers, and their union, with custodians and bus drivers and other contractors. Acutely sensitive to this bewildering universe of influences, the superintendent is also responsible for preparing a draft of the annual budget.

On town meeting day, when it comes time to vote on the school appropriation, it all boils down to whether you support the schools or not. The town's leaders have had some input along the way, and voters have read accounts of the budget battles district-wide in the local papers. We admire the local women and men who teach and perform services at Sanderson and Mohawk. We support "education," and we honor those who serve on the school committee, who, like loyal soldiers, rise in town meeting to explain and defend the proposed school budget. There is usually some talk about whether Ashfield is paying its fair share of the nine-town bill (usually, it seems, we are paying more than our share, but who knows for sure?). Sometimes there is a proposal to add a special appropriation (new computers? a specialty teacher?) for Sanderson Academy, but then someone argues that, as part of a nine-town district, we ought not to provide special advantages for just one school in the district. Someone moves the question, we vote the requested appropriation, and move on.

Perhaps it is just the philosophers among us, or in all of us, who wish for a more substantive discussion of the content of our children's education. But the sense of frustration over education is nearly universal.

"Ed Reform" comes to Ashfield

In 1994 Massachusetts enacted a major reform of public primary and secondary education, popularly called "Ed Reform." It provided "pothole money," special grants for districts that were struggling on the road to reform. To determine which districts were entitled to this assistance, state officials devised an arcane formula with more than thirty variables. Based on various measures of relative affluence, it was designed to insure quality public education even in poor communities.

As a select-board member at the time, I attended several sessions in which officials from the state's department of education explained the law and its formula to municipal officials from western Massachusetts. Each time I came away convinced that these bureaucrats were people of good will, but that their calculations were not meant to be understood by people like me. Given the complexities, we had no alternative but to trust them.

One major problem for the town over time was that it was impossible to predict how much state aid (including supplemental "pothole money") we would receive in a given year. From year to year, Ashfield's bill from the district varied wildly. One year it would go up by 8 percent, while a neighboring community had just a 2 percent increase. The following year our bill would go up by 3 percent; in the same next town, by 7 percent. There seemed to be no accounting for it. Each year, the towns that suffered would howl and sometimes vote not to ante up their shares. By another arcane formula, this one in the regional agreement, the budget passed if it had the support of seven or eight towns (depending on their relative population). If the requisite number of towns voted to accept the budget, the agreement forced the remaining towns to go along. If no budget obtained the necessary support, the school district would operate month-to-month, on one-twelfth of the previous year's budget, until a new budget could be prepared and adopted. That way lay chaos.

Several times during these debates at town meeting over school district budgets, a member of Ashfield's finance committee, a well-respected local realtor, would explain that the formula was unfair to Ashfield. Others would counter that, if we refused to meet our assessment, the district would be crippled and thrown into confusion, and if the budget failed to pass in the requisite number of towns by the end of the month, the district would be forced to proceed on a month-by-month basis. As supporters of education, the voters of Ashfield several times weighed these alternatives and voted to go along, but the whole process left a bad taste in many mouths.

Citizens react

So it went until the turn to the twenty-first century. As the national and state economies turned sour, the state legislature imposed severe cuts in aid for regional school districts. A bad situation for public schools suddenly got much worse. The regional school committee was forced to adopt a combination of two strategies: trim expenses, and seek more money from the constituent towns. Trimming costs meant cutting non-curricular expenses to the bone (laying off custodial and secretarial help, deferring maintenance). It also meant reducing curricular offerings (laying off teachers, especially in foreign languages and the creative arts), as well as sports and other extracurricular activities. The football team had to survive on funds raised at the town dump by collecting soda cans for redemption.

Despite these efforts, it became apparent that the district could not balance its budget solely by making cuts. The school committee began to consider closing one or two elementary schools. Which ones? Incredibly to Ashfield's voters, Sanderson Academy, housed in a practically brand-new building, began to appear on the list of schools ripe for closing. Declining enrollments had led to combined classes, sometimes across grade levels (for example, first and second graders were schooled together). As a result, several classrooms at Sanderson were vacant; at one time an entire wing was empty. And since the new building was well located and attractive, it was a prime candidate for sale or leasing for another use.

Confronted by turmoil and uncertainty, more than a few parents began to look for alternatives. By January 2008, out of 152 children in Ashfield who were eligible to attend elementary school at Sanderson, 10 were attending public schools outside the district (through the "school choice" program or at specialized charter schools), 17 were attending private or parochial schools, and 18 were being home-schooled. In other words, 45 youngsters, just under 30 percent of Ashfield's elementary-school children, were not attending the local public school. For Sanderson and the Mohawk Trail Regional School District, the result was catastrophic: a loss of $225,000 in state aid ($5,000 for each child). It was a classic Catch-22 situation. We were losing state aid because enrollments were down. Enrollments were down, in part, because of turmoil in the system caused by the loss of state aid.

I spoke to parents about why they had chosen not to send their children to Sanderson. One mentioned the rising student-to-teacher ratio: one year there had been eleven children in one section of the first-grade class and thirteen in the other. The following year there were twenty-six students in the single second-grade class. One mother responded by using the school choice option. Her daughter was now attending school in a town outside the district.

Another mother was home-schooling her children. She had never sent them to Sanderson. Why not? She found public education too regimented. Teachers told children what they needed to know. They did not follow where children's curiosity led them. What about socialization, I asked—weren't her children losing a chance to interact with peers? That is overrated, she replied. Kids at school are all the same age, and they do not have much time at school to talk, to get to know one another. Another factor for this family was that schedules were so rigid. Parents were discouraged from taking their children out of school for family trips. (On one trip abroad, her children had attended public school for several weeks and had a miserable time. They came home even more committed to home-schooling.)

I asked her how she felt about withdrawing from the community's effort to educate its young people. Wouldn't the community suffer if people like herself withheld themselves from the public project of educating the town's youngsters? At first she said that her primary responsibility was to her own children. But then she said that she would feel more inclined to help with the local school if Ashfield had greater control over it. Philosophically she was a locally oriented person. But public schools were so rule-bound, controlled by the state board of education and teachers' unions, that local teachers, parents, and school committee members had very little discretion.

For another perspective, I turned to a highly respected teacher who came to town in 1987 to teach at Sanderson. At the time there were 240 kids at the school, which serves kindergarten through sixth grade, and no teachers' union. Teachers in the Ashfield–Plainfield school district negotiated contracts with a local school committee and Sanderson administrators. By 2009 at Sanderson there were just 137 students attending classes there. (Twenty of them were students in this teacher's class.) Ashfield's secondary school students (85 of them, in grades 7–12) attend Mohawk Trail Regional High School in Buckland. Union leaders negotiate contracts with district administrators in Buckland, and they are adopted by a school committee elected from the member towns.

According to this teacher, regionalization has brought real benefits: efficiencies of scale (some shared administrators, coordinated bidding for supplies and services). She also values the opportunity to discuss curriculum and classroom challenges with a wide range of colleagues across the district. What has been lost is the sense of working within a community, with families and school committee members, toward a common goal. Now, she commented, "it is more like a job."

These trends may be exacerbated by the financial crunch that began with the stock market plunge of 2008. Regionalization was pressed on Ashfield and the other towns in part as a way of dealing with the inefficiency of having separate operations in each of these tiny jurisdictions. With further cuts in state aid, the search is now on for more efficiencies.[31] Some people think the remedy is further consolidations, even broader regionalization. Perhaps, some say, we should fold into a single district with Greenfield, the county seat, as the focal point.

Another development affects the curriculum more directly. In 1998, Massachusetts began a rigorous testing program, assessing students and schools against statewide standards.[32] MCAS, as it is called, has been highly controversial. Teachers and many parents complain about having to "teach to the test." But the teacher I spoke to in Ashfield was ambivalent about MCAS. On the plus side, she said, it had led to clearer expectations. It used to be, for example, that the solar system was taught in both the third and fifth grades, and not very thoroughly at either level. Now teachers knew where it should be taught and what material needed to be covered. The problem is that there is little room for a particular teacher's expertise and passion; as she remarked, "Everything is so scripted." Also, much time is devoted to test-taking. She spends a minimum of three weeks aiming at the tests, and the tests themselves take three full days. "Does even the bar exam take that long?" she asked.

She also noted the pressure on families. Test scores at Sanderson slipped in 2007. If that trend continued, the school and the district would suffer reduced funding. As part of an effort to repair the damage and head off sanctions, Sanderson administrators called parents in and explained the situation. Unless scores improved, they said, students would have to stay after school (some of them thereby losing opportunities to make money). Some parents reacted angrily to this pressure. It was difficult to get their cooperation without irritating or embarrassing them.

The bottom line for this teacher is that teaching is less fun for her personally because of these external pressures, although she recognizes the value of standards for the system as a whole. Mostly she regrets the loss of a sense of common enterprise with the local community.

The superintendent responds

Responding to these dangerous cross-pressures (cutbacks in state aid, inability of the towns to raise higher appropriations, declining enrollments), the district's superintendent, Michael Buoniconti, has been planning a new approach: forthrightly treating the district as a player in a market.

Buoniconti took the job of superintendent in 2005. A well-spoken, hard-driving man, a graduate of Yale who also holds an MBA, he was not long on the job before making a realistic assessment of the situation. He would try, as his predecessors had, to raise more money from the towns and from the state, but he thought there was little chance of success there. He would work hard to reverse the decline in enrollments, in part by using stronger marketing techniques. To this end, the district began an aggressive advertising campaign, depicting Mohawk district schools as safe learning communities in a nice rural setting.[33] School-choice students from outside the nine towns of the district, he pointed out, would bring $5,000 each into the district. Buoniconti was not deterred by howls of protest published in newspapers in the target communities, asking why public money was being spent to compete with other public institutions. He also adopted marketing techniques in outreach to the public. Until then, when families called the school to ask how to register entering students, the receptionist said simply to show up at the school on opening day. Now office personnel were told how to deal with such inquiries more actively. Buoniconti also began to hold information sessions in the towns, where teachers and coaches explained their offerings and recruited students to join them.[34]

Even if these programs worked, however, Buoniconti knew that the district faced an unsustainable future. He had a bolder idea. To survive and thrive, Mohawk would need to attract students who could pay tuition of $15,000 per year. Fifty tuition-paying students would yield $750,000 per year. Where could they be found? Buoniconti mentioned his own experience; when he was in college, he spent his junior year in Italy. He stayed in the home of an Italian family, developing his skills in the language. He explored Italy's rich heritage of the arts. Western Massachusetts has a number of private schools (Deerfield, Northfield Mount Hermon, Williston-Northampton, the Academy at Charlemont) that attract foreign students. Buoniconti dreamed of taking advantage of the artistic and cultural heritage of western New England and offering home-stays. He also hoped that wealthy families in Asia, Latin America, and the Middle East might see advantages for their children in spending a year or two in such a setting and that he might be able to interest foundations in such a program for urban youngsters in America.

The beat goes on, but the bottom line is that the people of Ashfield acting corporately have almost no role in determining how the town will come to grips with challenges in the education of its children.

Coda: Tearing down a schoolhouse

When the meat of an issue is taken away, it sometimes happens that attention and energies are directed to relatively trivial aspects. A recent controversy over what to do with the abandoned home of Sanderson Academy had nothing directly to do with educating children. Yet it seems somehow fitting that it occasioned a rather disheartening exercise in democratic citizenship.

It began when inspectors for the state department of education announced that the academy building was in violation of state standards. Many people loved the old wooden clapboard schoolhouse, but nearly everyone agreed that it would be impossible to bring it up to code. In any case, state officials declared that the commonwealth would provide no more funds for the old building, although it would contribute substantially to financing a new one.[35] This pronouncement touched off a process that led, by 1996, to a spiffy new building to house Sanderson Academy.

This left the question of what to do with the old building. The building itself was not antique, and it was certainly no treasure as a piece of architecture.

One sticking point was that a private body, the Trustees of Sanderson Academy, owned part of the land it stood on; as we've seen, their primary responsibility was to maintain a recreation area for the benefit of Ashfield's schoolchildren, and in 1939 they sold a small portion of the recreational field as the site of the new Academy.[36] A few years later, the school needed to build an addition to house more classrooms and an auditorium/gymnasium. Because the original parcel purchased by the school district from the trustees had no room for expansion, school district authorities had to obtain permission from the trustees to build on part of their land. By terms of a court settlement, the trustees reluctantly granted permission to build the expansion, but with the stipulation that the land would be used only for the education of the children of Ashfield and Plainfield.

During the half-century of the academy's occupation of land overlapping with the trustees' land, the school administration and the trustees had been good neighbors, assisting one another's mission. When it became known that the new school building would be built on a different site and that the town would inherit the school's land on Buckland Road, the trustees decided to seek recovery of its ownership of the land they had been forced to make available for the expansion of the school. Part of their concern was to insist that any reuse of the old building must respect the intent of the Fields' gift: that the land serve to enhance the education and recreation of Ashfield's children. Basically it was the trustees' position that the sundered land on which the old school had stood should be made whole again, under their control, for recreation.

Legally, the select board's power to act for the town on this matter was clear. At the end of each annual town meeting, voters routinely pass a resolution giving the select board power to dispose of property the town no longer needs. The present case may have involved more power than voters normally had in mind, but the resolution on its face clearly covered this case.

As for the substance of the matter, the select board was pretty passive through this period. My own view as a board member was that we should keep options open—don't let anyone take the building down—but otherwise let it play out. As it turned out, such passivity proved a poor substitute for responsible stewardship.

In a typical political maneuver, the board appointed a committee to explore reuse options. As chair we named a distinguished multigenerational resident. It was probably not a wise choice. Our hope was that he, if anyone, could lead townspeople to view the matter from the standpoint of the general interest. As a leading spirit among the Sanderson trustees, however, he had, as he readily acknowledged, conflicting interests. There were other good people on the committee, particularly a widely respected realtor who had long been an active participant in town governance, and a soft-spoken craftsman who, in the 1980s, had led a team that took down the tower from Town Hall and rebuilt and refurbished it, restoring an icon that is regularly used in the national press to illustrate stories about leaf-peeping tours to New England villages. These men were public-spirited, dedicated, and active, but, despite strenuous efforts, they were unable to lead the parties (trustees and town) to the high ground of the public interest.

After about a year of meetings, hearings, and informal conversations, the committee delivered its report. Basically the message was a counsel of despair. Given the constraints—principally, the trustees' unwillingness to permit any further encroachment on their land for any purpose other than recreation for Ashfield's children—any other use of the parcel seemed impossible. The committee produced a survey of townspeople's opinions about reuse. Not surprisingly, it was inconclusive. The Book of Proverbs declares that the people perish for lack of a vision. No one provided the necessary vision here. The select board asked whether the committee was unanimous in concluding that no reuse could be found. It was not. The realtor thought there were potential reusers who had not yet been approached. The chair of the committee, however, was genially adamant and offered to resign and let others search for a solution.

At this point the select board determined that we needed to talk directly with the trustees. We were informed that the trustees met only once each year, in August (several months hence), and that it would be practically impossible to arrange a special meeting. Nevertheless, we contacted another trustee, who was able to assemble a deputation of trustees for an informal, exploratory conversation. This group seemed in principle and spirit more conciliatory and open-minded, although they did not retract the trustees' voted position: that the land could be used only for the direct benefit of Ashfield's children. How about a land swap, we asked, with the town taking some land from the adjacent field for parking and elbow room, and the trustees in return getting land across the street or somewhere else in town? (The Sanderson Trust provided explicitly for such a transaction.) Here the spirit of the meeting seemed to stiffen. Clearly there was little enthusiasm for imagining another way. The trustees' stated position, however, was that the town had to be more specific. Tell us what you have in mind. They preferred (not unreasonably) not to answer hypothetical questions.

As it turned out, we—namely, the realtor on the committee and the select board—were unable to assemble a workable package in time. We did try. To spur exploration, the town backed our request for a small appropriation ($5,000) to engage a real estate agent in the area (not the man on the committee) to run advertisements nationwide to solicit interest in the property. Little if any of this money was ever spent, though, and nothing came of this effort.

At about this time, administrators from a nearby private school expressed interest in the property. The select board met a deputation from the school. The meeting seemed to go well. A few days later, however, we were told that the school's board had decided not to proceed. There was simply not enough room at the site for parking and for playing fields.

Several other potential suitors emerged during this period: a company that manufactured fishing tackle, a group that restored works of art, another group hoping to provide housing for Ashfield's elders. Each of these potential occupants was in turn frightened off, some by the condition of the building, but most by the muddled title and by the trustees' reluctance to negotiate. Without the cooperation of the trustees, problems of parking and access seemed insurmountable.

At this point, momentum began to gather for taking the building down. Those pressing this alternative (including some of the trustees) began to offer resolutions at town meeting setting deadlines and appropriating money for demolition. Even though (they allowed, somewhat disingenuously) it might be premature to take it down, it was not too soon to begin planning and setting money aside for that eventuality.

It was hard to resist this logic. The select board had not taken the position that the building should never come down. We believed, and now we argued explicitly, that it was not very expensive to keep it standing while we explored alternatives. It was costing about $7,000 annually for minimal security lighting and insurance. That translated into 7 cents on the tax rate (which stood at approximately $15 per $1,000 of assessed evaluation), not an exorbitant sum to preserve an option that might prove valuable, as housing for the elderly, recreational space, an incubator for light industry or arts organizations, or who-knew-what. On the other side, advocates of the demolition fund argued that the hulking, vacant building was an "attractive nuisance," as the lawyers say, a target for vandals and a fire hazard to its residential neighbors, and that it was rapidly deteriorating, full of asbestos and other horribles, and altogether a sick white elephant.

Underlying these public arguments were intense feelings about the Sanderson trustees, pro and con, including concerns about how they were managing their fiduciary responsibilities. The trustees and their many sympathizers bitterly resented a long, anonymous article in the *Ashfield News* impugning their integrity.[37] The trustees appealed to the select board to rebut it and were furious when we refused to do so (we thought it was their job).

Also deeply at play here were ardent feelings about the role of government generally. Many of the trustees were old-fashioned Yankees, "conservatives," and there were many people in town who agreed with them about this. They mistrusted any arrangement that involved the government, even one overseen by town meeting, managing the property. As the old cliché has it, just look at the post office. This latter point was critical for many people. They were Jeffersonians ("that government is best that governs least"). The bigger and more active government gets, the more cumbersome and remote it becomes, and the more likely it is to bungle or become corrupt. Anti-governmental views may not prevail generally in Ashfield, but many Sanderson trustees held them fervently, and they controlled this property. If they would not relax that hold, the town faced an indefinite expense, with no prospect, no vision, of a fruitful outcome. What could be done with that property, if the trustees were adamant about hanging onto what they owned and using it only for baseball and recreation? The town's property was land-locked, a 1.9-acre parcel with no frontage. The building on it slopped over onto the trustees' land. It was simply not viable, without positive, creative, flexible planning. The trustees had no interest in that.

In these circumstances, the town had no alternative but to tear the building down. Gradually that realization took hold. The decision was made by a new select board. Bill Perlman had been replaced by Susan Todd, probably a slight gain for the reusers. But my seat had been taken by Thom Gray, a solid victory for the demolishers. And Dianne Muller had been replaced by Rick Chandler. Chandler had the deciding vote on this issue, and he lucidly read the handwriting on the wall. Take it down. It was time to call this damaging game off.

Early in the morning on August 13, 2002, the long simmering quarrel ended with a crash heard across the village. A wrecking crew from a Springfield firm descended on town and turned loose its iron ball, ripping saws, and front-loading bulldozers on Old Sanderson Academy. For the proponents of reuse, it was a sad, frustrating denouement. But no one had any stomach for further conflict over this issue. And so, when the political leader of the demolishers crowed about a small grant he had gotten from federal funds earmarked for the restoration of brownfields, or sites contaminated with pollutants, such as asbestos (talk about abuse of government money!), and about accomplishing the demolition "on time, within budget," the other side simply bit its tongue.

The developments I've traced in this chapter show that Ashfield has lost control over the education of its children, a fundamental compromise of democratic authority.

At the founding, citizens hired teachers and watched over what was taught and how. We do none of these things now. We pay our share of the cost of public primary and secondary education, and we elect two members to the sixteen-member regional school board. But even this board has little actual control over the content and style of education in regional schools. Those matters are worked out mainly between the state's department of education, teachers' unions, and district administrators.

Those who know the history of public education in Ashfield generally believe that the education of Ashfield's children is superior now to what it was in 1960.[38] On the other hand, many residents do not accept this consensus. Even if this is true, they believe the current arrangements produce unsatisfactory education, and they have opted out, in favor of home-schooling, charter schools, or public schools in other districts.

Wherever they stand on this continuum, most citizens of Ashfield would agree that there is little they can do collectively about the education of the town's children as a public enterprise. This is what Ashfield's democracy has been reduced to, as far as the education of its children is concerned. Whether it would be wise to insist on greater local control in these complicated circumstances is a different question. I will save that question for the concluding chapter.

10

Finally, a Town Common

Our final story deals with citizens in Ashfield considering whether a democracy ought to impose on itself an ordinance that limits its own powers in a certain area.

At the turn of the millennium Ashfield had no town common. For several decades we had been using two acres or so of private land on Main Street, next to Town Hall, rent free, for festivals and other public events. This property was made available to us by the remarkable generosity of its owners, the O'Donnell family, and it disguised the fact that Ashfield had no common.

In chapters 2 and 3 we saw how it came to pass that Ashfield lacked a town common, that special mark of the New England village. The town began as a cluster of settler families on the remote frontier. In 1765, when the legislature incorporated the settlement into the town of Ashfield, it directed, as was customary, that the town designate one six-acre lot for a Protestant church and another for its pastor, and build (at public expense) a house of "publick worship" and pay the pastor. But Ashfield showed a pattern that would become a habit: taking its own sweet time to respond to dictates from Boston. Part of the problem was that the center of the town's population kept shifting. It wasn't until after the Civil War that Ashfield had a proper town hall on Main Street, and by that time there was no vacant land at the town center to set aside for a town common.

Saving the Fall Festival

On the south side of Main Street, at the center of the town, there was a privately owned, but blessedly undeveloped, piece of land. Each fall since 1965, over Columbus Day weekend, at the height of a fiery display of maple trees, the town has staged a festival that draws, when the weather is good, thousands of visitors, some from as far away as New York City and Boston. In the 1990s we feared that this precious open space at the heart of town would one day be bought by developers and converted into home sites or, worse, a strip mall centering on a Wal-Mart.

Preserving the Fall Festival site as open space became an obsession for many people active in Ashfield affairs. We communicated our concerns to the O'Donnell family, and they, who had generously made the site

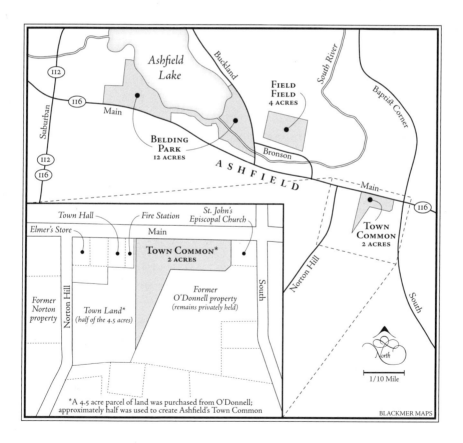

available for Fall Festival free of charge, were entirely sympathetic. They promised that while they owned the land we could continue to use it for the festival (and for parking for volunteer firefighters year-round). And whenever they decided to sell it, they would speak to the town first.

When the moment came, in 2003, for the O'Donnells to sell, I was no longer on the select board, but I followed the story closely. We all did. The legal owner was Angie O'Donnell, who was by then quite elderly. Angie had been active in town life for many years and was greatly beloved. Her children, no longer living in town, had the responsibility of caring for her. They had the parcel appraised. Not surprisingly, the land—enough under current zoning regulations for three prime building lots—was worth a pretty penny: at least $200,000.

There was some grumbling in town about this price. It seemed excessive; some even wondered if the O'Donnells were taking advantage of the town's determination to buy the property. On the other hand, people noted that the town had used the land over many years at no cost, and that Angie had allowed the fire department to park there. When several citizens agreed to raise as much of the money as possible through private fund-raising, opposition to the purchase collapsed. A special town meeting in November 2003 decided virtually unanimously to buy the land, amid warm expressions of gratitude to the O'Donnells.

As it turned out, the main issue surrounding the purchase was how to determine its use. The parcel bought from the O'Donnells was more complicated than it first appeared. Besides the site of the Fall Festival on Main Street, it included nearly three acres behind Town Hall, continuing all the way west to Norton Hill Road. This was the site of an old path that ran from Charles Eliot Norton's house on Norton Hill (now the house my wife and I own) to George William Curtis's house on South Street (at that time the O'Donnells' house). The fire department had long had its eyes on this land, to upgrade and expand its current facilities next to Town Hall. So did the staff at Town Hall, seeing a possible expansion of its cramped quarters and new parking space in the town center. Others imagined units of housing for the elderly on the site. Standing adamant against all these dreams was a determination by some people that the entire parcel should be left inviolate and undeveloped.

Development or conservation?

The select board reacted to this looming controversy as politicians always do. It appointed a committee to study the alternatives and make recommendations. The committee the board appointed was balanced and well-respected. It included two architects (one a specialist in landscaping), two carpenter/builders, an artist, a farmer, a community organizer, the chair of the planning board, a businessman, and one of the abutters. Some of these people could be counted on to oppose almost anything (which gave the committee credibility, if they finally accepted an idea). Some were sensitive listeners; others less so. There were two notable absences: no one from emergency services, although the fire department had its eye on room for expansion; and no one from the Town Hall staff, also looking to expand. These omissions by the select board must have been deliberate. But the appointees were shrewd folks, experienced in town government, well known to the community.

As soon as the committee got down to business, it became obvious that they knew what they were doing. They began by inviting ideas for the use of the space from everyone, and they adopted a host of strategies for soliciting these suggestions. They held open meetings where concerned citizens could express their hopes and fears. They took surveys to tap the opinion of people who could not attend, or preferred not to attend, public hearings. They specifically invited key people (the fire chief, abutters and other nearby neighbors, elder housing specialists) to present their views at open public meetings. They frequently exchanged views with the select board, in front of the local press, who kept readers informed of the deliberations.

It soon became apparent that the overwhelming majority who responded to their surveys and most speakers at the hearings were determined to prevent any development on the segment of the parcel that fronted on Main Street. The only issue here was how close to the fire station to draw the line of restriction, but that was not difficult to resolve. The line was drawn about where the Fire Department had already encroached for years onto the O'Donnells' land for parking.

But what to do about the land behind Town Hall, a little over half of the parcel? Most people agreed that the land close behind the fire station and Town Hall should be kept for expansion of those facilities, and for parking. How about the woods fronting Norton Hill Road? Here the advocates of housing for the elderly squared off against the most ardent preservationists. A sharp quarrel seemed in the offing, but it evaporated when an environmentalist's survey came in. It showed that most of the area in question was a wetland and thus would be unlawful to build on. This finding put a damper on the idea of building elder housing on it. With this protection against easy development, the committee decided to leave the matter open for the time being, confining themselves to delivering the environmental survey to the select board.

That left only the matter of defining the use restriction on the Fall Festival grounds, approximately two acres fronting on Main Street. This proved to be the toughest question of all. The devil was in the details. What activities, if any, apart from Fall Festival, should be allowed on the restricted portion? How about a monument to veterans? Benches for the elderly? A field for "town-ball" (a nineteenth-century precursor to baseball, played nostalgically in Ashfield)? How about a nice gazebo, for band concerts in the summertime? Or an arboretum, or a beautifully landscaped garden, or a poet's corner where local authors could sit on a bench and read to children?

To the committee, and to many others in town as we educated ourselves through a series of public meetings, this array of possibilities looked like a slippery slope. Gradually opinion began to harden: we must put a permanent restriction on the use of the land. In the words of the committee's flyer, distributed before a crucial special town meeting in April 2005, we ought to "maintain the land in the same condition we inherited—a flexible, open space available for community gatherings, festivals, and informal enjoyment." If we kept it "unencumbered by permanent structures, monuments and gardens," the space would remain available for the "greatest range of possible uses."

There was a paradox here. The committee insisted that there must be a permanent restriction on developing the site, in order to keep it "flexible"; as their flyer argued, "Any permanent structure will begin to limit the area of the common, restricting the range of uses and altering the character of this simple and unique open space. Incremental changes have cluttered commons across the state, obscuring their original open character and precluding many public uses." *Flexible* had a nice ring to it, but was it not misleading? A man who keeps his career options open by never taking a job has given up his principal option. That was the situation Ashfield was being asked to accept. Nor was that all. The committee was also asking us to agree not to trust ourselves to police this arrangement. State law required that, to impose such a restriction, we had to arrange for a "third party," not part of town government (not the select board, not the park commission), to assume responsibility for enforcing it.

Actually Ashfield had a situation right on Main Street, about a half-mile west of Town Hall, that illustrated the problem. In 1928 Milo M. Belding Jr., a philanthropist who summered in Ashfield, gave the town several acres on the south side of Ashfield Lake for a public park, for "passive recreation." Almost immediately the town highway department began storing equipment there. At first, it was unobtrusive. Belding himself saw it happening and apparently had no objection. Over the years, however, it began to loom larger and larger, with barns being built and mounds of sand and salt and spare parts and pipes being stored in open view. Finally, in the 1990s, someone who owned a house at the far end of the lake notified the attorney general's office of trusts that we were in stark violation of the terms of Belding's gift. The town had no alternative but to enter into an agreement with the state to buy another site for the highway department and move to it by a certain date. In the meantime, the town agreed to appropriate a sum of money ($10,000 a year for several years) to pay for the restoration of Belding Park.

In light of this history within living memory, it was not hard to persuade citizens that we needed a guardian. But who or what could fill that role? The committee proposed that we ask the state-chartered Franklin Land Trust, a "local, home-grown land trust—with offices across the street from the common," as they pointed out, to do it for us. They wrote, "Their proximity, their long connection with Ashfield, and their mission to save open space make them an optimal choice." And if the Land Trust should ever disband, we could provide in the restriction that the responsibility be assigned to a similar conservation organization.

What if we later changed our minds? Could the restriction ever be lifted? On this point the committee was reassuring. Conservation restrictions could be changed by a two-thirds vote of town meeting combined with a two-thirds vote of the state legislature. "Experience has shown that when there is a strong community consensus for change in such easements," the committee wrote, the legislature would concur and endorse the change. Furthermore, "minor changes that do not significantly alter the intention could be worked out between the Town and the Land Trust." How would this work? The restriction was intended to "retain said premises predominantly in its present condition in perpetuity." If anyone threatened this intention, the Land Trust would "have the right, but not the obligation, to enforce this restriction by appropriate legal proceedings," at the town's expense.

This, then, was the proposal of the committee, which the select board agreed to present to the town, first at a special town meeting on April 4, 2005 (where it passed, after a lengthy discussion, by an advisory vote of 50–11, with one abstention), and then at the annual town meeting on May 7, 2005, for a final, binding vote.

At the eleventh hour, just before the annual town meeting on May 7, Thom Gray, the former select-board member who belonged to one of the town's prominent families, weighed in with a thoughtfully worded letter in the *Ashfield News*. His argument took its stand on the town's commitment to democracy. Was it not somewhat arrogant, he asked, for voters today to bind future citizens of Ashfield? Was it wise to insist that our weighing of the value of open space versus other uses was better than any that a future generation might make? And why were we involving a third party in this? Weren't the town's citizens, now and in the future, able to settle this matter for and by themselves?

These were excellent questions, powerfully put. They went to the heart of our trust in democracy. Thomas Jefferson warned against "the dead hand of the past." Wouldn't future voters be as wise as we ourselves? They would certainly know more about their needs than we now do.

The other side of the argument, of course, is that democracies need to be wise enough to erect controls against their own passions and shortsightedness. That is why democracies impose the rule of law and bills of rights on themselves. We know the tendency, in the heat of passion, to squelch freedom of expression. We know that majorities sometimes wish to impose their religious beliefs and practices. We know that governments under stress sometimes want to round up suspects and torture them. We also know that such actions, however ardently passionate majorities may insist on them in the short run, undermine democracy in the long run.

Tipping the balance

The clinching argument at the May meeting came from Bill Perlman. He began with wry humor. While people in the past decade or so had enjoyed the services of a "good-looking, intelligent select board," he said, it would be foolish to count on good fortune indefinitely. Noting that he had been born and raised in New York City, he knew the pressures to allow development in Central Park, not all of which had been successfully resisted. The same was true for state and national parks. He also supported the idea of involving a third party in enforcement. It would reduce temptation. He compared it to the relief a teenager feels when he is able to respond to peer pressure by saying, "My mother won't let me." In his mind, the question was not whether to keep it open, but how to do it. Putting change beyond easy reach and asking the Franklin Land Trust to play a key role in the process made sense.

Most people in the room that day recognized that this was a remarkable argument. It came from a man who normally guarded the prerogatives of the select board and the town's voters jealously, one who was politically close to people who were wary of the Land Trust and its interference with the rights of landowners. If he was ready to accept the proposed arrangement, many others were inclined to follow his lead. Moments later, the article authorizing the conservation restriction on the newly acquired town common passed by voice vote, with just one audible voice in dissent.

The spirit that swept the town over all the obstacles on the road to creating a town common for Ashfield was beautifully caught in an article that John Snow, the retired minister I mentioned in the introduction, wrote for the *Ashfield News* in its January 2004 issue. Titled "Common," it deserves the last word.

> *Years ago, in the late [nineteen] forties, I used to drive by what I thought was the town common in Ashfield. I think perhaps for the next forty years I assumed it was the town common. I saw people walking their dogs on it. I saw firemen flooding it in the winter for skating, and later saw kids skating on it and grownups standing around tending a fire. It was not like any other town common I had seen. There were no cannons or statues or memorial plaques, no General Sherman tanks, nothing but green grass and open space. I liked it, and of course with the Fall Festival it became a Durer painting, a heart-warming tribute to our common life. Much later I*

discovered it was the O'Donnells' field, and a great sense of gratitude to the O'Donnell family flooded over me.

Ashfield has always been kind of slow to catch up. When a town in New England was founded, usually one of the first buildings to go up was the church. But not Ashfield. Years went by until the Baptists started a congregation which soon grew to a considerable size. The town fathers, all Congregationalists, felt ashamed, and built a town church and hired a fancy minister (Amherst, Yale Divinity School), and taxed the town, including the Baptists, to pay for it and the minister's salary. A few years later there was hell to pay.

But still there was no town common people could graze their animals on. Ashfielders killed themselves building inefficient stone walls to keep their cattle and sheep in, and spent a fair amount of their time and money suing each other for animal trespass. But still, we had no common.

Now at last we have a common, and it is a real common. We had a town meeting from 7 o'clock until midnight, and many people showed up to speak their minds. Old people, young people, new people, old-timers—a real cross-section of the town, and it was not easy. Buz Eisenberg, the town moderator, like Toscanini, conducted us as though we were a symphony orchestra. All said their pieces, some short, some really quite long, but all spoke. There was a vote. And now we have a common. No one can say they didn't have a say. The vote was overwhelming.

We used to live in a house at the end of South Street. It was surrounded by a large meadow in front and a forest behind. Looking out the front window, we could see people running by, jogging by, walking by, driving by with picnic equipment, snowmobiling, motorcycling, horseback riding, bicycling, even carrying rifles or shotguns sometimes. Even a young boy training a young team of oxen to pull together. Hunters and snowmobilers and many others asked our permission, God bless them. Others didn't. But no mind. I began to realize that many Ashfielders thought of Ashfield itself as a town common. The old days of animal trespassing and litigation were long gone. Few of us even post our land.

I remember one day in May, I thought I heard fairy music. I ran out of the house and down the hill and up another hill towards the high pasture and discovered a group of children dancing around a May pole and a young woman fiddling furiously. It was a beautiful moment. But we need a central, official town common symbolically to remind us of what we have in common, our will to govern ourselves, our willingness to share common responsibility, an openness to and concern for each other. You can't ask more of a town than that. But it's good to be reminded of it in the center of town.

Conclusion
Implications for Democratic Practice and Theory

In the introduction, setting up the argument of this book, I used Tocqueville's concept of the "point of departure." The origins of New England in colonial America included two important aspects: the physical situation (remote, hard, dangerous) and the cultural inheritance of the settlers (Protestant, self-reliant, egalitarian, law-abiding).

In this setting and from these elements, colonial New Englanders fashioned a way of governing themselves that centered on a particular set of institutions, namely, town meeting and a select board. In much of New England, particularly in the cities of Massachusetts, Connecticut, and Rhode Island, population growth eventually forced citizens to abandon these colonial institutions and move toward government by representation, city councils and mayors. But many communities in rural New England have retained their original form, more or less, to this day. These communities now offer a rare opportunity to observe direct democracy in action.

My argument here has been that democratic government works at the local level. Tocqueville was right. Middle-class people are capable of governing themselves. It is not utopia; human nature is not suspended when people choose to govern themselves democratically. Its imperfections are fully on display. But democracy works at that level. The kind of small-town self-government I've described delivers on the promise of democracy: that common people know what they need to know to govern themselves, that they will do so reasonably well, and that they will grow in the process.

The other part of the case for democracy is that, although far from perfect, it is better than any of the alternatives. That includes—let me be explicit now—government by elected representatives. Robert A. Dahl, a leading analyst of American democracy, discusses its adaptation to the problem of size in *On Democracy*. How can citizens participate effectively in large-scale units like cities and nations? How can they control the agendas in such places? Dahl recognizes that there is no good solution to these problems from the standpoint of democratic theory. He writes, "The only feasible solution, though it is highly imperfect, is for citizens to elect their top officials and hold them more or less accountable through elections."[1] To modern people, he adds, this accommodation may seem natural, but to our predecessors, it was not obvious at all. Theorists like Montesquieu and Rousseau thought that representative democracy was a contradiction in terms. Democracy could exist only in a town or small city. Such micropolities, when confronted by the military superiority of a large nation, were helpless. Drawing conclusions from these premises, these theorists tended to be extremely pessimistic about the prospects for genuine democracy.

The American founders knew this line of thought, and they shared its skepticism about democracy for a nation-state. But their argument went further. Not only was democracy not feasible; it was undesirable, at any level. In small polities, passions would make rational decision making virtually impossible. The solution was representation: it solved the problem of size, and it also addressed the moral problem inherent in entrusting government to human beings, who are by nature selfish. Representation would provide a filter. It would encourage the choice of more able people to assume the task of governing.

The other great advantage of representation, from the framers' standpoint, was that it was familiar. From colonial and state legislatures and from the Continental Congress, representation had become second nature. James Madison contributed the further idea that a large republic carried a great advantage: it could incorporate great diversity, many factions, thus diminishing the likelihood that any one of them would dominate and carry the nation away from the general public interest. With this understanding, the framers and ratifiers of the Constitution committed themselves to the idea of republican government on a continental scale.

Dahl suggests that Americans in 1787 and 1788 accepted this arrangement mainly because they had grown familiar with representation. I believe there was another factor. During the debates in the states over ratification, the founders of the American republic accepted the Constitution because they were convinced that it would not disrupt existing local arrangements. Southerners of course had their own "peculiar institution" in mind here, but New Englanders, too, studied the Constitution with local concerns in mind. If they had thought that local governments would be altered or disturbed by the national government created by the Constitution, they would certainly have rejected it. I am not guessing here. Recall the discussion, in chapter 3, of the ratification debate in Ashfield. Ephraim Williams, in defiance of town meeting, did finally vote to ratify the Constitution, but he would never have done so had he thought the national government would molest Ashfield's town meeting. And of course he was right: it did not, and it has not done so to this day.

Dahl concludes that, by the middle of the nineteenth century, the traditional concerns about representation being fundamentally at odds with democracy had vanished, or, "if remembered at all, treated as irrelevant." He gives John Stuart Mill, writing in 1861, the final word on this point:

> It is evident that the only government which can fully satisfy all the exigencies of the social state is one in which the whole people participates; that any participation, even in the smallest public function, is useful; ... and that nothing less can be ultimately desirable than the admission of all to a share in the sovereign power of the state. But since all cannot, in a community exceeding a single small town, participate personally in any but some minor portions of the public business, it follows that the ideal type of a perfect government must be representative.[2]

People in Ashfield would be far less ready than Mill, or Dahl, to accept this pale, spineless accommodation to the imperious demands of modernity, to "necessity."[3] We are not content with participation in small public functions. If we were told that we "cannot ... participate personally in any but some minor portions of the public business," we could not help but recognize the gravity of what we had given up, and we would not call what we are left with the "ideal type of a perfect government."

Republican government, government by elected representatives, takes us one critical step away from democracy, and thus away from Reinhold Niebuhr's famous aphorism in support of democracy. Democracy is possible, said Niebuhr, because of the human capacity for justice, but it is necessary because of the human inclination to injustice.[4] Anyone who has power, including elected representatives, will tend to abuse it.[5] This observation led Niebuhr to insist that checks and balances must be built into the structure of all governments.[6]

We've seen that there are checks and balances aplenty in Ashfield's government. They do not suspend human nature. They do not prevent or correct all mistakes. We still abuse police power. Our selfish quarrels blocked thoughtful consideration of opportunities for development in the reuse of Sanderson Academy. We built a sewer system that did not work as advertised and cost far too much. But we muddle along. We leave space for neighbors to love one another (or not), to worship (or not), to create or destroy within the limits of the law, to live and die in relative peace. Some of Tocqueville's modern admirers might think this is a pretty diminished list of human possibilities, but it is enough to expect of civic government for most of us who live in Ashfield. We are often frustrated and even angered by our local government, the time it takes, the pettiness, the triviality of its concerns, the nastiness we sometimes show toward one another. Many of us simply ignore it most of the time. But we would rise up angrily, virtually to a woman and man, against anyone who proposed to take it away from us, to substitute another form of government. Like Dartmouth College to Daniel Webster, it is a small thing, but we love it. We are invested in it, and we will fight against anyone who tries to take it from us.

Who governs?

As we have seen, Ashfield falls short from the standpoint of complete democratic participation.[7] Most of the town's citizens play no active part in its governance. Of perhaps thirteen hundred adults who are eligible to vote at the annual town meeting in May, rarely do many more than a hundred citizens attend. At times of aroused concern that figure can range upward toward three hundred or more, but far more typical is an annual meeting that begins with about 75 to 100 adults in attendance. Attendance may peak at 125 or so by midday, but after lunch it tapers off sharply, until there are typically around twenty-five or thirty citizens present to support a motion for adjournment.[8]

Special town meetings, held occasionally throughout the year on call of the select board (or, rarely, by petition of citizens), provide another opportunity for townspeople to engage in acts of governance. Between the annual town meetings, there are perhaps three or four of these special meetings each year. Most deal with routine, noncontroversial fund transfers and draw a small crowd: perhaps twenty residents (mostly from the groups directly affected by the proposed transfer). Sometimes, as with the two special meetings I described in chapter 4, matters on the agenda include items of more passionate concern, and for these, attendance typically comes close to that at annual meetings in May—still, though, only a small fraction (less than one in ten) of the eligible residents.

Another measure of citizen participation focuses on local governing bodies, the boards, commissions, and task forces, some elected but many appointed by the select board, that keep the machinery of democracy working. This is a significant measure of people's engagement in town governance. It represents in many cases a serious commitment of time, and it often puts people in a position to make decisions that have a real impact on life in town. The board of health, for example, supervises the work of the health agent, an official who inspects restaurants, monitors septic systems, and administers inoculation programs. The zoning board of appeals considers applications for variances from the town's zoning ordinance, deciding, for example, whether to allow a use that would otherwise violate a setback requirement. Legal guidelines and judicial precedents restrict the board's discretion, but hearings are often a pressure-cooker, raising messy questions about noise and parking in the neighborhood.

The town is administered by a select board and by perhaps twenty elected and appointed commissions and boards. A survey done in Ashfield in 2002 by select-board member Rick Chandler found as many as 250 different individuals serving on one or another of these bodies, or perhaps, in some cases, on several at the same time. That is about one adult in five, a higher percentage than in most American communities, but still nowhere near a majority.

What are we to say of the rest, though: those who never attend a town meeting or serve on a town board or commission? What is local democracy for them? Some are elderly or disabled. Many are distracted by personal concerns, or lack the temperament for communal decision making. Some briefly weigh the cost of attending and participating and find it less valuable, less interesting, than other things they might be doing at that time.[9] So they accept what their more active neighbors do in their name.

What have these stories revealed about democracy in action?

First let me list some things that this study has not established. Because it is a study of just one town, it is not comparative. Thus I have not considered whether Ashfield is typical or exceptional. Ashfield is a certain kind of place: most of its citizens are middle class, well-schooled, white, of European ancestry, and secular. It is fairly homogenous. Those characteristics probably bode well for the prospects of democratic politics. Would Ashfield's politics be different if more of its citizens were poor, or if they were members of religious or ethnic communities that were antagonistic toward one another? The principal division in Ashfield is between old-timers and newcomers. In other towns, that can be a major factor embittering local politics. It is sometimes a factor in Ashfield, but it has not made democratic accommodation impossible in Ashfield.

Moreover, I have not argued that democratic government will work everywhere as well as it has in Ashfield. Rather, I have examined how democratic government developed and works in one particular place.

Failures of local democracy

What, then, do our stories reveal about what is wrong with town-meeting democracy, as practiced in Ashfield?

First, they reveal a tendency to get personal, in ways that interfere with objective consideration of options before the town. Everything in a small town is personal.[10] That is an advantage in building social capital, but there is a cost, too. We saw this in the management of police affairs, when the consideration of a local applicant for police chief roiled relationships in Town Hall. We saw it in the assessment of solar aquatics, the innovative technology for treating wastewater. We saw it in the struggle over reuse of the decommissioned school building, Sanderson Academy, between the trustees and those who wanted to reuse a building that straddled property lines, provoking a painful eruption of tension between old-timers and newcomers.

Constitutional government depends on the rule of law, impersonal, objective, universal in application. Government in a small town is never a perfect practitioner of the rule of law. We know too much about one another. We want to temper strict justice with consideration of human needs and foibles; sometimes we favor friends. Sometimes that is a good thing, as when we work out an adjusted payment schedule for property taxes. Other times it leads us to close our ears to suggestions from people who irritate us, and that can be a bad thing.

A second conclusion that emerges from these stories is that voters at a town meeting suffer from a lack of expertise. When we must make decisions involving complex technical issues, we sometimes proceed in ignorance and make costly mistakes. Mistakes in selecting the wastewater treatment facility are the most obvious illustration here. As citizens, we were powerfully swayed by ideological considerations. What's worse, we failed to seek objective expert advice. Our consulting engineers were experts, and they were not shy about giving us their advice. The same was true of the state bureaucrats who oversaw the project. Both warned of the dangers in choosing the innovative technology—solar aquatics. Nevertheless, unwilling to forgo the chance to put our town at the forefront of applied green science, we chose it anyway.

That choice was not necessarily a mistake. The mistake was in doing it without seeking objective scientific counsel. Plenty of it could have been available to us, from faculty members and other scientists in our area, which is home to four colleges and a state university. To obtain sound, objective advice, we might have had to pay substantial fees. We failed to do it, and the costs of the system we chose far exceeded what we would have paid to obtain an objective assessment of it. Time pressures, including deadlines set in the consent decree, were partly to blame. The truth is, we did not insist on it. We should have.

So there is a remedy for citizens' lack of expertise, but amateur government is not always careful to avail itself of it.

The third lesson we can draw from Ashfield's experiences is that local governments often fail to take advantage of economies of scale. If we insist on reserving governance to the local level as far as possible, we risk missing out on these economies. Ashfield has found ways around this problem. We join with region-wide agencies to purchase fuel, highway materials, and inspection services. These arrangements are flexible; most of them preserve a measure of local control.

In one situation we have suffered despite trying to take advantage of economies of scale: primary and secondary education. Since the mid-1960s Ashfield has been part of a multitown regional school district. The state, by carrots and sticks, practically required that we enter into this arrangement. Judging by citizens' actions (protests by parents about conditions in our schools, recurrent battles over the formula for distributing the district's costs among the nine towns, enrollments in charter schools, and more recently a rise in home-schooling), the state's program of educational reform has not worked out very well for Ashfield. And as people move away from the public system, the burden of providing good public education only increases.

Fourth, our stories suggest that face-to-face governments often fail to learn from their mistakes. Ashfield still has a police department larger than many citizens want or think we need. Having been spared most of the cost of our mistakes on the wastewater treatment plant by federal and state grants that supported innovative technology, we may not have taken those lessons to heart, either.

This problem (inefficiency, disguised by abundant resources) is not unique to town-meeting democracies. The United States is a wealthy country. We command the temperate zone of a huge continent. We have abused our environment for many years, and only recently have we become concerned about the strain. Spending on national defense is hugely wasteful, but until recently we have been able to afford it. We have waged unnecessary wars, but as a nation we have absorbed the costs, both human and financial, without undue strain. Democracy, whether direct or representative, is not an efficient system of government, but our situation has been forgiving of waste.

There is reason to think that Ashfield's citizens may be better able to learn from experience than the nation at large. In a representative government, those who plead for wasteful expense, ignoring experience, can usually count on a short public memory. In a small town, the lessons of experience are more palpable, more visible to those who must pay public bills and for those who wish to remind us of our mistakes.

Fifth and finally, my tales of Ashfield show that the town does not keep pace with modernity. Our schools do not prepare our children to excel in competition with children in China, India, and Japan. We live in a place where many citizens have no access to high-speed Internet, which crimps communications. As a result, the children of Ashfield families often do not stay in town when they reach adulthood.

Residents are inclined not to worry too much about these shortcomings, to accept them as part of the cost for the benefits we enjoy from our separation from the troubles of modernity. Many of us do not lock our homes or cars. Our wives and children are safe on our streets, around the clock. It is relatively easy to arrange care for our children. Some things (homes, vegetables, entertainment) cost less. We live in a place of great natural beauty for six or seven months of the year (which months depending on your taste), largely unspoiled—at least so far—by cookie-cutter housing developments and big-box retailers.

Can local democracy plan?

I do not want to go too far afield in this conclusion, but I cannot resist the temptation to assess our findings in light of criteria set forth in Theodore Lowi's seminal analysis of the crisis of modern American government, *The End of Liberalism*.[11] Part 2 of that book, titled "Why Liberal Governments Cannot Plan," describes the major "clientele departments" of the federal government—at that time, Agriculture, Labor, and Commerce. Several others on this model have since been added: Transportation, Education, Housing and Urban Development, and Health and Human Services (originally Health, Education, and Welfare). Lowi contends that these departments display the fundamental defect of modern American government: a tendency to delegate the government's authority to interest groups. By their very titles, these departments designate a major sector of public activity. Affected interests are invited to determine standards and rules of conduct (including market conditions and prices, where necessary) for that sector. The government then enforces these rules as laws. Competitors who refuse to accept the rules are forbidden to operate, and violators are taken to court, tried, and punished.

Lowi's argument is that a government in the habit of acting this way not only cannot plan; it cannot govern. It cannot avoid gross waste in weapons procurement programs. It cannot conduct an effective war on poverty. It cannot mount a meaningful urban policy; it cannot end apartheid in housing. It cannot control expenditures or avoid deficits. All restraint, fiscal and moral, is lost. There is, effectively, no government, no authority. Iron triangles—networks grounded in interest groups, congressional committees, and federal agencies—replace the rule of law. And remember, Lowi published this analysis before most of us had even begun to use the term *earmark* in this connection.

Do Lowi's strictures apply to town-meeting democracy, as it is practiced in Ashfield? Certainly Ashfield's government has difficulty planning. The sewer case is the best illustration of that. The town was cited by the state government for polluting the South River for decades before anything was done about it. Town meeting did not act until the attorney general threatened to impose huge, daily fines if we failed to commit to a plan by a definite date.

But our sin in that case was not the one that Lowi identifies. We did not farm out the decision; we did not allow private interests to control it. We made big mistakes, choosing a system that was misleadingly sold and far too expensive to operate. We were gullible. We decided without consulting people who were knowledgeable and readily available to help us. But we never lost control. Our mistakes were our own—and we are now paying for them. The only way to share the blame would be to point out that the state—the attorney general's office—forced us to accept a consent decree that imposed short, inflexible deadlines that constrained our ability to examine adequately the technology we were considering. But that is a cop-out. We brought that bind on ourselves, by refusing to accept earlier warnings that we must stop polluting the river.

So yes, town-meeting democracy is defective in the ability to plan. It shies from imposing costs on itself now in order to avoid more pain later.[12]

Perhaps an aristocratic government, one led by philosopher-kings, would have been better at recognizing such trade-offs and taking advantage of the opportunity they offer. But authoritarian governments are rarely aristocratic. Advocates of government by town meeting prefer the inevitable human errors of democracy to the vagaries of rule by elites.

Another complaint one hears about government generally, and democracies in particular, is that, although they are not immune from the discipline of the market place, they tend to act as if they were. Their support comes from appropriations to a single-client provider, the government. If things go awry, there is a temptation simply to increase the amount of money being spent on the project.[13] One can see the logic in such criticism. But where the offending agency is accountable to an assembly of townspeople, one is less likely to get away with the argument that all that is needed is to raise more money.

Our preference for democracy is not moral

Charles Eliot Norton, the famed Harvard professor who summered in Ashfield during the last quarter of the nineteenth century, organized the series of gatherings known as the Ashfield dinners and used them as a forum for contrasting the ugliness of American cities with the virtues still found in the rural towns of western New England. In their oratory, Norton and his learned friends painted a bleak picture of a national culture inundated by immigration, urban blight, the rapacious greed of capitalists and the crazed lust of imperialists. At times these urbane critics seemed almost equally disheartened by the facts on the ground around them during their sojourns in the country. They spoke sadly of Ashfield's dwindling population[14] and of reports of "hoodlumism" in neighboring towns.[15] They saw this rural crisis as more than a local misfortune. Nothing less than the well-being of the nation was at stake in the recovery of the virtue of small-town New England: "How can we save Ashfield and all that it stands for?" Norton asked at one of these gatherings. "It stands for much. It is the image and type of towns that have been the wholesomest communities the earth ever bore, which by their intelligence have shaped the institutions of the nation, and largely directed its course, and by their virtues have set high the standard of democratic civilization."[16]

Norton's summertime neighbor and close friend, George William Curtis, put it this way: "The rugged hill-life of New England has set firm that triple rock—the Church, the Academy, the Town Meeting—on which our American liberty is established." These institutions ought to be "cherished as the glory and hope of New England." Much depended on it: "It cannot be too often repeated that it is from precisely such villages as these that the great characteristic structure of our American organization springs."[17]

I cannot emphasize too strongly that the Victorian sentiments underlying these remarks are not akin to the concerns that inspired my study of self-governance in Ashfield.[18] In examining town-meeting democracy, I have not been offering a model designed to counter the effects of pollution, illiteracy, the low supply of social capital, or whatever else afflicts American cities. My goal has been to examine democracy—community self-government—in action in a particular place. In contrast with those who addressed the Ashfield dinners, my purpose has not been primarily moral. It has been analytic. No doubt a moral preference has energized my work on this book. I believe in democracy, both for the egalitarian impulse that animates it and for its promise of human development. I have needed to be vigilant lest my commitment to democracy compromise my objectivity, and I hope my readers, too, will be alert for any distorting effect caused by my bias in favor of democracy. I want democracy to succeed, in Ashfield and wherever people practice it, but my goal has been to judge its performance in Ashfield candidly.

Looking beyond Ashfield

What then is the significance of our findings in Ashfield? What lessons can we properly draw? That democracy, hedged about with constraints grounded in law and enforced by higher authority, works in one tiny village, and that it might work in tiny villages similarly situated? Or does Ashfield's experience provide a more general model?

There are two dimensions to this question. One relates to the degree to which culture conditions the opportunity for the successful practice of democracy. The other relates to institutions, including the proper scope and agenda of politics in a community. In other words, even if we grant Mill's point, that some of the business of a modern nation must be accomplished by large units, and therefore by representatives and bureaucrats, are there not some parts that can be done locally and democratically?

Democracy on a Caribbean island?

Parts of this book have been written at our home on St. John, the smallest of the three main islands that compose the U.S. Territory of the Virgin Islands. The government of the territory is notoriously weak and badly administered. Its weaknesses stem mainly from the fact that sovereignty, by Article IV, Section 3 of the U.S. Constitution, rests ultimately with Congress, but Congress is most often inattentive. A related problem is that the judiciary of the islands derives its constitutional authority from an "organic act" of Congress, rather than from Article III of the U.S. Constitution. That means that territorial judges in the U.S. Virgin Islands serve for a renewable ten-year term, which makes them beholden to the president of the United States, who nominates them. For reasons explained by counter-arguments in *The Federalist,* no. 78, the political foundation of territorial judges' tenure makes the rights of Virgin Islanders precarious.

Right now, the U.S. Territory of the Virgin Islands is in the midst of a "constitutional moment." The U.S. Congress has authorized a territorial convention to draft revisions of the territory's organic act. Thirty elected delegates have been at work on the task. They met for the first time in January 2008, and after intense political maneuvering they managed to elect a chairman, a delegate from one of the large islands. He, a mortician, immediately announced that he had business to attend to elsewhere and would need to adjourn the convention by mid-afternoon. Needless to say, the delegates accomplished practically nothing that day.

Since then, delegates have spent most of their time in petty quarreling. Quorums are difficult to attain, due in part to delegates milling in the corridors, refusing to cooperate by stepping inside the room. Committees draft articles, but timely consideration bogs down as delegates battle over matters of mainly symbolic importance. (The principal issue so far has been whether governors must be native-born Virgin Islanders: is it wise to impose such a restriction, and is it consistent with the equal-protection clause of the Fourteenth Amendment?) Deadlines come and go; extensions are voted. The local press (a Pulitzer Prize–winning newspaper) covers each agonizing step with lively delight, emphasizing how much money the convention is spending and how little it has accomplished, despite real effort and commitment by some of the delegates.

What's wrong here? Why are these people having such difficulty figuring out how to govern themselves?

Partly the reason is that they have had almost no opportunity to practice the arts of citizenship. The constituent population of the Virgin Islands consists mostly of descendants of African slaves. A few of them own much valuable land, but most of them are poor. These blacks now share the islands with white residents, most of whom are in the tourist industry, one way or another. The tourist industry caters mostly to white "continentals" who use the Virgin Islands as a getaway.

This is not the place to enter deeply into a consideration of the culture of the Virgin Islands and its fitness for democratic self-government. Suffice it to say that the point of departure there is radically different from colonial New England. I am not referring to matters of religion, values, education, or social class. I am referring specifically to experience. Virgin Islanders have never been in a position either to practice or to demand self-government.[19] Now that Congress has provisionally, tentatively, given them a chance to do so, they hardly know where to begin. It does not help that powerful interests will probably draw back from the invitation if the people of the Virgin Islands go too far in claiming their right to self-government.[20]

Devolution

One is tempted simply to conclude, as many have argued, that neither democracy nor liberty can be imposed from above or outside. They must be seized by constituents, by citizens.

But here we come to the second part of our consideration of the relevance of Ashfield's experience to the larger problem of the possibility of democracy in modern nations. Might it not be possible to divide a territory (the Virgin Islands, or the United States) into small units, give these units control over some sources of revenue, and induce them to make, by majority vote in assemblies, appropriations and law for a limited set of local objectives (roads, police and fire departments, primary and secondary education)? The idea here would be to devolve functions of government to the lowest feasible level, and never to allow any function of government to be taken over by broader authority than is necessary for their proper accomplishment.

The future of democracy in Ashfield

Having devoted most of this conclusion to the shortcomings and problems of democratic self-government, I need to explain why Ashfield citizens are devoted to it. What do they find right about town-meeting democracy? Despite its errors and irritations, which they feel acutely, why do Ashfield's citizens feel so strongly about hanging on to it?

Basically we love it (and here I feel confident that I articulate the feelings of practically everyone in town, old-timer and newcomer alike) because it gives us who are active in it—and anyone who resides here is entitled to be—a measure of control in shaping our civic environment. It is hard, nay impossible, to imagine any consideration or eventuality that would dislodge our commitment to it. Old-timers are often dismayed by decisions made at town meeting and by the people we elect. Sometimes they cannot bring themselves to attend a town meeting that they know will make choices that are, from their point of view, foolish. Even so, they would not disavow their heritage. Newcomers, attracted here by the natural beauty of the place and by opportunities to practice, or at least to observe close up, an ancient way of life, join in the fun and the occasional agony of local democracy. Some watch it from a safe distance, but many enter into it with gusto. They are drawn into it because they wish to join in building a public environment for themselves. It provides an escape, an eddy outside of national and global currents where human agency sometimes seems to have little impact. Here in Ashfield, civic efforts have a measurable and immediate impact, on property taxes, on the size, equipment and operations of local departments (school, highway, police, fire, ambulance, library), on striking a balance between preservation and development.

The practice of democracy is basic to the promise of American life.[21] Democracy in a place like Ashfield is not a religion; it does not promise victory over death. It relates only indirectly to, and therefore respectfully stands aside from, the most important aspects of life, such as intimate personal relationships and our concern for ultimate things.

What it does do is draw us into a meaningful common life, one where we join in setting the agenda and the boundaries of our public lives. It is an arena where we can practice the craft of self-government, where it becomes a reality for anyone who wishes to participate in it. It is rarely glorious, but in Ashfield, at least, it is often a deeply satisfying human experience, and we insist on practicing it, to the best of our abilities.

Notes

Introduction

1. MassINC's self-described "mission" is to promote "a new commonwealth in which every citizen can live the American Dream." All quotations here are from the Summer 2002 issue of *CommonWealth*.

2. It should be acknowledged, with gratitude, that the current governor, Deval Patrick, adopts a quite different tone toward the western region of the commonwealth he governs.

3. People who own property in Ashfield—a vacation home, for example—but legally reside and vote elsewhere are not members of town meeting. Even their speech is restricted. They can address town meeting only by permission of a majority of legal residents attending that particular meeting.

4. Benjamin Ginsberg argues that elections tend to limit democratic participation: they limit the frequency and scope of participation, and they vitiate its intensity. See *The Consequences of Consent: Elections, Citizen Control, and Popular Acquiescence* (Reading, Mass.: Addison-Wesley, 1982).

5. Indeed, it is pretty clear that government in the United States *is* responsive to opinion, although perhaps less readily so than, say, the government of a parliamentary democracy like Great Britain. But to discuss that point would take us far afield.

6. This is the assessment of Harvey C. Mansfield and Delba Winthrop, translators of a new edition of Tocqueville's *Democracy in America* (Chicago: University of Chicago Press, 2000), xvii.

7. Robert T. Gannett Jr., "Bowling Ninepins in Tocqueville's Township," *American Political Science Review* 97, no. 1 (February 2003): 4.

8. I am not aware of any evidence that Tocqueville himself ever attended a town meeting in New England.

9. Hugh Brogan adds that Tocqueville "drew on [Sparks] so exhaustively . . . as almost to entitle him to be named as co-author." *Alexis de Tocqueville: A Life* (New Haven: Yale University Press, 2007), 182.

10. Brogan, *Alexis de Tocqueville,* 182. Sparks himself thought that Tocqueville's warnings about "the tyranny of the majority" were "entirely mistaken." In an 1841 letter to another

French author on American politics, Sparks wrote that Tocqueville's views on this point "are not verified by experience." Quoted in Herbert B. Adams, *Jared Sparks and Alexis de Tocqueville* (Baltimore: Johns Hopkins Press, 1898), 43–44.

11. Quoted from Tocqueville's journal in Gannett, "Bowling Ninepins," 5.

12. Gannett, "Bowling Ninepins," 5.

13. Adams, *Jared Sparks,* 10, translated in Gannett, "Bowling Ninepins," 5.

14. That phrase, Tocqueville thought, summarized what nineteenth-century France needed so desperately to develop.

15. See, for example, Frank M. Bryan's estimable book about town meetings in Vermont, titled *Real Democracy: The New England Town Meeting and How It Works* (Chicago: University of Chicago Press, 2004). Bryan is careful to explain why he claims the term for his subject (see esp. 3–4).

16. See, for leading examples, Robert A. Dahl, *Democracy and Its Critics* (New Haven: Yale University Press, 1989); Arend Lijphart, *Democracies* (New Haven: Yale University Press, 1984); and Adam Przeworski et al., *Sustainable Democracy* (Cambridge: Cambridge University Press, 1995).

17. For a penetrating analysis, see Robert A. Dahl, *How Democratic Is the American Constitution?* (New Haven: Yale University Press, 2003).

18. Of course, summers are not so lazy for farmers, road builders, and people who wring their living from the forests. For Ashfield's lumbermen, for example, the early twenty-first-century crash in the American home-building market was a disaster.

19. Many roads in Ashfield are unpaved, which sometimes presents a special challenge for the select board and road crew. One of my first lessons as a select-board member came when an elderly resident submitted a petition, signed by about thirty of her neighbors (virtually everyone who lived on the road), calling for the dirt road in front of her house to be paved. We queried some of the signers, who told us that, although they could not resist signing it when their neighbor presented it, they did not want the road paved. They valued the isolation it afforded. Our highway superintendent took me for a ride to show me the difficulties: the road was narrow, with rock cliffs on one side and a sheer drop on the other. Citing these problems, the select board decided not to approve the request.

20. Appearances even now are deceiving. A snowmobiler killed himself one winter after he left the Lake House tavern and crashed his vehicle headlong into a tree at the far edge of the frozen lake.

21. Frederick G. Howes, *History of the Town of Ashfield, Franklin County, Massachusetts, from Its Settlement in 1742 to 1910* ([Ashfield, Mass.]: Published by the town, n.d. [1910?]), 246–50. For a modern telling of this story, see Cameron Graves, "Mystery Surrounds Historic Ashfield Lake Drowning," *West County News,* November 1–7, 2007, 16. See also an account by Barnabas Howes in the Alvan Clark folder at the Ashfield Historical Society.

22. According to the U.S. Census, the population of Ashfield in 1860 was 1,302.

23. Based on Howes, *History of the Town of Ashfield,* 290–91.

24. Noah Gordon, *Shaman* (New York: Dutton, 1992).

25. Ashfield has (besides a highly popular pizzeria) two restaurants: Elmer's, which caters to sophisticated newcomers, and the Lake House, which serves a mostly blue-collar clientele. An older Ashfield resident, from a multigenerational family, told me that she had taken out-of-town guests to the Lake House (she does not feel comfortable at Elmer's). She was appalled at what she found there: a noisy, raucous atmosphere, lots of beer drinking, and no one she knew. "We have been invaded!" she exclaimed. Such people increasingly do not feel at home anywhere in Ashfield's public spaces.

26. Clayton passed away in the winter of 2008, but Ruth abides. These lines about them were written while both were alive and active.

27. Wilmore was presenting his book *Pragmatic Spirituality: The Christian Faith through an Africentric Lens* (New York: New York University Press, 2004).

28. At John's funeral in 2008, his daughter read from one of his sermons, delivered at a baptism in 1991. It read, in part: "When, at the baptism of Jesus, God said, 'This is my beloved son with whom I am well pleased,' God was addressing humanity. God was saying, 'If you want to know who I am, if you want to know what I have created and why, look very closely at the piece of history this baptism begins. This is the most complete answer you are ever going to get. . . . Look closely at this Jewish peasant standing in this dirty little creek. Keep your eyes on this man, listen to what he says, watch how he deals with the people around him. . . . See how he addresses the sick, the crippled, the blind and the deaf. See how he relates to outcasts and sinners. Listen to what he says to his enemies, to his persecutors, to the religious and secular authorities. See how he uses his time, what is important to him and unimportant. Watch him at weddings and funerals. See how he loves and cares about children. Pay attention to how he treats women and how quickly they understand who he is. Consider his attitude toward the use of force and violence. Notice his courage when he is afraid. Notice the things that make him angry, and pay attention to what they are. . . . And pay attention to how he dies, how his fear of pain and death do not stop his expression of love and concern for his friends and family, how alert he is to the pain of his neighbor, how he meets death itself as a completion and perfection of his life, and not as bad luck or a dirty trick." I did not hear John preach this sermon, but I have heard others he delivered, in tiny St. John's Episcopal Church in Ashfield. He spoke quietly and deliberately, but with great intensity and effect.

29. People in Ashfield were delighted and proud in 2007 when the Cranstons were picked by the National Christmas Tree Association to provide a tree for the vice president's residence in Washington, D.C. For Cynthia Cranston's charming account, see www.cranstonschristmastreefarm.com/christmastrees-wreaths.htm.

30. Prior to the dispute in Ashfield, the board of assessors in Chesterfield, a neighboring town, had consulted the state department of revenue about regulations governing the classification of land under Massachusetts laws that provide special treatment for agricultural and recreational land (chapter 61, 61a and 61b). They were told, in a letter from DOR dated February 24, 2004, that land "occupied by a dwelling or regularly used for family living" must be excluded from the parcels given lower rates of taxation. The letter further advised that the actual use of land was "determinative," and that assessors should use a "consistent 'houselot' area" in establishing these exclusions. (Letter, dated February 24, 2004, from Daniel J. Murphy, chief, property tax bureau, Massachusetts Department of Revenue, to Board of Assessors, Chesterfield, Mass., on file in Ashfield Town Hall.) The Ashfield board cites this letter as authority for shrinking the land excluded from 61a, as it was doing in 2006.

31. *Assessment Administration: Law, Procedures, Valuation,* published by Massachusetts Department of Revenue, Division of Local Services, 24, citing *Boston v. Boston Port Development Co.,* 308 Mass. 72 (1941). This manual is available from the Department of Revenue and is also on file in the assessors' office in Town Hall.

32. The best summary of the accusations against the board of assessors is "Town of Ashfield: Assessing Department Review," prepared by the Massachusetts Department of Revenue, Division of Local Services, Municipal Data Management and Technical Assistance Bureau, June 2007. This 14-page document, plus appendixes, takes Ashfield's board of assessors severely to task. The bureau's findings—including allowing a single assessor to modify property values without a vote of the board and without proper comparative analysis, placing land into 61a without setting aside a two-acre building lot for dwelling, not keeping adequate minutes of its meetings, consolidating parcels to decrease the value of properties without prior board vote and proper study, and not consistently following the open-meeting

law—are on pages 2–3 of the report. The report notes that Marilyn Browne, chief of the bureau of local assessment, ordered Ashfield's board to "restore all the combined parcels to their fiscal 2006 status" (that is, prior to the "sweeping property value changes" that the board had proposed for fiscal 2007). (Browne's order is on page 3; the "sweeping . . . changes" quotation is from the introduction to the report [no page number].)

33. On Italy, see Robert D. Putnam, with Robert Leonardi and Raffaella Y. Nanetti, *Making Democracy Work: Civic Traditions in Modern Italy* (Princeton: Princeton University Press, 1993). On social capital in the United States, see Robert D. Putnam, *Bowling Alone: The Collapse and Revival of American Community* (New York: Simon & Schuster, 2000).

34. The distinction here, between voluntary organizations and public jurisdictions (governments), is developed nicely and insistently by Gannett, in "Bowling Ninepins."

35. See Carlo Levi, *Christ Stopped at Eboli* (New York: Farrar, Straus, 1947); and Gao Xingjian, *One Man's Bible* (New York: HarperCollins, 2002).

36. The phrase is from Tocqueville, *Democracy in America,* book 1, chapter 17. *Habits of the Heart* is the title of a seminal study of American culture by Robert Bellah et al. (Berkeley: University of California Press, 1985).

37. The notion of *point de départ* was crucial for Tocqueville. For his argument, see *Democracy in America,* vol. 1, part I, chap. 2. For commentary, see Brogan, *Alexis de Tocqueville,* chap. 9, passim, especially 182. I will have more to say about this concept as this book develops, particularly in chapter 1.

1. Becoming Ashfield

1. This is the opening line of a novel, *The Go-Between* (1954), by L. P. Hartley. It has become almost proverbial for some historians; others find it annoying. William Cronon uses it as an epigraph in *Changes in the Land: Indians, Colonists, and the Ecology of New England* (New York: Hill and Wang, 1983), 172.

2. I cannot write these words without thinking of Edmund Morgan's teaching: that the concept of "the people" is a construct, a myth. See, especially, his *Inventing the People: The Rise of Popular Sovereignty in England and America* (New York: W. W. Norton, 1988); see also a review of Morgan's work by Russell Baker, *New York Review of Books,* June 11, 2009, 36–38.

3. For an excellent study of the role of the proprietors in settling Huntstown, see Mark Williams, *The Brittle Thread of Life: Backcountry People Make a Place for Themselves in Early America* (New Haven: Yale University Press, 2009).

4. Several studies have emphasized the monarchical aspects of colonial political culture, among them Richard L. Bushman, *King and People in Provincial Massachusetts* (Chapel Hill: University of North Carolina Press, 1985); and Brendan McConville, *The King's Three Faces: The Rise and Fall of Royal America, 1688–1776* (Chapel Hill: University of North Carolina Press, 2006).

5. Proprietors' minutes, Ashfield Town Hall.

6. There was a great deal of trading and speculation in the titles to these lots. Few, if any, of the original lot-owners, except Heber Honestman (for more on him, see chapter 4), actually migrated to Huntstown. Besides Williams, *Brittle Thread of Life,* for a general account see Roy Akagi, *The Town Proprietors of the New England Colonies: A Study of Their Development, Organization, Activities, and Controversies, 1620–1770* (Philadelphia: Press of the University of Pennsylvania, 1924).

7. Cronon, *Changes in the Land,* 48–50.

8. Rev. Thomas Shepard, for example, writing a sketch of the town's origins in 1834, says that he will trace developments "since the howl of the wild beast was alone heard through the forest." Shepard, "Sketches in the History of Ashfield, Mass., from Its First Settlement to the Year 1833," in Frederick G. Howes, *History of the Town of Ashfield, Franklin County,*

Massachusetts, from Its Settlement in 1742 to 1910 ([Ashfield, Mass.]: Published by the town, n.d. [1910?]), 13.

9. The best sources on the Native Americans of New England are the works of Neal Salisbury; see, especially, *Manitou and Providence: Indians, Europeans, and the Making of New England, 1500–1643* (New York: Oxford University Press, 1982); and *The People*, co-authored by R. David Edmunds, Frederick Hoxie, and Salisbury (Boston: Houghton Mifflin, 2007). Also useful is Charles Mann, *1491: New Revelations of the Americas before Columbus* (New York: Knopf, 2005).

10. Cronon, *Changes in the Land*, chap. 4.

11. Cronon, *Changes in the Land*, 57.

12. For a lively sense of how it felt to inhabit this "wilderness," see Shepard, "Sketches in the History of Ashfield," in Howes, *History of the Town of Ashfield*, 17–22.

13. But see John Demos, *The Unredeemed Captive: A Family Story from Early America* (New York: Random House, 1994), on the 1704 raid in Deerfield, the memory of which was still fresh at the time of the raid on Charlemont a half-century later.

14. Howes, *History of the Town of Ashfield*, 63–69.

15. My account of the impact of epidemic disease on the Native Americans of New England is based on Cronon, *Changes in the Land*, 85–92.

16. By some accounts, even earlier, long before 1620. See Mann, *1491*, 92–96.

17. Cronon, *Changes in the Land*, 91.

18. Quoted in Cronon, *Changes in the Land*, 90.

19. Fred Anderson, the author of a valuable account of this war, *Crucible of War* (New York: Random House, 2000), calls it the "Seven Years' War," to emphasize the larger European context. Young George Washington's failed attempt to dislodge the French from Fort Duquesne (modern Pittsburgh) happened in 1754, leading some historians to speak of the nine-year North American phase of the larger Seven Years' War.

20. Howes, *History of the Town of Ashfield*, 22, 62.

21. Howes, *History of the Town of Ashfield*, 70.

22. The September 1761 meeting was held at Richard Ellis's house, which was centrally located in terms of where settlers were then building, though in the northeast portion of the area thus far divided into lots.

23. Heber is listed in the proprietors' meeting of 1739 as having drawn nineteenth, for Josiah Prat. He chose lot number 1, in the northern part of the town.

24. Howes, *History of the Town of Ashfield*, 75. (Incidentally, ten rods, 165 feet, is a huge width for a road, then or now.) Howes follows with an account of where that road went, described in terms of home-ownership at the beginning of the twentieth century: from Conway village, over Baptist Hill to the Totman and Pfersick neighborhood, to Thomas Phillips's house, now Mr. Kendrick's pasture, then westerly to the sawmill near the present [now gone] Bear River bridge, then south to where Mr. Lanfair now lives, to the top of the hill. It was the first road in the new township. The Ashfield Historical Society has published, in its newsletter, an estimable collection of maps and accounts of these old roads. See, for example, Alden Gray, "Some Thoughts about a Road That Started at Heber's Fence," *Ashfield Historical Society Newsletter*, Spring 2005, www.ashfieldhistorical.org/newsspring05. html#fence.

25. Howes, *History of the Town of Ashfield*, 70, 76.

26. Howes, *History of the Town of Ashfield*, 56–57. Howes's implication is that some, perhaps most, of those who took lots in the first distribution in 1739 were speculators and may have intended from the outset to sell their rights, rather than to take possession of land in Huntstown. It is not clear how he knew that. Perhaps when he wrote, traditions were fresh enough to justify the surmise. Howes, though an amateur, was an unusually scrupulous chronicler.

27. Cronon, *Changes in the Land,* 129–30, 134–36. Cronon points out that a principal difference between colonial and Native American use of animals was that the colonials owned their animals. This simple fact led to bitter conflicts between native and colonial inhabitants of these forests.

28. Howes, *History of the Town of Ashfield,* 51, 71. This law calls to mind the apocryphal tale of a state legislature in the Midwest, impatient with obfuscation, enacting a law that simplified the value of pi. Soon buildings and bridges began falling down.

29. Howes, *History of the Town of Ashfield,* 71. Howes described Kellogg as a "noted surveyor" (59).

30. Howes, *History of the Town of Ashfield,* 50.

31. Howes, *History of the Town of Ashfield,* 72.

32. Howes, *History of the Town of Ashfield,* 74.

33. Records of this meeting are in Ashfield's Town Hall. See also Howes, *History of the Town of Ashfield,* 76.

34. Howes, *History of the Town of Ashfield,* 76–78. Ironically, the Plains cemetery, where the meetinghouse and Congregationalists' place of worship was sited, is on what is now called Baptist Corner Road. (See chapter 2, "Baptist Troubles.")

35. Howes, *History of the Town of Ashfield,* 255.

36. It would also serve as Ashfield's Congregational Church until 1814, when the new church on the hill was ready.

37. Howes, *History of the Town of Ashfield,* 251–52. The men on the committee were Edmund Longley, Elisha Billings, and John Hamlen.

38. Howes, *History of the Town of Ashfield,* 252. Other funds would come from the sale and rental of pews.

39. On changes in the use and appearance of New England meetinghouses, see Kevin Sweeney, "Meetinghouses, Town Houses, and Churches: Changing Perceptions of Sacred and Secular Space in Southern New England, 1720–1850," *Winterthur Portfolio* 28, no. 1 (Spring 1993): 59–93.

40. Howes, *History of the Town of Ashfield,* 260.

41. Howes, *History of the Town of Ashfield,* 250. Behind the building was a cemetery where many notable residents of the early years are buried, including Ephraim Williams, Nathaniel Porter, and Alvan Sanderson. The huge interior space of the building was originally a single room, with a gallery around three sides. In 1840 the building was divided horizontally into two large spaces, with the sanctuary/auditorium upstairs and meeting rooms below.

42. Quoted in Howes, *History of the Town of Ashfield,* 253.

43. This section on Knowlton is based largely on material at the Ashfield Historical Society, including an unpublished essay by Mary Lee Esty titled "Dr Charles Knowlton, a Biography." See also Robert E. Riegel, "The American Father of Birth Control," *New England Quarterly* 6, no. 3 (September 1933): 470–90. For Knowlton's significance in the history of American medical science, see Michael Sappol, "The Odd Case of Charles Knowlton," *Bulletin of the History of Medicine* 83, no. 3 (Fall 2009): 460–98.

44. Riegel, "American Father of Birth Control," 478–79. Sappol explains how Knowlton's implacable scientific curiosity led him to brush aside conventional scruples surrounding death and graves. Sappol, "Odd Case of Charles Knowlton," 476–87.

45. Knowlton traced his troubles there to Amherst College president Heman Humphrey's opposition to the philosophical doctrines of his book. Riegel, "American Father of Birth Control," 481–82.

46. This was the subtitle of the 1834 edition. The 1839 edition was subtitled "The Private Companion of Young Adult People." By then Knowlton apparently saw no need to restrict his advice to people who were married. Copies of these editions are at the American Antiquarian Society, Worcester, Mass.

47. Riegel, "American Father of Birth Control," 487. Riegel points out that very few copies of these early editions survive, presumably because they were "passed from hand to hand and read until they fell to pieces" (486). By 1839, there were already nine American editions of it.

48. According to Howes, many in town were "very bitter against" Knowlton. Howes himself, ever the discreet Victorian, never mentions the subject of Knowlton's book. For his account of the tensions and eventual schism of the Congregational Church in Ashfield, in which the controversy over Knowlton played a large part, see *History of the Town of Ashfield,* 163–65 and 368.

49. Riegel notes that, by the 1840s, Knowlton "had been accepted by the community, which was willing to overlook, at least, his intellectual wild oats, and to recognize him as a learned, intelligent, tolerant, and friendly neighbor." As for publishing, he by then confined himself to "case records, which he sent to medical journals, dealing with such safe professional subjects as erysipelas, puerperal fever, the pancreas, lumbar abscess, medical quackery, the fillet in breech presentations, and the autumnal fevers of New England." He died in Ashfield in 1850. Riegel, "American Father of Birth Control,"489.

50. This account is based on a talk by A. W. Howes to the Ashfield Historical Society. A. W. Howes's father had been a member of the moving committee of the Congregational Church. Quoted by F. Howes, *History of the Town of Ashfield,* 254–55.

51. Howes, *History of the Town of Ashfield,* 258–59.

52. This account of the half-century (1820–1870) of controversy surrounding Ashfield's Town Hall is based on Howes, *History of the Town of Ashfield,* 256–58, and on studies of deeds and other town records by Peter Wiitanen and me.

53. The building is still called "The Tavern." It is now an apartment house, diagonally across Main Street from St. John's Episcopal Church.

54. Howes, *History of the Town of Ashfield,* 257.

55. The ban lasted until the 1960s, when town meeting voted to allow package stores to sell alcoholic beverages and restaurants to serve them.

2. Baptist Troubles

1. As I began to organize my thoughts for this book, I came upon an essay by the political philosopher Bhikhu Parekh. "In the history of the west," he writes, "Athenian democracy, which flourished between 450 BC and 322 BC, was the first and for nearly two millennia almost the only example of democracy in action." ("The Cultural Particularity of Liberal Democracy," *Political Studies* 40, special issue [1992]: 161.) Two millennia after the flourishing of Athenian democracy would be the seventeenth century of our era, about the time that the towns of New England began to be settled. Parekh does not explicitly say so, but I could not help wondering whether he may have had these small rural democracies in mind when he wrote that sentence.

2. Frederick G. Howes, *History of the Town of Ashfield, Franklin County, Massachusetts, from Its Settlement in 1742 to 1910* ([Ashfield, Mass.]: Published by the town, n.d. [1910?]), 160. For further details on the law requiring towns to obtain and support a minister see William G. McLoughlin, *New England Dissent, 1630–1833: The Baptists and the Separation of Church and State,* 2 vols. (Cambridge: Harvard University Press, 1971), 1:531–32. For an extended discussion of the controversy in Huntstown over the meetinghouse and taxation to support the Congregationalist minister see Mark Williams, *The Brittle Thread of Life: Backcountry People Make a Place for Themselves in Early America* (New Haven: Yale University Press, 2009), 157–73.

3. Howes, *History of the Town of Ashfield,* 78–79. Here Chileab Smith sided with Jonathan Edwards, with whom he later consulted personally, against the Antinomians (believers in the doctrine that salvation was available to all people, not just the elect few). See William

G. McLoughlin, *Soul Liberty: The Baptists' Struggle in New England, 1630–1833* (Hanover, N.H.: University Press of New England, 1991), 149; see also chap. 5. Chileab may have inherited a sometimes cantankerous temperament from his father. It was rumored by a neighbor in Hadley that Chileab's father, Ebenezer, was using his own children to experiment with dental tools he had invented. His church in Hadley refused to defend him against these charges. Gregory Nobles, *Divisions throughout the Whole: Politics and Society in Hampshire County, Massachusetts, 1740–1775* (New York: Cambridge University Press, 1983), 92.

4. Howes, *History of the Town of Ashfield*, 149–50.

5. McLoughlin, *Soul Liberty*, 150.

6. Israel Williams was a leading "river god," one of the powerful men of the Connecticut River valley communities. Having inherited his uncle John Stoddard's political machine, he enhanced its power by placing members of his own extended family in strategic positions throughout the political and judicial machinery of Hampshire County. Nobles, *Divisions throughout the Whole*, 30–35. Later he would be suspected of loyalist sympathies and stripped of most of his power, but throughout this late colonial period he was the most powerful political boss in the area. On Williams's presence in the Connecticut River valley, see Robert Taylor, *Western Massachusetts in the Revolution* (Providence, R.I.: Brown University Press, 1954).

7. McLoughlin, *Soul Liberty*, 151.

8. McLoughlin implies that the influx of Congregationalists after 1762 was part of a deliberate effort to outnumber the Baptists there (*Soul Liberty*, 151). I know of no direct evidence of this, but I do not doubt it. Any migration of Massachusetts residents was bound to be heavily Congregationalist.

9. Rev. Thomas Shepard, "Sketches in the History of Ashfield, Mass., from Its First Settlement to the Year 1833," in Howes, *History of the Town of Ashfield*, 34.

10. Howes describes Chileab Smith as a "man with a tremendous disposition to have his own way. He had not the slightest doubt that his own opinion on any subject was right, and he would fight for his convictions with the courage of a lion." *History of the Town of Ashfield*, 151.

11. Howes, *History of the Town of Ashfield*, 81.

12. Howes, *History of the Town of Ashfield*, 80–86; McLoughlin, *Soul Liberty*, chap. 6. McLoughlin's book contains two remarkable documents, published in full for the first time: a poem written in 1771 by Rev. Ebenezer Smith, outlining the Baptists' case against the Congregational establishment of his town (139–45), and a statement of the case against slavery, also written by Ebenezer Smith and adopted by his congregation in 1773 (154–56). The latter was one of the first statements against slavery formally adopted by a church in America.

13. *The Acts and Resolves, Public and Private, of the Province of the Massachusetts Bay*, vol. 4 (Boston: Wright and Potter, 1890), 1035.

14. This may well have been true, although they did not constitute a majority of the active proprietors, i.e., owners of lots voting in town meetings in Hatfield, since fourteen of the nineteen families living in Huntstown in 1761 belonged to or attended Smith's Baptist church. McLoughlin, *New England Dissent*, 533.

15. *Acts and Resolves . . . of the Province of the Massachusetts Bay*, vol. 4, 1036–37, quote on 1036.

16. *Acts and Resolves . . . of the Province of the Massachusetts Bay*, vol. 4, 1040–41.

17. *Acts and Resolves . . . of the Province of the Massachusetts Bay*, vol. 4, 1037.

18. The Baptist records cited by Howes state that "the other society [presumably the Congregationalists] sold 400 acres of the Baptist lands for the support of their Minister and Meeting-House" (*History of the Town of Ashfield*, 150); McLoughlin gives the figure as 398 acres (*Soul Liberty*, 161).

19. On Hutchinson see Bernard Bailyn, *The Ordeal of Thomas Hutchinson* (Cambridge: Harvard University Press, 1974).

20. Howes, *History of the Town of Ashfield,* 85.

21. Howes, *History of the Town of Ashfield,* 85–86.

22. Howes, *History of the Town of Ashfield,* 150.

23. For more on the role of the Baptists generally in the struggle for religious liberty in America, see McLoughlin, *New England Dissent.* Also still valuable is Isaac Backus, *A History of New England, with Particular Reference to the Baptists,* 2nd ed., ed. David Weston (1871; repr., New York: Arno, 1969).

24. Note also the circumstances of voting in colonial Massachusetts: either by voice vote or by signed ballot; on this see Charles Sydnor and Noble E. Cunningham Jr., "Voting in Early America," *American Heritage* 4, no. 1 (Fall 1952): 6–8. In either case, voters' preferences were well known to their neighbors. Smith obviously had plenty of political support in Ashfield, which would have been unthinkable if he had had loyalist sympathies. For more on politics in Ashfield during the American Revolution, see chapter 3.

25. Howes, *History of the Town of Ashfield,* 213.

26. Ebenezer could have cited Luke 10:7, where Jesus declares that the laborer is worthy of his hire.

27. *Vital Records of Ashfield, Massachusetts, to the Year 1850* (Boston: New England Historic Genealogical Society, 1942), 263.

28. Howes, *History of the Town of Ashfield,* 151–52.

29. For a thoughtful analysis of the roots of America's dueling traditions about the relationship of church and state, see J. Judd Owen, "The Struggle Between 'Religion and Nonreligion': Jefferson, Backus, and the Dissonance of America's Founding Principles," *American Political Science Review* 101, no. 3 (August 2007): 493–504.

30. Andrew Murphy, *Conscience and Community: Revisiting Toleration and Religious Dissent in Early Modern America* (University Park: Pennsylvania State University Press, 2001) makes a useful distinction between toleration and tolerance and argues that religious toleration (not tolerance) in England and English America in the 1600s evolved, not so much from secular ideas about liberty, but from the clash of firmly held religious ideas.

31. Stanley Fish's op-ed in the *New York Times,* February 12, 2006, comments on the Muslim reaction to the caricature of the Prophet in a Danish newspaper and the inability of secular liberals to understand it. Is freedom of expression an absolute value? Here indeed is a "clash of civilizations," and some Christians cannot help wondering which side they are on.

3. Governing through a Revolution

1. Frederick G. Howes, *History of the Town of Ashfield, Franklin County, Massachusetts, from Its Settlement in 1742 to 1910* ([Ashfield, Mass.]: Published by the town, n.d. [1910?]), 228.

2. Articles of covenant, 1774, text and Ashfield signers; copy at Town Hall.

3. Rev. Thomas Shepard, "Sketches in the History of Ashfield, Mass., from Its First Settlement to the Year 1833," in Howes, *History of the Town of Ashfield,* 24–25. The terms of the article, in the warrant for the town meeting of October 20, 1774 (copy at Town Hall), directed that the town "chuse a number of men to settle and determine all matters relitive to Mobes, Rioates and Briches of the pece, within the Limets of said Town."

4. Robert Taylor, *Western Massachusetts in the Revolution* (Providence, R.I.: Brown University Press, 1954), 43–44. On the "river gods," see also Greg Nobles, *Divisions throughout the Whole: Politics and Society in Hampshire County, Massachusetts, 1740–1775* (New York: Cambridge University Press, 1983), 171–72 and passim.

5. Warrant [undated]; copy at Town Hall. By law and custom, warrants were issued two weeks before a town meeting. Though this warrant for the April 3 town meeting was undated, we can assume that it was issued around mid-March 1775.

6. Towns chose their own captains, who were in turn responsible to raise troops to fill their units.

7. Howes, *History of the Town of Ashfield,* 230.

8. Town Meeting minutes, June 1, 1775. All Town Meeting records cited in this chapter are at the Ashfield Town Hall.

9. Town Meeting minutes, August 22, 1775.

10. Town Meeting minutes, December 15, 1775.

11. The conflict surfaced again at a town meeting on December 25, 1775, which voted to give Lot 55 in the First Division to Rev. Porter, "to rectify an earlier mistake."

12. Letter from the Rev. William Emerson of Concord to his wife, July 15, 1775, quoted by Fred Anderson, "The Hinge of the Revolution: George Washington Confronts a People's Army, July 3, 1777," *Massachusetts Historical Review* 1 (1999): 28.

13. For a refreshing argument that American militia at the time of the Revolution fought according to the time-tested principles of European warfare, rather than "Indian style," see Guy Chet, *Conquering the American Wilderness: The Triumph of European Warfare in the Colonial Northeast* (Amherst: University of Massachusetts Press, 2003).

14. Victor Daniel Brooks, "American Officer Development in the Massachusetts Campaign, 1775–1776," *Historical Journal of Massachusetts* 12, no. 1 (January 1984): 8–18. See also Anderson, "Hinge of Revolution," 32.

15. Anderson's larger argument is that Washington was committed to the notion of a Continental Army, serving a Continental Congress and the nation. His vision was still inchoate, partial, blurred—but it eventually produced a powerful American army, serving the American nation. Anderson sees July 3, 1775, the day Washington arrived in Cambridge to size up his troops, as the "hinge of American history," a moment when we turned away from "embattled farmers" and began to mount a continental army. It did not happen quickly, but that, argues Anderson, was the turning point. Anderson, "Hinge of Revolution," 45–46.

16. Anderson, "Hinge of Revolution," 27 and 42–43.

17. Anderson, "Hinge of Revolution," 35–36. Anderson points out that British commanders-in-chief, like the Earl of Loudoun and General Jeffrey Amherst, despised the soldierly qualities of New Englanders (38).

18. Anderson, "Hinge of Revolution," 33–34, 39–40.

19. As early as 1645 the provincial legislature in Massachusetts authorized the governor to send members of the colony's militia to fight beyond the borders of the province even "without their [i.e, the militia's] free and voluntary consent." Jean Hankins, "Conscription for the Continental Army," in *The American Revolution, 1775–1783: An Encyclopedia,* 2 vols. (New York: Garland, 1993), 1:364.

20. General Washington's imposition of the ultimate penalty for desertions should be seen at least partially in the light of the hardships I mention here. On raising troops to fight the American Revolution, see Jonathan Smith, "How Massachusetts Raised Her Troops in the Revolution," *Proceedings of the Massachusetts Historical Society* 55 (1921–1922): 345–70; Robert A. Gross, *The Minutemen and Their World* (New York: Hill and Wang, 1976), 59–74; and John Resch and Walter Sargent, eds., *War and Society in the American Revolution: Mobilization and Home Fronts* (DeKalb: Northern Illinois University Press, 2007), 23–69.

21. After 1776, most soldiers fighting on the American side were not volunteers but had been drafted. States were forced to institute drafts when it became clear that men were reluctant to volunteer for anything except short terms. Hankins, "Conscription," 364.

22. Hankins, "Conscription," 364.

23. Howes, *History of the Town of Ashfield,* 236.

24. See Bill Baller, "Kinship and Culture in the Mobilization of Colonial Massachusetts," *Historian* 57, no. 2 (Winter 1995): 291–302. Baller's article describes the impact of the Revolutionary War on rural Massachusetts.

25. Howes, *History of the Town of Ashfield,* 227.

26. Howes, *History of the Town of Ashfield,* 227; for the list of names, see 231–37.

27. Town Meeting minutes, February 20, 1777.

28. Quoted in Howes, *History of the Town of Ashfield,* 229.

29. Quoted in Howes, *History of the Town of Ashfield,* 229.

30. Hankins, "Conscription," 363–66.

31. Hankins, "Conscription," 365.

32. Hankins, "Conscription," 366.

33. Town Hall records; see also Shepard's historical sketch, in Howes, *History of the Town of Ashfield,* 27.

34. Phillips was six years old when his family moved to town in the 1750s. A renowned hunter, he was reputed to have killed twenty-nine bears in one season. He would have two daughters and eleven sons, each son said to be over six feet in height, and all of them served in the town's militia. Eight Phillipses are named on Howes's list of Ashfield men who served in the Patriot army during the Revolutionary War. Howes, *History of the Town of Ashfield,* 235.

35. There is a marvelous sketch of Phillips in Howes, *History of the Town of Ashfield,* 219–20. It notes that, as a Tory, Phillips was forced to pay heavy fines for his refusal to join the Patriot army. Nevertheless, after the war he was elected Ashfield's representative to the state legislature and continued as justice of the peace for many years. In the latter post, record books in his own hand show that he was an inventive speller, but meted out justice with a firm hand. One entry tells of boys who were fined five shillings each for stealing "Water-millions." Several cases resulted in fines for "A salt and Batery." Joseph Lilly, whom Howes describes as "an odd character" best remembered as the man who "brought the guns back from Pelham in Shays' time," was fined five shillings for "uttering one profane oath." Lilly appealed for clemency, beginning his plea by saying, "Well now Squire, this is too D—n bad." "Be careful, Lilly," Phillips warned, "or I shall have to fine you again."

36. Howes, *History of the Town of Ashfield,* 228. Captain Bartlett's house was on the plain, near what is now Main Street (Route 116).

37. Town meeting, August 18, 1777.

38. Howes, *History of the Town of Ashfield,* 228.

39. Howes, *History of the Town of Ashfield,* 228.

40. Taylor, *Western Massachusetts in the Revolution,* 62–74.

41. Town meeting, January 1778. See also Howes, *History of the Town of Ashfield,* 229.

42. Shepard, "Sketches in the History of Ashfield," in Howes, *History of the Town of Ashfield,* 28.

43. The ancient Greeks, the other fountainhead of Western civilization, were similarly concerned about the link between personal piety and communal fate. Oedipus, the king of Thebes, to end a devastating plague, determined to rid his city of the scourge, only to discover that he himself, by immoral behavior (unwittingly killing his father and marrying his mother), was the source of it.

44. In the appendix to their large collection of documents, *The Popular Sources of Political Authority: Documents of the Massachusetts Constitution of 1780* (Cambridge: Harvard University Press, 1966), Oscar and Mary Handlin report that, after careful examination, they were unable to discover any correlation between the social characteristics of the almost three hundred towns in the commonwealth and the votes of their delegates at the ratifying convention of 1780. "The closest relationship is between grievances about Article III [obliging towns to provide, at their own expense, for the institution of the public worship of God, and for the support and maintenance of public protestant teachers of piety, religion and morality"] and the places where Baptists were numerous" (933). Of course, Baptists were not alone in resisting the claims of the established Congregational Church; many Anglicans and Quakers shared their opposition.

45. Quoted by Samuel Eliot Morison, *The Formation of the Massachusetts Constitution: An Address on the Occasion of the 175th Anniversary of the Constitution October 25th, 1955* (Boston: Massachusetts Bar Association, 1955; reprinted from the *Massachusetts Law Quarterly* 40, no. 4 [December 1955]), 1.

46. Oscar and Mary Handlin comment on the authentic tone they found in these documents reporting town-meeting reactions to the drafts of 1778 and 1780. "In these responses [from the towns], the polished phrases of the formal political essay dropped away and thoughts were expressed in the Biblical language that men of all estates heard in the meetinghouse." *Popular Sources of Political Authority*, 51–52.

47. Quoted in Taylor, *Colony to Commonwealth*, 43.

48. Quoted in Taylor, *Colony to Commonwealth*, 43.

49. Handlin and Handlin, *Popular Sources of Political Authority*, 52.

50. Handlin and Handlin, *Popular Sources of Political Authority*, 23; Taylor, *Colony to Commonwealth*, 49.

51. Shepard, "Sketches in the History of Ashfield," in Howes, *History of the Town of Ashfield*, 28. The threatening political atmosphere that underlay these preliminary proceedings, particularly in Hampshire County and the western part of the state generally, is strongly reflected in a set of resolves produced by a meeting of towns in Hampshire County on March 30, 1779. The resolves declared that every one of the legislature's enactments since the beginning of the Revolution was illegal: "We know of no Constitution in this state consented to by the people at large." A legislature can only be a "creature of the Constitution of a State." In this view, Massachusetts without a constitution was a lawless entity. Whoever delayed the framing of a bill of rights and constitution was attempting to "lull the people to sleep, or fatigue them other ways." They deserved not respect, but "to be treated with the severity due to a traitor." Such radical notions were widely held in Massachusetts at this time. A meeting held in response to this call drew representatives of twenty-three towns to a meeting in Northampton on April 20. In strong terms, it called upon the legislature to stop dithering and call a constitutional convention. The legislature finally did so, on June 15 (Taylor, *Colony to Commonwealth*, 110). The fine hand of Joseph Hawley, a firebrand from Northampton who during the Revolution had worked closely with the Boston radicals, can be detected in the ideas and language of these pronouncements, especially in the expression of animus against the existing state legislature. On Hawley's place in the politics of western Massachusetts, see Nobles, *Divisions throughout the Whole*, 63–65, 158, and passim.

52. Morison, *Formation of the Massachusetts Constitution*, 6.

53. Handlin and Handlin, *Popular Sources of Political Authority*, includes a table showing the taxes assessed from each town in the commonwealth (which then included Maine) by the law of 1780 (933–42). Using that table (in the absence of good population estimates) as a measure of weight, one can gauge the malapportionment of the drafting committee. According to Morison (*Formation of the Massachusetts Constitution*, 6), the committee totaled thirty men in all. Suffolk County, including Boston, was assessed by far the greatest share of taxes (£154,000 for Boston alone; approximately £419,231 for the county as a whole). Suffolk got three seats on the drafting committee. Hampshire County, where the wealthiest towns were Springfield and West Springfield, with about £16,000 each in assessed taxes, and the county as a whole was taxed £292,008 (Northampton was assessed £13,253; Ashfield, £4,981), also got three seats on the committee. Berkshire County, where Sheffield (assessed £13,813) and Lanesborough (assessed £11,970) were the wealthiest towns and the county as a whole was taxed £151,858, got two seats. Clearly the convention had bent over backward to accommodate the less populous western counties.

54. Morison, *Formation of the Massachusetts Constitution*, 6.

55. Article I of Adams' draft began, "All men are born equally free and independent." The convention revised this language to "All men are born free and equal." This clause was

the basis of the 1783 case (Quork Walker's case) in which Chief Justice William Cushing declared that slavery could not exist in Massachusetts.

56. Morison, *Formation of the Massachusetts Constitution,* 11–12.

57. Handlin and Handlin, *Popular Sources of Political Authority,* 432.

58. Morison, *Formation of the Massachusetts Constitution,* 13.

59. Handlin and Handlin, *Popular Sources of Political Authority,* contains 450 pages of returns from the towns. Morison remarks that he used to think the constitution of 1780 "went over" easily, that there had been no contest. "That is far from the truth," he admits, having examined the 188 returns from towns in the State Archives, plus forty more he unearthed himself. There was indeed strenuous opposition across the state, much of it traceable to Joseph Hawley of Northampton, the "Hampshire Cato," and the Rev. Isaac Backus, a Baptist minister from Middleborough and author of a three-volume *History of New England, with Particular Reference to the Baptists.*

60. The Ashfield return is printed in full in Handlin and Handlin, *Popular Sources of Political Authority,* 533–37. For the text of the constitution, as submitted and as declared ratified, see 441–72.

61. Ashfield explicitly approved the last paragraph of Article III. It stated that "every denomination of Christians, demeaning themselves peaceably, and as good subjects of the Commonwealth, shall be equally under the protection of the law; and no subordination of any one sect or denomination to another shall ever be established by law." Handlin and Handlin, *Popular Sources of Political Authority,* 533.

62. Morison, *Formation of the Massachusetts Constitution,* 17.

63. The quoted phrases are from Shepard, "Sketches in the History of Ashfield," in Howes, *History of the Town of Ashfield,* 29–30.

64. An 1827 letter, "Visit to the Shaker Village," by Margaret Hall, a visitor from Edinburgh, gives a vivid impression of Shaker worship. xroads.virginia.edu/~HYPER/DETOC /FEM/religion.htm#hall.

65. David Newell, an Ashfield resident who owns a remarkable collection of primary-source material on the Shakers and has studied their history carefully, offered a summary of their visits to Ashfield: "The first converts to Shakerism in the Ashfield region 'embraced the faith' during the summer of 1780. There were scattered converts in the Baptist Corner area, as well as a few in neighboring Buckland and Shelburne Falls. When Ann Lee embarked upon her missionary tour (1781–1783), she spent considerable time in central Massachusetts. While she was there, hundreds of Shaker converts from New York and western Massachusetts were constantly visiting her. The commonly used route went from Pittsfield to Cheshire, Ashfield, Montague, Petersham, and so forth. These towns had numerous resident converts who offered boarding and meals to the travelers. Sometimes they made a nuisance of themselves by their noisy worship. It was these 'travelers' that Ashfield authorities particularly objected to, 'straggling tremblers' who would come and go, outsiders, religious fanatics. Note that Ashfield's town meeting stopped short of warning the local Shakers. The select board's 'warning' was not enforced during this first visit. In the Shaker 'Testimonies,' it is recorded that Mother Ann asked the 'believers' not to visit her in Ashfield. There may have been a 'compromise' of some sort, reached just prior to her arrival. A second town meeting in late March appointed a 'committee of safety' to deal with the Shakers. Asa Bacon, a Shaker himself, had been appointed one of the town constables just prior to this."

66. [Rufus Bishop and Seth Y. Wells, eds.], *Testimonies of the Life, Character, Revelations, and Doctrines of Mother Ann Lee and the Elders with Her* (1816), 2nd ed. (Albany, N.Y.: Weed, Parsons, 1888), 106. The account here and in the following paragraph is based on Howes, *History of the Town of Ashfield,* 371–74, supplemented by documents in the private collection of David Newell (see previous note). Newell offers the following summary of their sojourn in town: "Mother Ann and her entourage returned to Ashfield (November 1, 1782), stay-

ing at Asa Bacon's place for a full half year. This time, they encouraged 'believers' from all quarters to visit. Several thousand did so at various times. The report that there were six hundred there at one time is credible. In November, 'all hands took hold' and constructed a log meeting house which served as a place of worship, a dining hall, and, with the lofts above, as sleeping quarters. It was called the 'Log Sanctuary.' It was built adjacent to Asa Bacon's home, which was on an old road (long since discontinued), near the juncture of Baptist Corner and Pfersick roads."

67. According to the Shaker account in *Testimonies of the Life, Character, Revelations, and Doctrines* (chap. 16), Asa's brother Daniel, an early convert but now an apostate, in high dudgeon brought his wife to the Bacon compound and left her there. Mother Ann, sensing trouble, ordered the hapless woman returned to her husband, which apparently, judging by the band that came charging over the hill from Shelburne the following spring, infuriated Daniel Bacon all the more.

68. Howes, *History of the Town of Ashfield*, 373. See also *Testimonies of the Life, Character, Revelations, and Doctrines*, 110. The account in *Testimonies* says that the meetings at these venues occurred in the reverse order, but the difference is not material.

69. *Testimonies of the Life, Character, Revelations, and Doctrines*, 106–10.

70. Howes, *History of the Town of Ashfield*, 374.

71. *Testimonies of the Life, Character, Revelations, and Doctrines*, 109.

72. Andrew Murphy, in *Conscience and Community: Revisiting Toleration and Religious Dissent in Early Modern America* (University Park: Pennsylvania State University Press, 2001), develops a distinction between toleration and tolerance and argues that, in England and America in the 1600s, one often finds instances of religious toleration, even in the absence of a general culture of tolerance. In other words, toleration resulted, not from a culture imbued with secular and universalistic values, but from practical accommodations between conflicting groups.

73. Town meeting, 1782.

74. Shepard, "Sketches in the History of Ashfield," in Howes, *History of the Town of Ashfield*, 30–31.

75. On the convention generally, see Thomas H. O'Connor and Alan Rogers, *This Momentous Affair: Massachusetts and the Ratification of the Constitution of the United States* (Boston: Trustees of the Public Library of the City of Boston, 1987). Sadly, on p. 103, Ephraim Williams's name is misspelled.

76. All's well that ends well. The constitution was soon amended by the addition of a bill of rights. As for Williams, he subsequently served as a member of the board of selectmen and in a number of other local positions of responsibility and trust.

4. Transformation

1. I am speaking here in shorthand. I am ignoring native Americans, people of African origin, and those with roots in other European countries (particularly Germany and France). What I mean to emphasize is the cultural and political dominance in much of the United States, at the founding and well into the nineteenth century, of Protestants from the British Isles and northern Europe, followed by a gradual shift in the direction of greater diversity, at first slowly, then with gathering momentum.

2. *History of the Town of Ashfield*, vol. 2, *1910–1960* (Ashfield, Mass.: published by the Town, 1965), 8. This continuation of the town's history beyond the years covered by Frederick Howes, published in 1965 to mark Ashfield's bicentennial, was "written by the citizens of Ashfield" and illustrated by Elice D. Pieropan. A third volume, projected for 2015, is now being planned, under the direction of the Ashfield History Project.

3. Frederick G. Howes, *History of the Town of Ashfield, Franklin County, Massachusetts, from Its Settlement in 1742 to 1910* ([Ashfield, Mass.]: Published by the town, n.d. [1910?]), 104–6.

4. Opinion on Norton seems finally to be shifting. Compare a vicious review of James Turner, *The Liberal Education of Charles Eliot Norton* (Baltimore: Johns Hopkins University Press, 1999), by Richard Poirier (*New Republic*, May 8, 2000, 25–33), with a more recent positive assessment by Linda Dowling, in *Charles Eliot Norton: The Art of Reform in Nineteenth-Century America* (Hanover, N.H.: University Press of New England, 2007). There are several marvelous vignettes of Norton in books by Van Wyck Brooks, including *The Flowering of New England* (New York: Dutton, 1937) and *New England: Indian Summer, 1865–1915* (Cleveland: World, 1940).

5. His was the seventh generation of Halls to occupy the farm on which he grew up. G. Stanley Hall, *Life and Confessions of a Psychologist* (New York: D. Appleton, 1924), 53.

6. Hall, *Life and Confessions,* 148–50.

7. Hall says that the payment was five dollars, but it is unclear from his account whether that sum was for each lecture or for the whole series of twelve lectures. See Hall, *Life and Confessions,* 217.

8. Hall, *Life and Confessions,* 217.

9. Hall, *Life and Confessions,* 219. His dissertation, titled "The Muscular Perception of Space," jumped into the middle of a dispute then raging about whether Immanuel Kant's ideas about time, space, and causality might save religion from its scientific debunkers.

10. For a modern example of the kind of contempt Hall endured from Harvard, see Louis Menand, *The Metaphysical Club* (New York: Farrar, Straus and Giroux, 2001). Calling Hall "an intent reader of academic signals: . . . not a man who regarded his intellectual interests and his professional prospects as necessarily exclusive concerns," Menand remarks that "when Hall was no longer dependent on James's patronage, the competitiveness in their relationship ceased to be latent" (268). Earlier, Menand reports, while studying in Germany, Hall "worked with nearly every German celebrity in the field" (270). As a young "philosopher manqué at Antioch [College]," he put himself forward as a candidate for an appointment at Johns Hopkins and began "bombarding Gilman [Daniel Coit Gilman, president of Johns Hopkins] with unsolicited letters of recommendation" (271). "In the beginning," Menand writes, "he advertised himself as a hard scientist," but when he "figured out that this was not the note Gilman was hoping to hear," Hall wrote again, noting that he was a "graduate in divinity, & without agreeing entirely with all I hear, am in the habit of church-going, & indeed am still a nominal church member I believe" (271). These are indeed embarrassing words to read. Hall was not always a smooth academic politician, but he was more than a careerist. Later in life, he founded the American Psychological Association. He is also credited with bringing Sigmund Freud to America, to give a series of lectures at Clark University in 1909, during Hall's tenure as president there. Given Freud's reputation at the time, sponsoring him in America was not the act of a craven sycophant. Menand's book is full of brilliant exposition and balanced judgment, but his generosity deserted him when he came to Hall.

11. Hall, *Life and Confessions,* 175.

12. The story of the demise of the Ashfield dinners is sensitively told in a superb pamphlet by Betty and Edward Gulick, *Charles Eliot Norton and the Ashfield Dinners, 1879–1903* (Ashfield, Mass.: Ashfield Historical Society, 1990), 15–21; quotes in the text are taken from the excerpted addresses in the appendix (24–35). Ed Gulick taught history and international relations at Wellesley College for many years; he and his wife retired to neighboring Conway.

13. That may seem like a sexist remark, but older women in town, some of them quite fiercely feminist, assert it as an empirical fact. They tell of the town's telephone operator using her switchboard to monitor local gossip, then sharing it with favored friends.

14. For an account of the rigors of farming in rural western Massachusetts, see Mark Kramer, *Three Farms: Making Milk, Meat, and Money from the American Soil,* (Boston: Little Brown, 1980). One of Kramer's three farms is the Totman dairy farm in Conway, Massachusetts, just down the road from Ashfield.

15. For a particularly valuable account, see Mary Beth Norton, *Liberty's Daughters: The Revolutionary Experience of American Women, 1750–1800* (1980; repr., Ithaca: Cornell University Press, 1996).

16. There are, of course, wonderful exceptions, like Abigail Adams and Mercy Otis Warren, but Warren's travails, in particular, prove the rule. See Norton, *Liberty's Daughters,* 116 and 121–23. Another exceptional case was Elizabeth Murray, a Scottish immigrant shopkeeper in Boston who executed tightly drawn prenuptial agreements with her second and third husbands (*Liberty's Daughters,* 147–51).

17. The committee in Ashfield appointed to prepare the town's response to the 1780 draft state constitution voiced no objection to confining active, public citizenship to men. It goes without saying that the committee consisted entirely of men.

18. See Louise L. Stevenson, "Women Anti-Suffragists in the 1915 Massachusetts Campaign," *New England Quarterly* 52, no. 1 (March 1979): 80–93.

19. Harriet Jane Hanson Robinson, *Massachusetts in the Women's Suffrage Movement: A General Political, Legal, and Legislative History from 1774 to 1881* (Boston: Roberts Brothers, 1883), 108.

20. Robinson, *Massachusetts in the Women's Suffrage Movement,* 108–9.

21. On the referenda see www.primaryresearch.org/suffrage. The result was the same that year in three other eastern states: New Jersey, Pennsylvania, and New York.

22. Originally, in 1995, town meeting voted to appropriate $4,500 for the Youth Commission. By 2002, the amount had grown to $10,000. The funds paid a director's salary and supported trips to Red Sox games and museums in Boston, mainly during the summer months. Hard questions about who benefited from some of these activities, plus an intensifying fiscal crunch, led to a sharply reduced appropriation in 2007, and in 2009 the commission was discontinued.

23. This spirit endures in the early summer baseball leagues (Pee-wee, Bantam, Little League, and girls' softball). They are entirely locally administered and support themselves by donations and by selling refreshments at the games. Young families of all descriptions are heavily involved in these leagues. They provide one vital locus where the town's various elements meet, compete, and play together on a level field.

24. In Massachusetts, when you register to vote, you are asked if you choose to identify with a political party. It used to be (as recently as 2005) that in order to vote in a party's primary you had to be enrolled in that party, although if you were unenrolled on primary election day you could enroll in any party simply by asking for the ballot of that party. To recover your status as an independent, you had to ask to be restored to "unenrolled." Now, unless you choose to identify with a political party, you are automatically restored to "unenrolled" after you vote. Thus, even people who normally vote for candidates of a particular party and regularly vote in that party's primaries are nevertheless listed as "unenrolled" unless they deliberately choose to register with a party. The result is that the number of political independents in Massachusetts tends to be inflated in the official records. Over the years, a steady 60 percent of those registered to vote in Ashfield have not been enrolled with either party.

25. It is worth noting that Nixon's running-mate that year was Henry Cabot Lodge, whom JFK had defeated in his first run for the Senate in 1952. We should also to bear in mind that it was the pre-Watergate Nixon who ran in 1960. Nixon was never an appealing figure to many Democrats, but nationally he ran very strongly among Republicans. Many, including Nixon himself, believe that he won the presidential election of 1960. It was one of the cases detailed in his *Six Crises* (Garden City, N.Y.: Doubleday, 1962).

26. Senator Ted Kennedy, who had been filling his brother's unexpired term, ran for re-election in 1964. He ran much better this time, losing in Ashfield by just 239 to 285. State-wide he won again by a large margin.

27. This election marked the debut of John Olver, at the time a professor of chemistry at the University of Massachusetts Amherst. Olver lost to incumbent state senator John Barrus in Ashfield in 1972, but prevailed in the district, launching a career that took him through several successful campaigns for the state senate, then on to the U.S. House of Representatives in 1991. In the 1991 Democratic primary to replace Silvio Conte, Olver won practically every town and city in the district, including Ashfield, where he won by 135 to 105.

28. In the 1994 race for his seat in the U.S. Senate, Ted Kennedy bested his Republican challenger, Mitt Romney, by 475 to 291, but Ashfield voters continued to split their tickets. Republican William Weld triumphed in the gubernatorial race over Mark Roosevelt, the Democratic nominee, by 490 to 272.

29. Known as "Yankee Rowe," it was the third commercial nuclear power plant built in the United States and the first built in New England.

30. Town Meeting records, 1988, 352. All Town Meeting records cited in this chapter are at the Ashfield Town Hall.

31. The proposed legislation on the treatment of domestic farm animals did not find favor statewide, either, falling by a margin of over 2 to 1. That same year, 1988, Ashfield also came down hard, 155 to 597, against a proposed ban on handguns; and by an even greater margin, 45 to 665, against the idea of increasing the salaries of statewide elected officials.

32. Town Meeting records, 1982, 249.

33. Town Meeting records, 1984, 279.

34. Town Meeting records, 1986, 319.

35. Town Meeting records, 1990, 391.

36. This was still short of the peak, 1809 persons, reported in the 1810 federal census. Howes, *History of the Town of Ashfield,* 102.

37. The exact figure for the increase in population between 1960 to 2000 is 59.2 percent, according to the decennial federal census. Among neighboring towns in Franklin County, only Conway (nearer to Interstate 91, with quicker access to Greenfield, Northampton, Amherst, and Springfield) grew faster. Between 1980 and 2000, Conway's population expanded from 1,213 to 1,809 (49.1%), narrowly passing Ashfield in total population.

38. Barbara Kingsolver, in *Animal, Vegetable, Miracle* (New York: HarperCollins, 2007), writes about her family's project of living for a year on food produced locally, wherever their travels took them. One stop was Ashfield, where she visited two thriving enterprises: Side-hill Farm, operated by Amy Klippenstein and Paul Lacinski (118–23), and the New England Cheesemaking Supply Company, founded and operated by Ricki Carroll (131–36).

39. The income figures are from a compilation of 2000 U.S. Census data, available at www.city-data/zips/01330.

40. Curiously, the percentage of children in single-parent households is higher in Ashfield than in neighboring towns in Franklin County. I do not know why.

41. *2003 State of the People: For the Pioneer Valley,* a report prepared by the Pioneer Valley Planning Commission (West Springfield, Mass.), 62–63. The report is available at www.pvpc .org/resources/infopolicycenter/State of the People report.pdf.

42. This account draws on articles "exploring the future of dairying," published in the *West County News,* a local weekly. The series, written by Faye Whitney, an Ashfield journalist, appeared in the summer of 2007.

43. "APR [Agricultural Preservation Restriction] Program: Eligibility Criteria & Considerations," from the Web site of the Massachusetts Department of Agricultural Resources, www.mass.gov/agr/landuse/APR/criteria.htm.

44. Only 4 percent speak a language other than English at home (compared with 18 percent across the United States). These figures on education and other "social characteristics" are from the 2000 U.S. Census.

45. *2003 State of the People: For the Pioneer Valley,* 36–37.

46. Heber Honestman was sometimes listed as Heber Negro on old deeds. Howes quotes the *History of the Town of Easton* as saying that Heber was formerly a slave, given his freedom by his master. He joined the church in Ashfield in 1763. Howes, *History of the Town of Ashfield,* 55 and 61. For more, see Nancy Gray Garvin, "Who Was Heber Honestman?" *Ashfield Historical Society Newsletter,* Spring 2005, www.ashfieldhistorical.org/newsspring05.html#heber.

47. Special town meetings are called at the discretion of the select board, and normally there are about three or four of these each year. The select board is obliged to call a special meeting if ten citizens sign a petition asking for one, however.

5. Town Hall and Town Meeting

1. These figures are based in part on Joseph Zimmerman, *The New England Town Meeting: Democracy in Action* (Westport, Conn.: Praeger, 1999), 27; cf. 54.

2. There is a statewide code of practice, published by the Massachusetts Municipal Association, and there are mandates in state statutes, including the requirement that towns with fewer than six thousand inhabitants must have an open, rather than representative, town meeting (see www.sec.state.ma.us/cis/cistwn/twnidx.htm). As we will see in the next several chapters, however, many state guidelines are ignored, sometimes deliberately. Since ancient Athens, democracy has often been impatient with precedent and sometimes a bit restless under the rule of law.

3. Frank Bryan, *Real Democracy* (Chicago: University of Chicago Press, 2004), provides an excellent survey of these various styles and their implications as experienced in Vermont.

4. Challenges to the moderator's discretion are extremely rare in Ashfield; I cannot remember the last time it happened. Zimmerman (*New England Town Meeting,* 54) says that the same is true throughout the commonwealth.

5. As we've seen, state law in Massachusetts has various provisions privileging agricultural land. Although of course the town must abide by these laws, the select board in recent years has decided to make no further distinction between types of property: residential, commercial, agricultural, industrial.

6. Another minor exception appeared in the 1990s, when we learned that a state program to loan money for home improvements contained a provision that returned repaid loan money to the towns. Under state regulations, the funds could be spent at the discretion of the select board. This program eventually returned over $100,000 to Ashfield. When we became aware of it, the select board announced that, as a matter of town policy, no money from this windfall would be spent without a positive advisory vote of town meeting. Reportedly, however, toward the end of the first decade of the twenty-first century, the select board occasionally spent these funds without consulting town meeting.

7. The same is true for the board of assessors and the finance committee.

8. The current state open meeting law was enacted in 1976. It replaced an ineffective, much vaguer statute passed eighteen years earlier. Many believe it still needs tightening.

9. There are some exceptions, such as for a discussion of matters that might invade a person's privacy. Under the open-meeting law, a board could go into executive session to deal with such matters.

10. Toward the end of her tenure, the town began to receive some critical evaluations from auditors for these practices.

11. In 2008 town meeting faced controversy about financing the purchase of a new truck

for the highway department. The voters decided to do it by a method known as debt exclusion; state law allows towns temporarily, for capital expenditures, to exceed the state-imposed limit (2.5%) on overall spending increases in a given year. But the town-meeting resolution was contingent on passage by ballot vote, which was not obtained. A special town meeting then voted to take the money for the truck from reserve funds. The people of Ashfield have various ways, apart from town meeting, to impose their will.

6. Tinkering with the System

1. At that time, the board of selectmen served ex officio as the finance committee.

2. Both of the quoted phrases are from *Administrative Management in the Government of the United States* (January 1937), 5. The report was prepared by the President's Committee on Administrative Management, chaired by Louis Brownlow. The popular TV drama *West Wing*, which ran from 1999 to 2006, offered a chance to assess the fruit produced by the adoption of these recommendations. One character, Leo McGarrah, the president's original chief of staff, seemed sincerely to want anonymity, but his successor, C. J. Cregg, sometimes leaned in the direction of McGeorge Bundy or Henry Kissinger.

3. Since I left the board, members have been working on cooperative arrangements for ambulance service, for example. A shared public health nurse and housing for elderly persons were other ideas we thought worth exploring.

4. Compare the city of Boston: with a population of 589,141 in 2000, a similar proportion of people serving on municipal boards and commissions would have meant over 100,000 people (113,296, to be exact).

7. Building a Sewer System

1. Twenty years earlier, a town meeting discussed what could be done to clean up "Sewer Brook," as South River was already being called, but nothing came of it.

2. As we will see, calling it "innovative" was critical. It was the basis for getting demonstration grants from federal and state environmental agencies.

3. In an interview with me in 2007, Ed Scott remembered these repeated modifications in the state's regulations as a particularly vexing part of this story.

4. In a telephone conversation we had in November 2007, Andrea Ash, manager of environmental resources at Ben & Jerry's, told me that the company "removed this technology" from the Waterbury plant in 1994. She reported that it had proven not well suited to the extraordinary demands of the effluent produced by an ice-cream factory.

5. Despite these alleged forerunners, MassDEP was exploring new territory in reviewing the Ashfield project. This project would have made tiny Ashfield the first municipality in Massachusetts to use solar aquatics for treating its wastewater.

6. Four years earlier, Olver had defeated me (along with several other candidates) in a hotly contested Democratic primary to fill the district's seat in Congress, vacated by the death of Silvio Conte. Olver and I had been political allies before the sudden primary, and we quickly resumed our alliance as Olver mounted his general election campaign. I strongly supported him in the subsequent campaigns of 1992 and 1994 as well, and by 1995 we were once again firm friends.

7. Half of the additional $656,000 would come in the form of a grant from the U.S. Department of Agriculture; the other half was a loan from the same agency.

8. The consent decree was not lifted until 2003. The factors that prompted the seven-year delay were questions about the technology (and whether we would stick with it) and issues of financing.

9. The town's taxpayers—including the users, of course—would receive their portion of the break from the reduction in the town's debt for construction as relief in property taxes.

10. For a good statement of the case in favor of solar aquatics, see "Scapegoating Solar-Aquatics," by Ken and Ethel Kipen, at www.purplepanthers.com/rx2.htm.

11. In April 1999 the select board reported having received a study conducted by an independent investigator, Margaret Hamel. Titled "Independent Assessment of the Ashfield Wastewater Treatment Plant," it concluded, according to Bill Perlman, that the plants in the tanks and greenhouse did not play a significant role in the treatment of the water.

12. After leaving the select board, Perlman was elected to the sewer commission, replacing Delaney.

13. Tilley's report, titled "The Ashfield Wastewater Treatment Problem," was given as a PowerPoint presentation. A copy of the presentation file is on deposit at the Ashfield Town Hall.

14. Oddly, I do not remember having heard that name during the 1990s. It may have been mentioned, but if so, it did not register with me.

15. It was rumored at the time that one of the regulators had the proverbial "son in the business"—in this case, the business of marketing and building conventional treatment systems.

16. Tom Cranston, chair of the finance committee through this process, was not appeased by the argument that most of the expense was borne by the federal and state treasuries. That's our money, too, he reminded me. Tom Carter, a conservative Republican, was more sardonic. With all the malfeasance surrounding the Big Dig in Boston, he said, and all the corruption in Washington, wasn't it high time we got a little government money ourselves?

17. Democracy, Churchill said, is the worst form of government imaginable, except for the alternatives.

8. Controlling the Police

1. Max Weber, "Politics as a Vocation" (speech originally given at Munich University, 1918), in *From Max Weber: Essays in Sociology,* ed. and trans. H. H. Gerth and C. Wright Mills (London: K. Paul, Trench, Trübner, 1947), 78.

2. This is a paraphrase of Reinhold Niebuhr's famous aphorism (to which I return in the concluding chapter): "Man's capacity for justice makes democracy possible, but man's inclination to injustice makes democracy necessary." From the foreword to *The Children of Light and the Children of Darkness: A Vindication of Democracy and a Critique of Its Traditional Defence* (New York: Charles Scribner's Sons, 1944), xiii.

3. In 2009 the police chief was elected to the board of health, and his wife was elected to the board of assessors. It was unusual, for Ashfield at least, to have both the police chief and his wife running for and winning elective office on the same ballot.

4. The town could not expect to get off scot-free, of course, since insurance premiums are often raised after such a settlement.

5. When I ran in the primary for U.S. Representative a year earlier, a neighbor asked why I had not run for a local office first, to which I replied that, having studied national politics all my life, I felt ready to serve in Congress, whereas at that time I knew practically nothing about local affairs. Indeed, the idea of running for office in Ashfield had never occurred to me. My initial reaction to the chief's invitation had been dismissive, but he persisted, others joined in his effort, and eventually I agreed to run.

6. This critical attitude toward the state police became a staple of local discussions. No one in town seemed ready to stand up for them, whereas several families benefited directly from the practice of using local people as part-time reserve officers. I sometimes wondered whether we were getting all sides of that issue. We never heard directly from the state police. They apparently felt no need to justify themselves.

7. As of late 2009 the hourly rate was between $38 and $40.

8. Traditionally the power of choosing officers to work construction detail belonged to the regional state police headquarters, but in the 1990s Ashfield's town meeting passed a unique local ordinance giving the police chief exclusive power to name officers to work detail in the town. As was routine procedure, the ordinance was submitted to the state attorney general, who let it pass. Shortly thereafter, Bill Perlman attended a meeting at the regional state highway headquarters and announced that, for the project then under discussion, in Ashfield, our chief would appoint the detail, and anyone who tried to interfere with our chief's appointees would be issued a summons. After recovering from their astonishment, people at the meeting agreed to modify their usual procedures when working in Ashfield.

9. Cops Fast became a signature Clinton administration program, pandering to the public's desire for security and to the police unions' hunger to grow. It may have met a serious need in some places, but it was an invitation to waste and corruption in others.

10. Compare James Madison's dictum: "In framing a government which is to be administered by men over men, . . . you must first enable the government to control the governed; and in the next place oblige it to control itself." He adds: "A dependence on the people is, no doubt, the primary control on the government; but experience has taught mankind the necessity of auxiliary precautions." These propositions, in *The Federalist* no. 51, provide an introduction to his discussion of the U.S. Constitution's separation of powers.

11. Political scientists, following E. E. Schattschneider, speak of the "contagion of conflict," that is, the tendency in democracies for the arena in which an issue is thrashed out to expand when controversy breaks out. Ashfield's summer of 2009 provided a vivid illustration of this phenomenon. See Schattschneider, *The Semisovereign People: A Realist's View of Democracy in America* (New York: Holt, Rinehart and Winston, 1960), esp. chap. 1, 1–19; the quoted phrase is on page 5.

12. Diane Broncaccio, "Gun Play among Charges against Ashfield Chief," *Recorder* (Greenfield, Mass.), August 11, 2009, 1.

13. Diane Broncaccio, "Ashfield Selectboard Chair Resigns," *Recorder,* August 12, 2009, 1.

14. Henry Steele Commager, "The Defeat of America" (review of *Roots of War* by Richard J. Barnet), *New York Review of Books,* October 5, 1972, 7.

9. Educating Children

1. To be exact, in 2005 town voters appropriated $1,902,708 for educational expenses, in a total budget of $3,576,583. Of that, $1,618,279 was for operating district schools, $165,000 for vocational education, paid to schools in the area on a pro rata basis (for each child who elects to attend one of the vocational high schools), and $118,529 for capital costs.

2. This account of the early evolution of primary and secondary education in Ashfield is based mainly on Frederick G. Howes, *History of the Town of Ashfield, Franklin County, Massachusetts, from Its Settlement in 1742 to 1910* ([Ashfield, Mass.]: Published by the town, n.d. [1910?]), 175–80, 185–89, 191–93, 196–200, and passim.

3. Most of these buildings were quite primitive, but one, called "The Round," was hailed as "sui generis" by Eugene C. Gardner, a prominent Springfield architect who transcribed his recollection for Ashfield's historian sixty years after the schoolhouse was built. "I do not believe there ever was another schoolhouse like it in this world," he wrote. It accommodated up to seventy pupils in its single room, "eight [during the winter of 1848] from the Leonard family alone (no twins)." Its circular shape enabled students to sit along the wall, on slightly raised platforms, and face the school's single teacher (usually a male), who stood in the central well, or arena, as Gardner described it. Howes, *History of the Town of Ashfield,* 178–80.

4. G. Stanley Hall, *Life and Confessions of a Psychologist* (New York: D. Appleton, 1924), 110–11; Hall offers there his impressions of these "masters," recorded in his personal journal of these years.

5. Howes, *History of the Town of Ashfield*, 191.

6. Hall says that John 11:35, "Jesus wept," was a favorite "because of its brevity, and it was never disallowed." *Life and Confessions*, 112.

7. Sumner, a champion of the antislavery movement, had been beaten nearly to death in the Senate chamber three years earlier by a congressman from South Carolina. Reelected to the Senate by the Massachusetts legislature in November 1856, by 1859 he had apparently recovered sufficiently to resume his career. His appearance in Greenfield must have been pretty dramatic.

8. Hall, *Life and Confessions*, 118–19.

9. Hall, *Life and Confessions*, 123.

10. Howes, *History of the Town of Ashfield*, 193.

11. Dawes was remembered as a "good disciplinarian." Howes records that, when "one of the smart village boys attempted to play one of his favorite tricks upon [Dawes]," he found himself "in a horizontal position so suddenly that, as he afterwards expressed it, he didn't know how he came to be there." Howes, *History of the Town of Ashfield*, 194.

12. Dawes's intention in proposing the legislation, he wrote to supporters in Boston, was to "arouse the Christian sentiment of the country" against the oppressive policies of the U.S. Department of the Interior and to absorb Native Americans into the mainstream of the United States. Ironically, the effect of the program was to put the vast majority of tribal lands in the hands of white speculators. For background, see Frederick Hoxie, *A Final Promise: The Campaign to Assimilate the Indians, 1880–1920* (Lincoln: University of Nebraska Press, 1984).

13. Howes, *History of the Town of Ashfield*, 196–97.

14. One of my sources here is Betty and Edward Gulick's excellent pamphlet, *Charles Eliot Norton and the Ashfield Dinners, 1879–1903* (Ashfield, Mass.: Ashfield Historical Society, 1990).

15. Howes, *History of the Town of Ashfield*, 197–99.

16. Howes, *History of the Town of Ashfield*, 199.

17. Howes, *History of the Town of Ashfield*, 200.

18. Howes, *History of the Town of Ashfield*, 202–3.

19. *History of the Town of Ashfield*, vol. 2, *1910–1960* ([Ashfield, Mass.]: Published by the town, 1965), 56–57.

20. The willingness of many women to work for lower salaries than male teachers encouraged the trend toward female teachers. See Wayne J. Urban and Jennings L. Wagoner Jr., *American Education: A History*, 2nd ed. (Boston: McGraw Hill, 2000), chap. 4.

21. See chap. 8 ("Education") in *History of the Town of Ashfield, 1910–1960*.

22. *History of the Town of Ashfield, 1910–1960*, 58.

23. In 1929 Sanderson established a regular course in home economics; it began with an enrollment of twenty girls.

24. *History of the Town of Ashfield, 1910–1960*, 58.

25. *History of the Town of Ashfield, 1910–1960*, 59.

26. *History of the Town of Ashfield, 1910–1960*, 60. Another straw in the wind was that by 1957 ten high school students from Ashfield were attending vocational high schools (only seven had done so in 1949), and by 1960 the number had risen to fourteen. *History of the Town of Ashfield, 1910–1960*, 60.

27. *History of the Town of Ashfield, 1910–1960*, 64–65.

28. The figures for 1940 exclude the capital cost of the new Sanderson Academy building.

29. *History of the Town of Ashfield, 1910–1960*, 60.

30. One town kept its elementary school out of the system. Rowe, formerly the site of

a nuclear power plant, is practically afloat in federal funds, which it spends on lavish public works, including its own elementary school. Students in the higher grades attend Mohawk Trail Regional High School. Rowe has one non-voting member on the regional school committee.

31. In 2008 the Greenfield Community College Foundation funded a review of local primary and secondary education. The report, titled "Creating a Sustainable and Quality Education System in Franklin County Public Schools: Study of Potential Efficiencies," is available at www.frcog.org/pubs/general/misc/FRANKLINCOUNTYSCHOOLSREPORT.pdf.

32. The Massachusetts Comprehensive Assessment System (MCAS), a statewide standards-based assessment program, was developed in response to the Massachusetts Education Reform Act of 1993. This act predated the federal No Child Left Behind program by almost a decade.

33. These efforts suffered a cruel setback in the spring of 2008 when three boys were found at the regional high school toting a handgun. Shades of the ghastly incident in Columbine, Colorado, haunted some local imaginations. Buoniconti moved aggressively to contain the damage, removing the boys from Mohawk and putting tough new regulations in place.

34. A former school committee member from Ashfield, whose daughter "school-choiced" into Greenfield when the second grade at Sanderson Academy combined into a single section, spearheaded these efforts to improve the marketing of Sanderson and other district schools.

35. This kind of strategy is typical of the method by which state authorities coerce local action.

36. As I mentioned earlier, the trustees also administered a small endowment to support scholarships. It was not very actively or aggressively managed. The trustees' main job, as they saw it, was to maintain the old academy's playing fields, now home to a summer baseball league for area youngsters.

37. At about this time, a resident, not a member of the board of trustees, attended the annual meeting of the trustees and sought recognition to ask questions about its funds and how they were being managed. The reception was frosty and produced no adequate answers. The trustees, a private body, were under no obligation to open their books, and they had no interest in transparency.

38. This was the clear conclusion of a conversation between leading local educators convened by the Ashfield History Project during the summer of 2008.

Conclusion: Implications for Democratic Practice and Theory

1. Robert A. Dahl, *On Democracy* (New Haven: Yale University Press, 1998), 93.

2. Dahl, *On Democracy*, 95, quoting Mill's *Considerations on Representative Government*.

3. Necessity, as Milton wrote, is "the tyrant's plea."

4. Reinhold Niebuhr, *The Children of Light and the Children of Darkness: A Vindication of Democracy and a Critique of Its Traditional Defence* (New York: Charles Scribner's Sons, 1944), xiii.

5. I've avoided burdening this book with references to classical political philosophy, but it may be worth noting that John Locke bases his argument against autocratic power partly on the notion that no one can be trusted to exercise power benevolently (see, for example, the *Second Treatise on Civil Government*, chap. 9, section 125). Note also, incidentally, Rousseau's argument, in chap. 15 of *The Social Contract*, that "Sovereignty . . . does not admit of representation."

6. Niebuhr believed that communism's failure to incorporate a system of checks and balances made it demonic. See, especially, *The Irony of American History* (New York: Charles Scribner's Sons, 1952), chap. 5.

7. I borrow the title of this section from Robert Dahl's study of New Haven, *Who Governs? Democracy and Power in an American City* (New Haven: Yale University Press, 1961).

8. Average attendance at annual town meetings in 136 towns across Massachusetts in 1996 was 13.72 percent of all registered voters, based on responses to questionnaires mailed to each town with an open town meeting (the rate of return on this question was 52%). Joseph Zimmerman, *The New England Town Meeting: Democracy in Action* (Westport, Conn.: Praeger, 1999), 54.

9. I know this from my own observations, but also from a survey done for me by Smith College students in 2003. Unfortunately, we were not able to complete enough interviews to make our survey scientifically useful.

10. Arthur J. Vidich and Joseph Bensman, *Small Town in Mass Society: Class, Power, and Religion in a Rural Community* (Princeton: Princeton University Press, 1958; rev. ed., Urbana: University of Illinois Press, 2000), a classic of political sociology, looked hard at the drawbacks of public life in a small, face-to-face community in upstate New York.

11. Theodore Lowi, *The End of Liberalism: Ideology, Policy, and the Crisis of Public Authority* (New York: W. W. Norton, 1969).

12. A vivid example came in May 2008, when Ashfield's annual town meeting avoided hard decisions (sharply reducing funds for road repairs or for the police department) by using reserve funds. Voters supported articles that drew down its rainy-day fund from $300,000 to $100,000. As a result we stood, and still stand at this writing, exposed to an emergency—what would we do, for example, if the state spotted violations at the town dump? We need to raise taxes to re-fund our reserves; instead, we continue to draw them down. Recessionary times are not a good time to raise taxes, but we are not planning prudently. But then presidents and Congress are not paragons here, either.

13. I owe this observation to my friend Roger Hanlon.

14. Norton's friend William Dean Howells put it this way: "The loneliness of country work adds a burden that lies heavily on the hearts of the young. They long to go anywhere, to do anything to escape it." Instead, he thought, yeomen should pore over books as they plowed. "The future is yours as much as it is that of any young man or woman in New York, Washington, or Chicago; nay, even more, as we all know, who know American history, and who recognize the springs of life and power. It was such as you who made America, and it will be your own fault if you do not continue to make it." Quoted in Betty and Edward Gulick, *Charles Eliot Norton and the Ashfield Dinners, 1879–1903* (Ashfield, Mass.: Ashfield Historical Society, 1990), 24–25.

15. Norton offered a bizarre proposal for dealing with the threat to public order posed by local toughs: "the organization of a body of the better citizens in each of our towns and villages to give definite support to the town officials in their work of suppressing lawlessness in all its stages, of stamping out the rough and the hoodlum, the savages of our civilization, and worse enemies of society than the Indians of two centuries ago." He believed that "such an organization of even a dozen honest men, known by some simple name, such as 'Good order men,' ready to advise with the officials in regard to difficult cases, to act if need be as special constables, . . . might be a most efficient instrument in the maintenance of a right public spirit and in the repression of lawlessness. Difficulties might arise in the actual working of such a scheme, but there are none which seem insurmountable. At any rate it is manifest that it is the duty of all our country villages and towns to take more effective measures for the restraint and correction of the reckless and vicious members of the community." Norton, at the 1897 Ashfield Dinner, quoted in Gulick and Gulick, *Charles Eliot Norton and the Ashfield Dinners*, 28–29.

16. Norton (1890), quoted in Gulick and Gulick, *Charles Eliot Norton and the Ashfield Dinners*, 26.

17. Curtis (1880), quoted in Gulick and Gulick, *Charles Eliot Norton and the Ashfield Dinners,* 24.

18. I call them Victorians, not only because they lived during Queen Victoria's reign, but because the men who spoke at the Ashfield dinners, and especially Norton himself, were frequent travelers to England and friendly with leading Britons of that period, whose culture they warmly shared. Van Wyck Brooks, *New England's Indian Summer* (Cleveland: World, 1946), presents a vivid picture of these deep and extended interactions.

19. In 1733 the enslaved Africans on St. John did mount a heroic rebellion, but its moment of triumph was tragically brief. A novel by John L. Anderson, *Night of the Silent Drums* (New York: Scribner, 1975), recreates the story.

20. Sadly, although perhaps predictably, the territory's constitutional assembly became ensnarled in a conflict over whether to confine certain basic civil rights to what the proposed new constituton terms "heritage" Virgin Islanders, that is, persons who are themselves, or are descendants of, residents of the territory before 1925. Several delegates tried vainly to block these provisions, and in 2009 the governor refused to forward the draft that included them to the U.S. Congress. The whole enterprise seems likely to collapse under the weight of this disagreement.

21. My phrase here echoes Herbert Croly's title, *The Promise of American Life* (New York: Macmillan, 1909). Croly's argument, however, is different from mine. He sought to ground Progressive politics on Hamiltonian principles. I am tying the promise of American life explicitly to democracy and using the latter term in the sense suggested by its elements from the Greek language: rule by the people. To put it another way, I believe Tocqueville was right: rural New Englanders have shown, and continue to show, that the middle classes are capable of governing themselves.

Index

253

DONALD ROBINSON was educated at The Kent School, Yale College, and Union Theological Seminary (New York); he earned his doctorate at Cornell University. He is the author of *Slavery in the Structure of American Politics, 1765–1820*, winner of the Anisfield-Wolff Award in 1971, *"To the Best of My Ability": The Presidency and the Constitution*, and, with Ray Moore, *Partners for Democracy: Crafting the New Japanese State under MacArthur* and was a panelist on the PBS series *The Constitution: That Delicate Balance*. Robinson retired from the faculty of Smith College in 2004, where he had taught government and American studies since 1966. In 1983, he and his wife, Molly, with their four children, moved to Ashfield, Massachusetts, where he served on the select board from 1991 until 2000.